M000291213

to my father

The texts initialed (fb)
are by Fiorella Bulegato

www.electaweb.com

© M. Huber, R. Savignac, E. Sottsass by SIAE 2015

© 2015 by Mondadori Electa spa, Milan
All rights reserved

food design in italy

product development and communication
alberto bassi

Electaarchitettura

Contents

design and communication
of the food product

Food design is a word that has become rather ubiquitous in recent years to mean "the process of designing food actions," intending, in the wider sense, everything that has to do with the conception, preparation, realization, production, communication, distribution, sales and enjoyment of food.

The context it defines is therefore so ample that it becomes difficult to develop accurate analyses or detailed studies, considering furthermore that food is a theme with a great many implications, which offers many opportunities for investigation.[1]

To be more precise, and without delving into the merits of the word design,[2] a distinction can be made between design "with food" (for example, a specific way of making recipes or food dishes), design "for food" (any product of any kind pertaining to eating or serving food, from cutlery to pots and pans, and drinking glasses) and the design "of food," to which this book is dedicated: *food product design.*[3]

The ambition of the book is to analyse the food artefact[4] as a total project: from the organoleptic properties to the form, from the technological systems and organization of production, to the strategies of development, communication and consumption built around the product, and the management of its life cycle. These are, basically, the same elements that define the birth, life and end-of-cycle for all other goods (product/object/artefact, system or service).

For architect and designer Ettore Sottsass, "because eating is a linguistic process—where language means the visual transformation of signs—and a cultural act, it is subject in a certain sense to a creative action which means that eating necessarily involves a

→**Advertising billboards in Piazza San Babila in Milan, 1936 (Galbani Historic Archives).**

[1] "Food remains an 'elusive' theme yet at the same time, it continues to offer new implications and reveal new approaches" (P. Sorcinelli, *Gli italiani e il cibo. Dalla polenta ai cracker*, Bruno Mondadori, Milan 1999, p. 3). Massimo Montanari confirms: "Food appears to be a simple object, but it isn't because it contains everything" (M. Montanari, "Cibo, storia e didattica," in P. Floris D'Arcais, C. Petrini, C. Scaffidi (edited by), *Il cibo e l'impegno, Quaderni di Micromega*, 2, Gruppo editoriale l'Espresso, Rome 2004, pp. 164–65).
[2] The designer and intellectual Enzo Mari sustains that it has become a "suitcase word," a container in which everyone puts meanings that can be very different but are all labelled the same way (E. Mari, *La valigia senza manico. Arte, design e karaoke*, Bollati Boringhieri, Turin 2004, p. 11). For an introduction to the discipline, see A. Bassi, *Design. Progettare gli oggetti della vita quotidiana*, Il Mulino, Bologna 2013.
[3] The references this historical study is based on include research studies by anthropologists, sociologists and economists, as well as scholars of food, who explore "how food is created, how it is distributed, consumed, conceived, through the mechanisms that cover an extremely long and complex process, that involves environmental concerns, production methods, techniques, social and political relations, economic structures, mental biases." (M. Montanari, *Cibo, storia e didattica*, cit. pp. 164–65) Much information and knowledge may also be found in the works of aficionados and connoisseurs for the general public, as well as in company archives and museums. The interest of design historians and critics has been scant so far.
[4] Tomas Maldonado writes: "If we can say, generically speaking, that artifice is the result of *techne*, of state-of-the-art making to the state of the art, then the artefact is its tangible product. The material culture of a society is the sum total of the artefacts that this society has created" (T. Maldonado, *Critica della ragione informatica*, Feltrinelli, Milan 1997, pp. 140–41).

→C.A. Crespi, *Kitchen with
Cooks and Parmigiano Cheese*,
Galleria del Seminario vescovile,
Bedonia (PR), eighteenth
century (Museo del Parmigiano-
Reggiano, Musei del cibo della
provincia di Parma).

creative process. In this sense it lies within the realm of the design profession".[5]

This history of food product design intends to examine the general context and global systems, leading to and including the "design of the form," that developed in Italy in relation to product design with the onset of the industrial age in the mid-nineteenth century. Not only the aspects that concern production (which span manufacturing by hand, by machine, in automated processes; in one-of-a-kind, limited editions or standardized production), but the necessary components and dynamic processes that go hand in hand with production (which remains important to company identity, but has long ceased to be decisive in constructing the mechanisms that determine the value of goods) and which, among other things, include functional, aesthetic and symbolic factors, and those that lie within the collective imaginary. It should therefore be emphasized that even food was caught up in the critical changeover brought on by the development, in the wake of industrialization, of an economic, technological, productive and cultural system in which we are still fully immersed today, despite the many transformations that have taken place over the decades.[6]

At different moments in time for the different economies of the world, a new general industrial framework emerged, which often grew alongside the existing systems and was absorbed into them.

This complementary coexistence is very clear in the area of food, especially in Italy. The attention to and preservation of a "traditional" culinary identity based on the quality of food and on the ingredients, which was reflected in the profusion of small food shops and *trattorie* or restaurants, coexisted with the advent of industrial food products and mass distribution, with a new approach to domestic organization, with the introduction of self-service cafeterias and fast-food restaurants. In this sense what happened in the food industry revealed innovative dynamics, linked for example to the growth of new markets and consumer awareness with respect to quality, safety and sustainability, as well as the role of design.

There is yet another specific aspect of the production of artefacts in Italy worthy of note, which is common to many different manufacturing sectors: the capacity to introduce variations to an existing archetype, to produce an ample range of products that are just slightly differentiated, to build a large number of entrepreneurial ventures around the same product typology. The cluster system—which lies at the origin of part of the country's industrial development, of the small to medium-sized companies that represent Italy's family-based

[5] E. Sottsass, "La simbologia dell'oggetto," F. Burkhardt (edited by), *Cibi e Riti, atti del seminario di progettazione svoltosi all'IDZ di Berlino gennaio 1981*, printed by A.F. Lucini, Milan 1988, p. 60.
[6] "The origins of this design history significantly cross paths with the history of the organization of the industrial process, and many food products have emblematically represented the diverse and contradictory aesthetic questions of the form and structure of the industrial object" (G. Bosoni, "Cibo: l'ingegneria genetica prende il comando," G. Bosoni, F. Picchi (edited by), "Food design. Il progetto del cibo industriale," *Domus*, 823, 2000, p. 72).

→*Discritione del paese di chucagna dove chi manco lavora più guadagna*, engraving, Stamperia Remondini, Bassano del Grappa, seventeenth century (Museo del Parmigiano-Reggiano, Musei del cibo della provincia di Parma).

capitalism, and of the so-called "pocket-sized multinational corporations"—began with and based its growth on this approach, on the "variable series" or as we would call it today, on *custom design*, on tailor-made projects. This is as true in furniture and fashion, as it is in the mechanical and automotive industries, and of course the food industry. In this field, it has led to an amazing variety of foods, ingredients and products, even within individual typologies (with countless cheeses, types of pasta, confectionery products, wines, etc.).

Though it is guided by a minimum of "good taste" and some expertise in the matter of food, this study does not deal in the strictest sense with specific organoleptic content or the complex question of "taste," in the sense of whether a product is good or not, or whether its quality is high or low. In this case, it seems appropriate to point out the cultural factor that underlies our perception and judgment, so all in all—as food scholars Massimo Montanari and Alberto Capatti might say—the organ dedicated to the pleasure of fine food must be considered the mind rather than the tongue. Taste is generated by history and evolves over time, in its twin significance as "flavour" ("the historical experience of food is irrevocably lost to us") and "knowledge" ("the experience of a culture is the result of a tradition and an aesthetic conveyed to us by society from the very moment we are born"[7]).

Food design in Italy is structured on the basis of two levels of scholarship, reconstruction and interpretation. An analysis of context and systems has delineated four fundamental phases in time, each of which represent different approaches to the conception, production, distribution and consumption of food; at the same time, they offer a synthesis of the elements that can help to understand the various domains involved in the design of the food product.

Chapter one deals with Italian food in the phase prior to the advent of industry, and hence with the necessary and intrinsic conditions for the existence of the products, which can help to recognize the implicit, spontaneous and "natural" processes and practices of design. Chapters two and three address the industrial "interpretation," around the turn of the twentieth century, of many products that already existed within an artisanal context (not limited to production); and with it the rise, during the modern and Modernist eras, of food industries and new products.

Chapter four talks about the contemporary condition, and the awareness that there are many different ways to conceive the design and fruition of food. That a different notion of food systems (organic, slow, traditional, typical and so on) has emerged and taken such a strong hold, particularly in Italy, can help shed a light on the significant

[7] A. Capatti, M. Montanari, *La cucina italiana, storia di una cultura*, Laterza, Rome–Bari 2005, p. 99. See also L. Vercelloni, *Viaggio intorno al gusto. L'odissea della sensibilità occidentale dalla società di corte all'edonismo di massa*, Associazione Culturale Mimesis, Milan 2005.

transformations that have changed the economic system and the marketing of food products, and the role of design.

In the intent to offer a second level of interpretation, each temporal and logical phase is completed with a sort of Inventory, in which the products are identified in terms of their historical relevance, and are examined from the perspective of design based on research conducted on historical documents.[8] On the basis of the material at hand (documentary, iconographic, archival, museum and oral sources), we sought to construct an overall intelligibility and provide indications that could help understand not only the product, but its specific context as well: the culture of the designer, the manufacturer, the industrial cluster or a technological or social point in time.

It seems obvious to observe that the contributions to the design came about in many different ways: at times the authorship is explicit, but in most cases it is the result of anonymous or team work by entrepreneurs, company employees, industrial researchers, designers, graphic designers, advertisers and so on. Depending on the different conditions, the contribution might involve a complete project or merely individual elements, such as the packaging, the visual design, the design of the form or of the food content.

In some cases, the stories appear sufficiently complete, in others they summarize the state of the art of knowledge (frequently embryonic, especially where design is concerned), sometimes they represent an initial attempt at a case study and organize the first information available on the theme. The Inventory is therefore a selection based on a series of choices, some of them objective and necessary, others more subjective and representative. And finally, the methodological approach and criteria led to the consolidation of some material, sometimes immediate, sometimes functional to the development of the historical proposition, and to some forced exclusions.

There were choices made in certain directions, well aware that—as Joseph Rykwert wrote—"to be a historian is to develop a project. Through the questions he asks his material, which is the past, the historian must build a story. There is no history that is not also a story… the essence of the story is selection."[9]

[8] Jules D. Prown makes the following distinction: "Scholars from different disciplines, who share an interest in the material culture, are distinguished between those who prefer the "material" and those who dedicate their interest primarily to "culture." This distinction sets "farmers" against "cowmen." The "farmers" studied, gathered and ordered data and information systematically [...] and deal in diachronic influences and developments. They concentrate their attention on the characteristics intentionally attributed to objects by the very people that made them. The process is mostly deductive. The "cowmen" pay little attention to the primarily physical elements of the artefacts; they are interested in the synchronic conditions of thought more than in the facts and events; they explore those aspects that express the underlying models of thought in a non-intentional manner [...] and generally operate by induction" (J. D. Prown, "Cultura/Materiale. 'Agricoltori' e 'allevatori' possono continuare ad essere amici?," R. Riccini (edited by), *Imparare dalle cose. La cultura materiale nei musei*, Clueb, Milan 2003, p. 118).
[9] "Il progetto della storia," interview by J. Rykwert with V.M. Lampugnani, *Domus*, 683, May 1987.

→Pasta from Naples,
advertisement, early twentieth
century (Buitoni-Nestlé Historic
Archives).

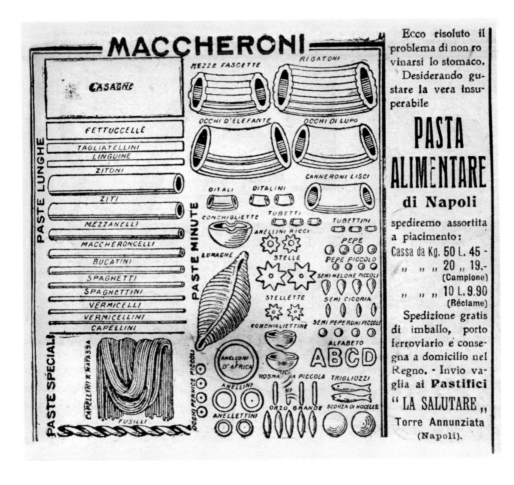

→Drying rack for spaghetti,
1910s (Barilla Historic Archives,
Parma).

The History of Material Culture, the History of Things, Design Histories

The design of food products may be correctly considered part of the history of the material culture.

Without purporting to be exhaustive, or even to elaborate on the themes or the methodological and theoretical issues in the history of the material culture, artefacts and design, this book will simply present some concepts underlying the work of a historian and critic.

As archaeologist George Kubler wrote: "Let us suppose that the idea of art could be expanded to the entire range of man-made things, including all tools and writing in addition to the useless, beautiful and poetic things of the world. By this view the universe of man-made things simply coincides with the history of art. It then becomes an urgent requirement to devise better ways of considering everything men have made."[10]

The scholar therefore introduces the idea of the "history of things," which "is intended to reunite ideas and objects under the rubric of visual forms: the term includes both artefacts and works of art, both replicas and unique examples, both tools and expressions—in short all materials worked by human hands under the guidance of connected ideas developed in temporal sequence".[11]

From the perspective of historiography, writes art historian Giovanni Previtali, this is a "radical change from the point of view from the human to the object, from the creator to the artefact".[12]

A fundamental concept in the "history of things" (and within it, the more specific history of design artefacts), is Kubler's idea of "sequence," as a "connected series of solutions to the same problem," originating from "prime objects" that represent a substantial breakthrough in relation to their predecessors and create the conditions for replicas to follow.[13] This fracture within the sequence is determined by and linked to innovation: "In our terms, each invention is a new serial position... The technique of invention thus has two distinct phases: the discovery of new positions followed with their amalgamation with the existing body of knowledge".[14]

Kubler's position, published in 1962, attempts to shine a light on the historical—but still relevant—issue of the relationship between invention and replication, between innovation and conservation, between manufacturers or designers who choose to be *first movers* or *followers*: "The replica relates to regularity and to time: the invention relates to variation and to history. Human desires in every present instant are

[10] G. Kubler, *The Shape of Time. Remarks on the History of Things*, Yale University Press, New Haven and London 1970, p. 1.
[11] Ibidem, p. 9.
[12] G. Previtali, "Introduzione," G. Kubler, *La forma del tempo. Considerazioni sulla storia delle cose*, Einaudi, Turin 1976, p. XII.

[13] See A. Leroi-Gourhan, *Gesture and Speech*, MIT Press, Cambridge, MA – London 1993); *L'homme et la matière. Évolution et techniques*, I, Albin Michel, Paris 1943, vol. 1, *Milieu et techniques. Évolution et techniques*, II, Albin Michel, Paris 1945.
[14] Ibidem, p. 64.

torn between the replica and the invention, between the desire to return to the known pattern, and the desire to escape it by a new variation."[15] And again: "A signal trait of our own time is an ambivalence in everything touching upon change. Our whole cultural tradition favours the values of permanence, yet the conditions of present existence require an acceptance of continual change."[16]

The change of perspective that he proposes opens innovative directions in research that can help to place design history in a more appropriate context. The extension of the field, and the need for tools of criticism that can bring the concept of innovation into sharper focus, the identification of prime artefacts and replicas in the construction of formal sequences, requires rethinking the methods and measures of history and criticism, and adopting an open approach, free of prejudice. As sustained by Siegfried Giedion, one of the few design historians and critics to deal with food: "For the historian there are no banal things… He has to see objects not as they appear to the daily user, but as the inventor saw them when they first took shape. He needs the unworn eyes of contemporaries, to whom they appeared marvellous or frightening. At the same time, he has to establish their constellations before and after, and thus establish their meaning."[17] In his fundamental book *Mechanization takes command*, written in 1948, and subtitled "a contribution to anonymous history," he explores the mechanization of the bread-production and meat-butchering processes: the new system and context of production that would change food forever, along with the quantity and quality of people's lives.

From the point of view of the "history of things," the study and interpretation of design artefacts requires a methodological approach that takes into account a comprehensive process common to all of them, which starts with the development of the concept and the design, branching out into a variety of different contexts and systems (geographical, cultural, technological, market-driven) that determine a plurality of theories and practices. Not just one design process but many, each with its own specific characteristics to be explored, clarified and explicated by historians and critics, who build the tools to make them intelligible for professionals in the field, and more in general for users and the public.

Design and the work of the designer involve different elements depending on the sector of production, on the organizational, economic and financial characteristics, on the market position with respect to competitors and so on. There are many different types of manufacturers, in terms of scale and expertise in technology and produc-

→**Applying black tincture to the Parmigiano cheese wheels, c. 1940 (Museo del Parmigiano-Reggiano, Musei del cibo della provincia di Parma).**

on the following pages
→**Leonetto Cappiello, Cirio, advertising poster, 1923 (Cirio-Conserve Italia Historic Archives, San Lazzaro di Savena).**

→**Leo Lionni, Caffè Cirio, advertisement (from E. Persico (edited by), *Arte Romana*, suppl. to *Domus*, 96, December 1935, inside front cover).**

[15] Ibidem, p. 72.
[16] Ibidem, p. 64.
[17] S. Giedion *Mechanization Takes Command*, Oxford University Press, London 1970, p. 3. And "but no more in history than in painting is it the impressiveness of the subject that matters. The sun is mirrored even in a coffee spoon. In their aggregate, the humble objects of which we shall speak have shaken our mode of living to its very roots." (Ibidem, p. 3).

IL SUPERIORE CAFFÈ
CIRIO È VERO BRASILE

IL BRASILE È UN
GRANDE PAESE AMI-
CO DELL'ITALIA
NON HA ADERITO
ALLE SANZIONI E
ACQUISTA PRO-
DOTTI ITALIANI

2.000.000 DI ITALIANI
VIVONO IN BRASILE

→The Saclà factory, 1950s
(Saclà Historic Archives, Asti).

tion, attitude, openness to research and design, entrepreneurial quality and management. Designing for industry and artisanal production are two entirely different things; different manufacturing systems can frequently be complementary, however, and new manufacturing methods crop up and develop all the time. Within the framework of a comprehensive approach, the product must be conceived to reach the consumer market (with operational strategies for communication, distribution, promotion, etc.), but also to provide necessary services (management, monitoring or maintenance, for example) until disposal at the end of its life cycle.

It becomes increasingly clear that the profession of the designer is no longer a solitary endeavour, but a team practice, structured to combine different areas of expertise, roles and responsibilities. The designer must work with entrepreneurs, engineers, marketing and communication specialists, experts in technology, production systems, materials, and so on.

From this point of view it is therefore essential to work within a notion of *design histories*, simply because there exists a diversity of possible methodological points of view and ways of understanding and practicing the "different types" of design. This methodology and definition of the field are undoubtedly challenging but are essential to contextualizing design history, even in its vital critical dimension, within the framework of scientific research, of the design culture and the vital mechanisms of the economy.[18] In the seminal words of Enrico Castelnuovo: "Telling the story of design means telling many stories. The story of economics, of industry, labour, commerce, ergonomics, technique, technology, society, patterns of behaviour, education, of the artistic, scientific, technical and visual cultures, of perceptive methods and conventions, the history of art, architecture, and one could go on. There are so many different histories: like strands in a rope, they intersect, intertwine and overlap as they unfurl." He continues: "The history of design brings into question the autonomy of the various spheres and the various series and it can't help but be an inter- (or at least) multidisciplinary undertaking, in the sense that it does not emerge from the juxtaposition of many histories, but from an encounter between them. And the places where these events come into contact and interact are its most interesting and symptomatic nodes."[19]

[18] See A. Bassi, "Nuovi approcci alla storia del design," *Il design e la sua storia*, Proceedings of the AisDesign conference, Milan, 1–2 December 2011, Lupetti, Milan 2013, pp. 75–82.
[19] E. Castelnuovo, "For a History of design," E. Castelnuovo (edited by), *History of Industrial Design. 1750-1850 The Age of the Industrial Revolution*, vol. I, Electa, Milan 1990, p. 8. On the historiography of design see, among others, VV. AA., *Design: storia e storiografia*, Progetto Leonardo, Bologna 1995; K. Fallan, *Design history. Understanding theory and method*, Berg, Oxford–New York 2010; M. Dalla Mura, C. Vinti, "A Historiography of Italian Design," G. Lees-Maffei, K. Fallan (edited by), *Made in Italy. Rethinking a Century of Italian Design*, Bloomsbury, London 2013, pp. 35–56.

In 2007 I published my book entitled *Design anonimo in Italia. Oggetti comuni e progetto incognito.*[20] It was a survey of objects that were well-designed, sold well and lasted over time, thanks to the contribution of the many people who took part in a wide-ranging process of design, development and realization.

All of them possess that which, in a precise synthesis—within the context of a more general analysis of Achille and Pier Giacomo Castiglioni's design methodology—Sergio Polano (borrowing from Ray and Charles Eames) indicated as the *Uncommon Beauty of Common Things,* "for the intelligence that has coalesced over time in "common things," for the logical rationale of "anonymous design" that eschews redundancy and waste, for the understated knowledge expressed in the best solutions to be found within the repertory of utensils, tools, and objects we use everyday."[21]

Their process of acknowledgment was not built primarily on an emphasis of its authorship, of the name of the designer or the brand (which in recent decades has been considered to be one of the most effective ways of enhancing the desirability of products), but on the delineation of a well-articulated interdisciplinary design process, within broad contexts and systems. Some of these anonymous objects allude to the domain of technical culture because they are the result of an innovation, which may even have been patented; others are the result of accumulation and small improvements, coming out of a long tradition of production that generates a definitive model; others again represent original product typologies that respond to newly-arising needs.

Some of the artefacts that were selected at the time for *Design anonimo in Italia* were food products, from the ice-cream cone to the packaging of Barilla pasta, from the Chianti flask to the bottle for Campari Soda.

If food is examined from the perspective of design, many analogies with anonymous design will come to light. For most food products, the author is unknown; digging under the surface however, authorship does emerge, from a series of contributions, expertise in various fields or accumulated knowledge. This viewpoint makes its possible to widen our scope and to consider the food artefact (like the anonymous object, the utensil, the technical object, etc.) within the context of people's everyday lives, which will also help to methodologically re-establish "a" history of design, not as a sequence of isolated "auratic"

[20] A. Bassi, *Il design anonimo in Italia. Oggetti comuni e progetto incognito,* Electa, Milan 2007. Over time critics and designers have dedicated their thoughts to this subject. Among them, P. Antonelli, *Humble masterpieces. 100 Everyday Marvels of Design,* Thames & Hudson, London 2006; N. Fukasawa, J. Morrison (edited by), *Super Normal: Sensations of the Ordinary,* Lars Müller Publishers, Zurich 2007; *Diid-disegno industriale,* 55, 2012; F. Clivio, *Hidden Forms. Vedere e capire le cose,* Skira, Milan 2014.

[21] S. Polano, *Achille Castiglioni, tutte le opere 1938-2000,* Electa, Milan 2001, p. 10; see also "Le cose invecchiano," *Multiverso,* 3, 2006, pp. 42–45.

→Mario Labò, poultry shop
in Genoa (from M. Labò,
*Architettura e arredamento
del negozio*, Hoepli, Milan 1936,
p. 180).

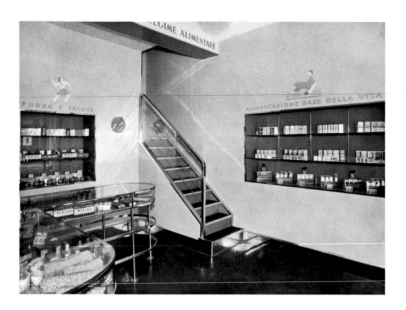

→Gio Ponti, pasta shop in Milan;
Federico Seneca, confectionery
shop in Milan (from M. Labò,
*Architettura e arredamento del
negozio*, Hoepli, Milan 1936,
p. 171 and 175).

→Erberto Carboni, Barilla stand
at the VIII International
Exhibition of Preserves and
Packaging in Parma, 1953, built
by Medardo Monica (Barilla
Historic Archives, Parma).

episodes, with some degree of authorship, but as a survey of "every-day products" (that may be the carriers of different "values," such as design, technical and production quality, social function and so on). And in this specific case, within a "history of things" dedicated to food.[22]

Food Design Histories

The considerations we have made about design as a collective and/or anonymous process within a more broad-based history of the expressions of material culture, therefore appear particularly relevant in the case of the history of food product design. Capatti and Montanari sustain that "if we must relate it to something, that would be to the knowledge and techniques of material culture, the rituals and needs of everyday life, the shapes of taste."[23]

Within the greater story of food, and of individual food products, the lens will be focused on design thinking, that is to say on the process that leads to the formulation of a concept of handmade/industrial artefact as the outcome of a functional and/or technological and/or aesthetic "intuition" or in response to a market need, and to the choice and development of its technological and formal characteristics in relation to the possibilities and economies of production, distribution, communication, consumption and end-of-life cycle.

Within the overall system of the industrial age, food responds to the logic and the practices that are characteristic of design. First, it is designed to be replicated at a large scale, with identical organoleptic qualities. The exact replication from a technical and alimentary point of view requires the utilization of machines, forms and moulds, control systems, guaranteed sanitary conditions, and so on. Design takes into consideration raw materials, specific production technologies and legal standards, the issue of a limited lifespan, the needs of preparation and preservation. It also deals with formal aspects, specific fabrication systems, communication strategies, packaging and more. It takes into consideration mass or niche consumer trends and diverse markets, and is influenced by different social, economic, cultural, entrepreneurial-technological-production conditions. There is also an aspect of teamwork in the design process, that can involve many actors-protagonists-contributors: the entrepreneur, the designer, the engineer, the communicator, the marketing professional, the distributor, the retail store, etc.

→Diffuser that automatically refilled the pipes for the production of spaghetti, 1960s.

[22] Addressing this theme in the catalogue of the exhibition *Progetto cibo*, which he curated at the Mart museum in Rovereto in 2013, Beppe Finessi underlines that it is "possible to learn to interpret the design (of food) based on the beauty and intelligence of "anonymous" products, which have no recognized author, because they descend from a tradition that has passed them down to us." He continues: "After learning (again) to perceive the power and rationale behind a design that officially has no designer, or better yet for which the designer is unknown, one can understand the equally intelligent variety of teachings that "industrial food" has to offer" (B. Finessi (edited by), *Progetto cibo. La forma del gusto*, Electa, Milan, 2013, p. 12).
[23] A. Capatti, M. Montanari, La *cucina italiana…* cit., p. VIII.

→Colussi factory at Petrignano
di Assisi (PG), 1970s (Colussi
Archives, Milan)

→Mould for the Mulino Bianco
Macine biscuits, 1990 (Barilla
Historic Archives, Parma).

on the following pages
→Arrigoni, double-page
advertisement (from *L'Italia
nel Mondo*, 3, March 1942,
pp. 158–59).

The same is true for products that are not manufactured within the mass-production system. The production method, and even the factors that determine the food properties of the products (natural, organic or locally-produced), become an element of identity and a sign of quality, which acquire their full significance and value when contextualized within the logic of the capitalist system and consumer society that evolved out of the industrial era.

Food products have other specificities, for example their constituent elements are necessarily complementary and must be immediately evident: from the identification of the product as food and merchandise, to the general entrepreneurial strategies and how the various instruments of design concur to their development. The food product exists as a unitary whole. The food-content is not loose but is placed inside a container, a form of packaging designed ad hoc, and more or less directly connected to materials-technology-form. The identity of the brand and the visual communication are developed on the packaging, but they may frequently be found directly on the product: the label and brand, information on the organoleptic content and ingredients, and instructions for use.

Thus the food product represents a "total design proposal" which is, as Ampelio Bucci writes, "the design of all the elements used to make contact with possible consumers (in addition to the product and its communication properties, the packaging, the image, the brand, the venues and methods of purchase, etc.). This is the innovative factor that more than any other distinguishes the marketing of aesthetic and niche products from that of mass consumer products."[24]

This structure provides the framework for a general history of the design of food products in Italy and *food design histories.*[25]

In focusing on the relationship between the material culture, the construction of a food system and the role of design, sociologist Franco La Cecla sustained that Italy is a country with a fine tradition of attention to form ("The culture of poverty in Italy is a culture that responds to critical conditions by elaborating forms") and that "an example of popular culture that pays attention to form is the development of the food system in our peninsula." He concludes by saying that "the concept of 'Made in Italy' first arose within the food system."[26]

[24] A. Bucci, "Dal prodotto alimentare all'offerta globale," *Diid-disegno industriale*, 19, 2006, p. 13.
[25] It is easier to find texts on food products that deal with design in international publications. For an initial selection see *999 Phaidon Design Classics*, 3 vols., Phaidon, London 2006. In this sense, exemplary essays in terms of historiographical method and analysis are the following by S. Polano, "Strategie di comunicaione del più grande brand," *Diid-disegno industriale*, 3–4, April 2003, pp. 66–95; "Coca-Cola storie di un marchio," *Casabella*, 711, May 2003, pp. 45–49.
[26] F. La Cecla, "La forma che il cibo può assumere racconta dell'Italia e delle sue profonde differenze geografiche," *Domus*, monograph issue *Food*, 913, April 2008, p. 47.

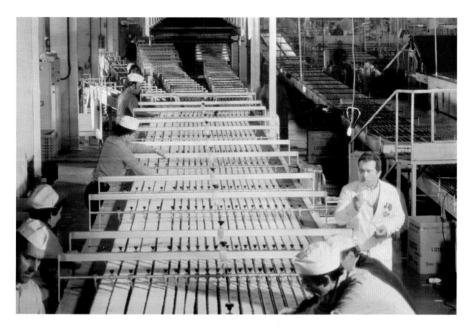

ARRIGONI

TRIESTE

PRODUCE IN ITALIA, VENDE IN TUTTO IL MONDO

ΛRRIGONI

TRIESTE

PRODUCE IN ITALIA, VENDE IN TUTTO IL MONDO

traditional italian food artefacts

Food Culture and the Urban Context

To understand how such an important tradition and culture of ideation, design, production, communication and consumption of food artefacts developed in Italy, there are many different factors to be taken into consideration: from the eating habits, based on the availability of natural ingredients for foods and recipes, to the ways the products were consumed.

The subject of this chapter is the lengthy phase that began with the dawn of the Mediterranean civilization and ended with the transition from an artisanal to an industrial system around the turn of the twentieth century, which in fact coincided with the progress of scientific and technological research, the advent of mechanized and standardized methods of factory organization and production and, to meet the needs of a consumer market, systems for "artificial" food preservation, as well as specific instruments and professional figures for the design of food products.

To understand the phase that preceded this industrial breakthrough, it is important to examine the role of the city-states over the centuries, the true drivers of social, economic and cultural forces, constantly engaged in virtuous rivalry and proud competition. As John Dickie writes, "Italian cuisine is city cuisine."[1]

Because food was produced by artisans (and/or in the home), the central question remained what to do with "fresh" foods, or foods meant to be aged with "natural" artifices that would preserve their integrity, and eliminate the problem of spoilage. Like many foods in the Italian tradition, systems for preserving foods often came down from Antiquity: some of them were based on processes of transformation (that directly affect the foods, as in the case of milk, wine or olives) others on drying (as in the case of grain or legumes), others again on a combination of foods and natural ingredients (such as, for example, salt or spices used on meats and cheeses).

The history of Italian food delves its roots in the Roman agricultural civilization, which also originated what is known as the Mediterranean diet, when populations began to settle and became sedentary. They raised livestock, and learned to cultivate fruit trees, grapes and olives, as well as vegetables and grain (wheat in particular, developing processes and foods made from flour, such as bread, flatbreads and sweet or savoury pies).

→*Gioco della cucagna che mai si perde e sempre si guadagna,* **engraving by Giuseppe Maria Mitelli, 1691.**

[1] J. Dickie, *The epic history of the Italians and their food,* Simon and Schuster, New York 2010. And also "The heritage of fine foods is usually identified and recognized in reference to the identity of a city" (A. Capatti, M. Montanari, *La cucina italiana, storia di una cultura,* Laterza, Rome – Bari 2005, p. XIX).

→**Meat processing room
at Citterio, Rho, c. 1935.**

→**Hams hanging outside to dry,
Luppi company at San Vitale
Baganza (PR), c. 1950.**

In his book dedicated to the Mediterranean, a seminal work in the history of the material culture, Fernand Braudel described wheat, grapes and olives as the "plants of civilization."[2]

The Roman model of food production learned from the Celtic model, characteristic of nomadic populations who practiced pastoral livestock herding, from which they derived products such as meat, milk, lard and butter, along with beer and beverages made from grain, which are short-term cultivations and can adapt to nomadic lifestyles. Over time, these differences faded, leading to the rise of the European agrosilvopastoral civilization, which developed common homogeneous characteristics.

During the Medieval age, a common identity began to emerge in Italy, though it was based on a plurality of "languages," as may be seen for example in the recipe collections, which were the expression of a broad-based food culture. Montanari takes them as a demonstration of the existence of "a national culinary heritage."[3]

The next phase, occasioned by the introduction of new foods and ingredients between the fifteenth and seventeenth centuries, brought with it a sea change in the Italian identity. In the fifteenth century, rice was first imported from the Arab world, the sixteenth century brought buckwheat from the Black Sea, and corn from the Americas (both of which were used to make *polenta*, a food staple for all classes of society), but more importantly, potatoes and tomatoes.[4]

These products were instrumental in shaping one of the most original aspects of our cuisine, the core value of vegetables and grains: this was undoubtedly consequent to the strict constraints of the humble diet, consisting primarily of vegetable soups and grain-based *polenta*, on which the vast majority of the population relied for its basic survival.[5] The situation only partly improved with the introduction of pasta and rice, followed by oil and wine.

And so a national model gradually came into existence, defined by a network that represented the sum total of many local realities gravitating around the urban contexts, the centres for the construction and transmission of a local and national culinary culture. For lack of an aristocracy with the power to coordinate broader regional contexts, the city grew to express a dominant identity that exercised its influence

[2] F. Braudel, *Civiltà e imperi del Mediterraneo nell'età di Filippo II,* Einaudi, Turin 1953, pp. 166–68 (orig. ed., *La Méditerranée et le monde méditerranéen à l'époque de Philippe II,* Paris 1949). See also S. Guarracino, *Mediterraneo. Immagini, storie e teorie da Omero a Braudel,* Bruno Mondadori, Milan 2007, pp. 28–39.
[3] M. Montanari, *L'identità italiana in cucina,* Laterza, Rome – Bari 2013, p. 31.
[4] See A. Saltini, *I semi della civiltà. Frumento, riso e mais nella storia delle società umane,* Nuova Terra Antica, Bologna 1996; S. Guarracino, *Mediterraneo. Immagini, storie e teorie da Omero a Braudel,* cit.
[5] A. Capatti, M. Montanari, *La cucina italiana...,* cit., p. 51.

over the countryside.[6] Again there are recipe collections—from the Renaissance period, such as those by Martino De Rossi, Bartolomeo Sacchi, Bartolomeo Scappi—that substantiate this situation, which was localized on the territory but could count on a trans-urban (and later trans-regional) network with unitary characteristics.[7]

This two-fold condition (identity and unity) is the underlying feature of the complex dynamic relations between city and countryside, between the popular and elite food culture, between a humble and a rich cuisine, in a meshing of techniques and traditional skills, because the kitchen—suggest Capatti and Montanari—"is the place of exchange and cross-fertilization *par excellence*, rather (and more) than of origin. If a product may be considered the expression of a territory, the way it is used in a recipe or a menu is basically the result of hybridization."[8] Of course, it is essential to emphasize that the roots of food and cuisine in Italy are predominantly popular.[9]

"There is nothing in human history that is as profoundly determined by class disparity as food—explains Paolo Sorcinelli, reasserting the need for an objective examination of the agricultural-farming roots of traditional Italian food—differentiations crumble into a tangle of expedients, falling back on increasingly mediocre ingredients as resources become more and more limited."[10] This condition proved extremely difficult for a very long time for ample portions of the population in rural Italy (and later for Italy's urban proletariat). And—he continues, underlining the need to discredit certain pervasive stereotypes on the theme—these social classes "usually dedicated little time and attention to preparing their food; they ate at the workplace without sitting down… at home the preparations were equally hasty and frugal… Instead of the usual image of the good old days… when food was healthy and natural (who could actually afford it?) it sounds like there was far more affinity with the pace of today's fast food and sandwich shops."[11]

Fresh and Dry Foods

Natural ingredients can be used in different ways, and they determine the specific characteristics of foods: they can be eaten as they are, used to make recipes, transformed to preserve them.

This book is interested in examining how foods are processed to be eaten fresh or preserved by means of natural systems, which are the result of a "design," that is to say a process of ideation and physical transformation of the original state in which they are found in nature.

---

[6] M. Montanari, *L'identità italiana in cucina*, cit., p. 8, who further specifies: "Regional cuisine is an invention created to fit the demands of politics, trade and tourism. These are not cultural demands…the cuisines may be referred to as "local," "regional," urban. And as a national circuit that connects them into a network….But the regional model proved to be a more

successful strategy, because it was easier to handle, easier to communicate," and was supported and exported in cooperation with the food industry (p.80).
[7] A. Capatti, M. Montanari, *La cucina italiana…*, cit., p. 10.
[8] Ibidem, p. VIII.
[9] "Cuisine, rather than an invention of the ruling classes, is a need of theirs, satisfied

Vegetables and fruit may be consumed after they are harvested, just like milk after it is drawn from the animal. At the same time, "production" processes can be set in motion for ingredients and raw materials deriving from crops (from wine to oil, from fruits to vegetables) or livestock (from meat to milk).

Most fresh foods can be eaten without needing to be processed for preservation or transportation, or to construct mechanisms of identity and communication, such as labels, graphics or packaging: they are generally prepared in or near the places where they will be consumed (locally grown produce—"from farm to fork").

From the perspective of product design, "fresh foods" exist in relation to the challenges they represent to their own limits of physical substance and duration, and to the production system (and global industrial system) with which they are scarcely compatible. To be consumer-ready they go through a minimum number of steps in the product development and marketing process: what counts is the taste, the freshness, and that they be affordable, available and easy to find.

The category of fresh products—often available in "dry" versions produced naturally through drying, cooking, aging or other processes—includes many foods that are important to the Italian and Mediterranean diet, such as cheese, pasta and bread (made with water and various types of grains and flours).

These three examples lead directly into considerations regarding the "variety" of food products in Italy: there are in fact a remarkable amount of different types of bread, pasta, cheese (as well as cakes, liqueurs, or wines) that have come down from a long tradition rooted in specific territories.

Almost every city or region has its own type of bread with distinctive characteristics, from the *michetta* in Milan to Tuscan bread, or the *pugliese* from the Puglia region. Then there are the dry and flatbread versions, which during the industrial phase were adapted to be processed, cooked, preserved and then packaged: from the *piadina* to *grissini torinesi*, from *carasau* bread to *taralli*. It is important to emphasize that none of them ever built a strong overall image over time (for example identifying with a manufacturer, or achieving worldwide distribution): in most cases they simply remain a local variety of fresh food.[12]

Different types of flour are used to make savoury or sweet flatbreads or tarts ("the tart is Italian as a type," sustains Montanari[13]), the most famous archetype of which is undoubtedly pizza.

by the art of the people" writes Giovanni Rebora (quoted in C. Petrini, *Il cibo e l'impegno*, in P. Floris D'Arcais, C. Petrini, C. Scaffidi (edited by), "Il cibo e l'impegno," *Quaderni di Micromega*, 2, Gruppo editoriale l'Espresso, Rome 2004, p. 9).
[10] P. Sorcinelli, *Italiani e il cibo. Dalla polenta ai cracker*, Bruno Mondadori, Milan 1999, p. 127.

[11] Ibidem, p. 62.
[12] This is an issue that also concerns many other food products which may perhaps be famous but have often struggled to emerge from anonymity or from being identified with a generic name, such as *limoncello* liqueur or *gorgonzola* cheese.
[13] M. Montanari, *L'identità italiana in cucina*, cit., p. 18.

Tarts are made with filled hard dough, that is to say an edible wrapping that contains the filling. This dough can both contain and be baked at the same time; possible examples are fruit pies, tarts or *tortelli* (halfway between pasta and tarts) which, among other things, can be an answer to the popular need for recycling leftovers or, in the best of cases, excess food. From a design perspective, they are food containers, which are themselves edible.

As mentioned earlier, many fresh products are also available in a dry version, obtained by cooking or other processes that ensure preservation. Pasta is an excellent case in point. Widely known since the Ancient Romans and produced at the time as a larger form of lasagne, by the Middle Ages pasta was readily available in a range of different varieties: the long *vermicelli* and the short tubular *maccheroni*, filled pasta (such as *ravioli* and *tortelli*), sweet and savoury, fried or boiled. The identification of pasta in terms of typology and merchandise category (divided into two basic types: long like *spaghetti* and short like *maccheroni*), the production based on machine systems (the mechanical pasta press was invented in the mid-seventeenth century), and the adoption of moulds to produce identical replicated series of a "type," the drying process for long-term preservation, the consequent need for a container to enable transportation, recognisability and communication, all represent steps in the process of creating an industrial product. Though it was long just another food typology, as a result of these technological-productive developments pasta became a truly popular food, the basic staple of a daily diet, especially for more impoverished urban dwellers.[14]

More than pasta in and of itself, it is the project for pasta as a product that is emblematically Italian, and in particular "the variety of types and formats, that multiply as a result of the many different overlapping culinary traditions."[15] It is obvious that the profusion of pasta types (or of any other food product) could only have developed in a territory with the culinary culture to conceive them, and to appreciate their many different forms. Inspired by the *Lunario della pastasciutta*, a book written by Gustavo Traglia in 1956 that lists two hundred and ninety eight different types, Franco La Cecla sustains that "this inventory reflects, on the one hand, the extraordinary flexibility of the manufacturing industry and, on the other, the incredible competence of consumers who have the capacity to distinguish the qualities and opportunities offered by one form rather than another."[16]

A natural and cultural quality that Italy demonstrates in many other fields, such as fashion: Italians know how to eat, how to dress, and we might add, how to "make," if we look at the artisanal matrix of Italian design companies, often more important than their economic-commercial vocation, in the fields of furniture and mechanical manufacturing.

[14] Ibidem, p. 50.
[15] "That pasta is Italian… is indisputable" (Ibidem, p. 46).
[16] F. La Cecla, "La forma che il cibo può assumere racconta dell'Italia e delle sue profonde differenze geografiche," *Domus*, monograph issue *Food*, 913, April 2008, p. 47

→Tapping and analysing
the Parmigiano wheel, c. 1940
(Museo del Parmigiano-
Reggiano, Musei del cibo della
provincia di Parma).

→Weighing the Parmigiano
cheese, 1930 (Museo del
Parmigiano-Reggiano, Musei del
cibo della provincia di Parma).

The "Natural" Packaging of Aged Products

The most successful "typical" products in the history of Italian food," write Capatti and Montanari, "are those with the greatest industrial vocation (pasta, *parmigiano*, tomato sauce). The ones that are best-suited to circulate.[17]

The success and diffusion of products also depends on their potential for emerging from their local dimension and boundaries to seek appreciation in larger markets. To make this possible, especially in the pre-industrial era when there were few means of information and communication other than visibility or physical presence, it was important that these products be portable so that they could be traded. Charcuterie and cheeses are food specialities with a commercial vocation, because they last long and can be transported. Clearly, fresh foods are also marketable, "but preserved products are the ones that guarantee the continuity of transactions, the sedimentation of shared habits, practices and tastes."[18]

In the phase that preceded the introduction of "artificial" systems typical of industry (from vacuum-packing to frozen foods), preservation was ensured with "natural" methods: drying, cooking or stewing processes, or aging with natural ingredients such as salt.

In Antiquity, these methods were perfected in meat products derived from cattle, sheep or pig-farming, primarily to get through the times when food was scarce, but later to use them for trade.

Italy developed a rich variety of different types of charcuterie (a term used to define foods made from raw or cooked meat, almost always containing added salt, animal fats, herbs and spices, and possibly other ingredients and preservatives): there are the hams (*prosciutto* and variations such as *bresaola, speck,* lard, etc.) made from salt-dried pork legs; and there are the cured sausages (*salame, mortadella,* etc.), meat packed into "containers" generally made of animal gut.

Capatti and Montanari write: "For a long time charcuterie was an essential part of the cuisine. Cured meats and "salsiccioni" were ways of preparing the meat, a staple more than a preserved food"; and "The chapter on charcuterie may be seen in the context of the economy and culture of food preservation, a strategic node in building a culinary model, because it makes it possible to distribute specialities made from local products with techniques and traditional skills from all over the country."[19]

Natural food preservation systems, such as salting or meat curing, were harbingers of food product design, as they developed both a morphology and a type of packaging. The salting process, for example, was the basis for a production process that shaped the contents into a recognizable identity-defining "aesthetic" (*prosciutto crudo*

---

[17] A. Capatti, M. Montanari, *La cucina italiana...*, cit., p. 314 and ff.
[18] Ibidem, p. 92.

[19] M. Montanari, *L'identità italiana in cucina*, cit., p. 35.

→Annibale Carracci, *Vende formaggio parmigiano*, engraving by Simon Guillain, 1646 (Museo del Parmigiano-Reggiano, Musei del cibo della provincia di Parma).

→Advertising panel, 1950s (Auricchio Historic Archives, Cremona).

shaped like a "chicken thigh" was from Parma and the one shaped like a "guitar" was from San Daniele). At the same time it created a partly rigid "packaging" that protected the product from spoilage and breakage, but also displayed the communication which was fire-branded onto it. Just like for sausages, the component elements (animal interiors) and "tools of production" (the strings with which they were bound and hung on racks) determined the form and identity of the product.

The same is true of the aging processes for cheeses, in the case of cheeses that are bound and hung up to age (such as *caciotte* or *provole*), and in the case of cheese aged in moulds (such as Parmigiano Reggiano and Grana Padano). Here too, the hard sturdy crust serves as packaging and as a communication surface to be fire-branded.

The hams and cheeses selected for the Inventory (there are of course many more to choose from within the variety that is typical of Italian products) constitute a typological archetype, in terms of production processes, the resulting form of the product, and the potential they offer for preservation, marketing and communication.

The design of a food artefact is the outcome of ideas and methods that have sedimented over time to form a "definitive" system, a "standard" that opens a "series"—to quote Kubler—followed by an infinity of variations.

From the point of view of the relationship between the food product, the context in which it is used and its fruition, we agree with Capatti and Montanari's considerations on "taste," as a meeting point between the popular and elite cultures: "Preserving or storing food has always been a crucial strategy in warding off hunger. But the excess of labour and culture that is expended in so many ways on natural products becomes a precious opportunity to please the palate."[20]

Bruno Munari and the Good Design of Natural Products

For scholars studying food and its "natural" design (both implicit and explicit) from a historical point of view, it seems only fitting to acknowledge the intelligence contained in a small booklet that offers an innovative and unexpected perspective on the design of the food product.

In 1963 Bruno Munari, an artist, visual and product designer, author and educator, published *Good Design* for Vanni Scheiwiller's All'insegna del pesce d'oro ("n. 7 in the series with the small square format").[21]

Inspired by the elegant irony that distinguishes most of his work, the author proposed to interpret several artefacts "manufactured" by Nature from the perspective of good design: the evolutionary process, in fact, has perfected morphologies that have become easy to use

→Drying rooms, Pastificio Voiello, early twentieth century (Barilla Historic Archives, Parma).

→Drying racks for skeins of egg noodles, 1910s (Barilla Historic Archives, Parma).

[20] A. Capatti, M. Montanari, *La cucina italiana...*, cit., p. 94.
[21] B. Munari, *Good Design*, All'insegna del pesce d'oro – Scheiwiller, Milan 1963 (later Corraini Edizioni).

→Erberto Carboni, Boschi Luigi
& Figli, advertising poster, 1926
(Museo del Pomodoro,
Musei del cibo della provincia
di Parma).

and are perfectly adapted to their function and taste, even from an aesthetic point of view.

Oranges and peas are illustrated with their constituent and functional characteristics, which are perfectly consistent with those of a well-designed object in terms of form, use, dimensions and so on. Both have external packaging that is easy to recognize by its bright colour and shock-resistant structure ("the packaging, he specifies, as is the custom today, need not be returned to the manufacturer, but is disposable"); inside it contains standard elements, with geometric and ergonomic shapes, easy to eat or to take in hand and, in the case of the orange, complete with seeds: "This is a little gift that the producers offer the consumer just in case he should wish to start his own personal production of these objects."

And as he discusses fruits and vegetables, between the serious and the facetious, Munari raises questions that are important to design: "One of the typical characteristics of these productions is the variation in the series." And wonders: "In the design of a mass-produced object must we take into account the tastes of the public and propose possible variations to the model in order to increase production and satisfy the greatest number of consumers? In the production of peas, for example, there may be an excess of variation." An excess that he attempts to attribute to errors in market research or the negligence of a bureaucracy that ordered a single type of packaging for any hypothetical number of peas: and what if someone wanted just one pea, does he have to buy the entire container?

Munari also raises the question of projects containing elements that are neither rational nor functional, such as the rose. He is especially concerned with the thorns, which he deems to be incongruous and unnecessary, though they do carry "a certain degree of suspense perhaps, he asks, to create a contrast between the sweet scent and the aggressive claws?" He believes however that this object is "absolutely useless to man… unjustified… that invites workers to daydream. An object that can even be called immoral."

An analogous design process, based on natural elements and components, and on the gradual development of productive, technical and formal solutions for preserved foods (such as the hard crust of cheese, or the process of making sausage out of animal interiors or salt-curing meat), may be found in many traditional food products.

Pizza Margherita

Various producers, Naples

late eighteenth–early nineteenth centuries, then 1889

On June 11th, 1889, Camillo Galli, Master of the Household for the Savoia family, who was responsible for supervising the food services of the Royal Household, wrote to Raffaele Esposito, a pizza-maker from Naples: "Dear Sir I confirm that the three types of Pizza that you prepared for Her Majesty the Queen were found to be delicious." This letter, still on display in Raffaello Esposito's pizzeria, now known as Brandi and located in Salita Sant'Anna di Palazzo, is considered to be the origin of the name Margherita, used to describe a pizza made with tomato sauce, fresh basil, salt and oil, both a tribute to the colours of the Italian flag and to Queen Margherita of Savoia. When the royal family came to inaugurate the new urban and architectural accomplishments of the Regeneration of Naples and to stay at the royal summer palace at Capodimonte, three different versions were prepared for them of a traditional savoury dish on a base of dough made with flour, water, salt and yeast, and flattened by hand, known as *pizza*—as it was called in a book published in 1858 which described the life and customs of Naples, but the term, which had previously appeared in a written document dated 1799, probably existed as far back as the Middle Ages to describe other types of flatbreads as well: the first was topped with oil, cheese and basil; the second with "cecenielli" (or whitebait, the young of sardines); and the third with mozzarella cheese and tomato sauce. Esposito's personal contribution remains a historic controversy: he might have added the tomato sauce or the leaf of basil—which some say was his wife Maria Giovanna Brandi's idea, inspired by the colours of the Italian flag—or have codified a dish made of a few simple ingredients, and given it the name of the Queen who had so thoroughly enjoyed it.

Given that a pizza with these three ingredients probably existed since the early years of that century, "Esposito's stroke of genius," wrote Antonio Mattozzi, who also described his early managerial spirit, culminating in his request to use the name "the Queen of Italy's pizzeria" for his own establishment, "was not the 'creation' of this type of pizza, but his idea of giving it a name, of calling it 'Margherita'."

In this manner, a traditional recipe was ultimately "stabilized," with specific characteristics, thus initiating a sort of standardization process for the dish. Furthermore, by naming a food product that until then had been identified simply by its general typology, it was given an identity and became recognizable, ushering in a new phase in the history of pizza. No longer was it the anonymous and random output of a "pizzajolo"—cook and/or baker— but the result of a specific process required to "produce" the Margherita, recognized as such by consumers who could find it anywhere, in a more or less similar version.

Identified more generally within a typology of food prepared with a water and flour-based dough, then baked on a pan or in the oven, "Neapolitan pizza"—starting with the type commonly known as "marinara," made with soft durum wheat, tomatoes, garlic, oregano, basil and olive oil—was known since the early eighteenth century and had been conceived as a dish made with modest ingredients, clearly popular in nature. It could be found outdoors at stands positioned in the narrow streets of Naples outside the bakeries, and could be eaten on the go or standing up, folded in half as was the custom for the version known as "calzone." The eighteenth century also witnessed the advent of specific venues that served pizza; they soon became widespread, contributing to the popularity of this dish, even though, writes Mattozzi again, conveying how hard it is to achieve historic certainty—

"the precise date on which the first pizzeria opened in Naples is unclear, nor do we know when the first *pizzaiuolo* was referred to by that specific name."

Pizza remained a prevalently local phenomenon until the mid-twentieth century, when it spread throughout Italy and the rest of the world in countless variations, becoming an icon of Italian food. Made with simple and modest ingredients, though absolutely natural, this dish is pleasing to the eye, delicious to eat, nutritious and satisfying, and typical of the "Mediterranean diet."

Since February 5th, 2010, pizza has been officially recognized as a Traditional Speciality Guaranteed (TSG) of the European Community, a geographical appellation introduced to protect quality agricultural products and foodstuffs that have a "specificity" linked to their method of production or recipe that refers to the tradition of a geographical area.

E. Rocco, *Il pizzajuolo*, in F. de Bourcard (edited by), *Usi e costumi di Napoli e contorni descritti e dipinti*, vol. 2, Stabilimento Tipografico Gaetano Nobile, Naples 1858, pp. 123–27 (available online at http://books. google.it/books?id=SuMnAAAAYAAJ&pri ntsec=frontcover&hl=it#v=onepage&q&f =false); R. Minervini, *Storia della pizza*, Società Editrice Napoletana, Naples 1973; G. Benincasa, *La pizza napoletana. Mito, storia e poesia*, Guida, Naples 1992; F. Salerno, *La pizza*, Tascabili Newton, Rome 1996; A. Mattozzi, *Una storia napoletana. Pizzerie e pizzaioli tra Sette e Ottocento*, Slow Food Editore, Bra (CN) 2009; Associazione Verace Pizza Napoletana, *Farina acqua lievito sale passione: vera pizza napoletana*, Malvarosa Edizioni, Ischia (NA) 2013.

→L. Bianchi, *Pizzajolo*, engraving, 1834 (Civica Raccolta delle Stampe Achille Bertarelli, Castello Sforzesco, Milan).

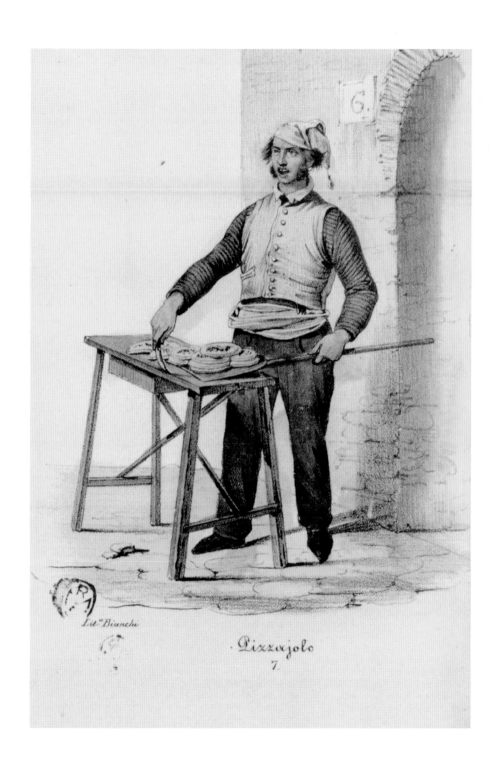

Lit.ª Bianchi

Pizzajolo
7.

Parmigiano Reggiano and Grana Padano Cheese

Various manufacturers, Po Valley

Middle Ages; then second half of the nineteenth century

Many typologies of cheese are distinguished by their rounded shapes that correspond to the containers or moulds used to make, age, cook and later preserve them. The aging process in particular, which is the last of several phases in the cheesemaking process, takes place inside a special form that gradually hardens to create a sturdy rind on the outside, which hence becomes the "place" inside which the cheese is produced, but also its packaging, which preserves it from spoiling and makes it easy to transport. Throughout the cheesemaking process and until it is ready, this cheese both produces and packages itself.

The round shape and hard rind of cheeses such as the *Parmigiano Reggiano* or the *Grana Padano* therefore represent a perfect example of "natural" product packaging. These two cheeses, which are emblematic of the Italian tradition, appeared in Antiquity in neighbouring geographical areas of the Po Valley. They are both hard cheeses, aged slowly, with similar shapes, organoleptic properties, production systems and processes, shaped inside two moulds known today as "fascere," and fire-branded; the difference between them lies essentially in what the milking cows are fed, how often they are milked every day and the length of the aging process, which is longer for the Parmigiano Reggiano.

Historic sources are unclear about which of the two came first. The specific qualities of a cheese originating in the area around Parma, with characteristics similar to those of today's *parmigiano*, were recorded in the Roman era and praised by Columella, Varro and Martial, whereas those of *grana*, the name of which derives from its typical granular consistency, seem to originate in a process developed in 1135 by the Cistercian monks of the Abbey of Chiaravalle, south of Milan. The most ancient grana is considered to be the *lodesano*, from Lodi, but other varieties originate in Milan, Parma, Piacenza and Mantua as well. Basically, the spreading practice of animal husbandry in areas with an abundant water supply led to the development of an expedient that could preserve the surplus of milk and maintain its nutritional properties. The refinement of the aging process—facilitated by the fact that the salt required for the cheesemaking process was easy to procure—guaranteed not only the preservation, the fragrance and a flavour that was both salty and sweet at the same time, but also the consistency needed to transport and sell the product. It therefore became a prized course in the banquets of the Renaissance aristocracy, as well as a cornerstone of the farming economy and the popular cooking tradition. Starting in the late seventeenth century and for a century and a half, the production of *parmigiano* declined as a result of the agricultural crisis that swept the Duchy of Parma and Piacenza, while hundreds of *grana* producers resisted in lower Lombardy. *Parmigiano* made a comeback after the Unification of Italy when, as a result of the abolition of import duties, growing trade and the diversification of crops from wheat to hay, which led to an increase in the production of milk, the cheese industry began to expand. The city of Bibbiano, in the province of Reggio Emilia, an area with significant livestock and cheesemaking industries, decided to publicize its local product by participating in national and international industrial expositions: in 1867 the *Società anonima bibbianese* was founded to trade in cheese, buying the production of local manufacturers and branding it as Sab, marking the beginning of a modern "industrial" system similar to the one that exists today. *Parmigiano* and *grana* are distinguished today on the basis of the provinces that provide the milk used to produce them: *Grana Padano* originates in the zones left of the Po River, all the way to the Trentino and Piemonte regions, while *Parmigiano Reggiano* comes from the zones on the right. The need to protect the qualities of similar cheeses had led as early as 1934, in Reggio Emilia, to the constitution of the *Consorzio volontario interprovinciale del grana tipico*, a consortium gathering manufacturers of *parmigiano* and *reggiano*, which worked with the government to officialise the name Parmigiano Reggiano in 1938, and in 1954 the *Consorzio volontario interprovinciale del grana tipico*. The Convention between European cheese manufacturers dated June 1st, 1951, and the later Decree of the President of the Republic no. 1269 dated October 30, 1955, defined the characteristics, production processes, zones of production and names: "Grana Lodigiano," which later became "Grana Padano" and "Parmigiano Reggiano." In 1996, both won recognition of the DOP brand (Protected Designation of Origin) from the European Community. (fb)

E. Sani, *Il Parmigiano-Reggiano dalle origini ad oggi*, edited by the Consorzio del formaggio parmigiano-reggiano, Editrice Age, Reggio Emilia 1958; M. Zannoni, *Il Parmigiano-Reggiano nella storia*, Silva Editore, Parma 1999; O. Parisi, *Il formaggio grana*, 4th edition revised and expanded, Mucchi, Modena 1966; F. Bonilauri (edited by), *Il Parmigiano-Reggiano. Un simbolo di cultura e civiltà*, De Luca, Rome 1992; N. Panzani, *Formaggio grana*, Eta, Vignola (MO) 1994; M. Iotti, *Storia del formaggio di grana "Parmigiano-Reggiano"* (1200–1995), 2nd ed., Futurgraf, Reggio Emilia 1996; G. Arlotti, Bibbiano. *Nella Culla del Parmigiano Reggiano*, Comune di Bibbiano, Bibbiano (RE) 2008; www.museidelcibo.it/parmigiano.asp.

→Wheels of Parmigiano-Reggiano cheese (Consorzio Parmigiano Reggiano).

→Brining room and storerooms
for the Parmigiano-Reggiano
(Consorzio Parmigiano
Reggiano).

→Gino Boccasile, Caseificio
Tavella, poster, 1940 (Consorzio
Parmigiano Reggiano).

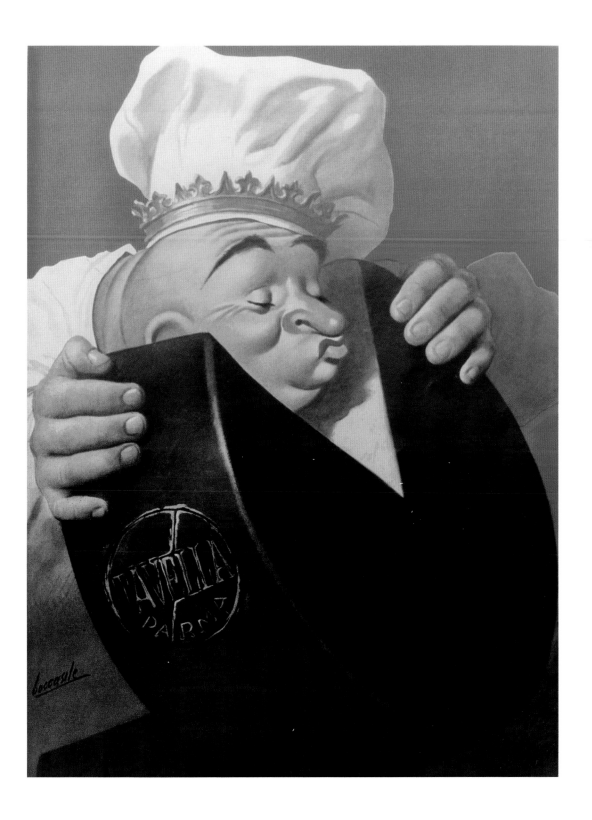

Auricchio "Provolone" Cheese

Auricchio, San Giuseppe Vesuviano (Naples)

1887

Stretched-curd cheeses, either the fresh variety such as mozzarella or the variously-aged varieties such as *provola*, *provolone*, *scamorza* and *caciocavallo*, have a characteristic shape, imprinted by the strings that bind them during their forming or aging phases, which may be considered as an early and, strictly speaking, unwitting packaging scheme.

Founded in 1877 in San Giuseppe Vesuviano in the province of Naples by Gennaro Auricchio, within a vast context of small cheesemakers, the Auricchio company, initially known as *Società corrente*, was one of the first to achieve a scale of production, organization and communication that could effectively address the new phase in the history of food products, which in Italy began around the turn of the century.

The distinctive contribution of Auricchio's *provolone* to the traditional locally-produced cheese was, apart from its protracted aging process, the addition of a "spicy curd," known as "don Gennaro's secret," which gave it a unique flavour. By the end of the nineteenth century it was being exported overseas, thanks to the shape which made it easy to transport without the risk of spoiling. Given the growing market demand, which became impossible to satisfy with the local production of milk alone, his son Antonio moved the business to Cremona, a fertile area, well-stocked with milk cows and cheesemakers whom he introduced to the production of a type of cheese that was virtually unknown in the area. The founding of the first company branch in 1913 was followed by the development of other production units that set in motion a process of expansion, culminating in 1949 with the constitution of a joint-stock company.

While focusing on the development of the alimentary properties of the product, and its recognizable formal aspect based on the pattern of the strings and the brownish colour of the texture, from the very beginning Auricchio also constructed identity strategies, starting with the factory trademark that the owner himself patented around 1910 (no. 10613). The red A crowned with an anchor and the name of the company were transformed in the advertising campaigns into a stylized human figure or a mascot that promoted the cheese, creating a total correspondence between the typology of the product and the company, in the figure of the logo-mascot.

In the seventies, in response to the changes in milk preservation and transportation methods, the company modernized its facilities at Pieve San Giacomo (Cremona) and opened a plant in the United States, in the state of Wisconsin; in 1994 it renovated the production plant at Somma Vesuviana, resuming the production of Auricchio *provolone* cheese in the place where it originated.

Il Buon Paese. Inventario dei migliori prodotti alimentari d'Italia, Slow Food Editore, Bra (CN) 1994, p. 548; *Auricchio 1877-2007: 130 anni di storia*, Litograf 5, Reggio Emilia 2007; C. Ruggero, *L'oro d'Italia. Storie di aziende centenarie e famigliari*, vol. 2, Maggioli, Sant'Arcangelo di Romagna (RN) 2012, pp. 131–38; Archivio centrale dello Stato, Italian Patent and Trademark Office, no. 10613, filed 16.06.1910, reg. 16.08.1910.

→Auricchio trademark (Auricchio Historic Archives, Cremona).

→Advertisement, 1950s (Auricchio Historic Archives, Cremona).

→Production and aging
of provolone cheese, early
twentieth century (Auricchio
Historic Archives, Cremona).

Prosciutto Crudo di San Daniele and Prosciutto Crudo di Parma

Various manufacturers, San Daniele del Friuli (Udine) and Parma

**Roman and Celtic eras;
then second half of the nineteenth century**

Before developing the meat preservation systems typical of the industrial era, many were the methods devised over time to produce and preserve products deriving from the process of butchering and preparing meat products from animals, beef and pork in particular. The quantity of solutions they generated was considerable: cured meats—aged (such as salami), cooked (such as *mortadella* or *soppressata*) or fresh (such as sausage), and products preserved by cooking, sun-drying, marinating or salting (such as ham, bacon, lard, *speck* or *bresaola*).

One property of salt, in particular, is that it maintains the organoleptic qualities of meat over time and reduces moisture, thereby preventing the growth of microbes.

Many different varieties of *prosciutto crudo* may be found in Italy, but there are at least two historic areas of production that were established as far back as Antiquity: San Daniele del Friuli and Parma.

The Celtic peoples who settled in Friuli around 400 B.C. were familiar with techniques for curing pork with salt. Experienced cattle farmers and salt traders found that the area around San Daniele provided the right micro-climatic conditions to establish meat-curing ventures, which lasted through the centuries. Sixteenth-century documents record the characteristic flattened "guitar-shape" of the ham produced there, the result of pressing, a treatment that consisted in laying the hams down on wooden planks, and applying uniform pressure with other planks, essentially with the purpose of thoroughly draining the femoral artery, and ensuring that the liquids formed during the salting process were pressed out. This traditional technique, which was once common throughout Italy but was abandoned when less laborious procedures were developed,

was kept alive in San Daniele, making the form of the ham unique and exclusive, like the trotter that remains on the end of the leg, and helping to drain the moisture from the more problematic areas.

Expertise in pig farming and skill in salt curing, given the vicinity to salt-mining locations, were factors in the origin of ham production around Parma in the Roman Era. When it became a speciality in the Middle Ages, its production became the domain of the lard-makers from Parma, the guild of workers dedicated to preparing and selling cured meats and fats: the processing method was gradually regulated, leading to the production of the classic ham in the shape of a "chicken leg," with its unusual sweet and savoury flavour.

A truly industrial approach to the process was introduced in the early twentieth century when production achieved year-round continuity, independent of the seasons, thanks to the installation of refrigeration systems in the production plants which artificially maintained the proper temperature in the cells where the hams were preserved, leaving the traditional characteristics of the product unchanged.

The institution of the *Consorzio del prosciutto di San Daniele* in 1961 and two years later of the *Consorzio volontario fra i produttori del prosciutto tipico di Parma*, as well as later laws and provisions—leading to the recognition in 1996 of PDO (Protected Designation of Origin) status by the European Community—progressively defined the areas of origin of both the pigs and the production: the *prosciutto di San Daniele* is made exclusively within the municipality of San Daniele, while *prosciutto di Parma* is produced within a delineated hilly area of the province, south of Via Emilia, at an altitude below 900 metres.

The designations were strictly defined and univocal rules were established for the entire supply chain, in order to protect the quality of the raw materials and the proper implementation of the curing process to guarantee the quality of the finished product.

In addition to the typical configuration that distinguishes them, another recognizable signature element is the fire-branded seal on the rind, issued as a certification of authenticity by the Consortiums: for the *prosciutto di San Daniele* it is a stylized silhouette enclosing the initials "SD" and surrounded by the phrase "Prosciutto di San Daniele," for Parma the five-point crown with an oval base that contains the word "Parma." (fb)

E. Faccioli (edited by), *L'eccellenza e il trionfo del porco. Immagini, uso e consumo del maiale dal XIII secolo ai nostri giorni*, Mazzotta-Comune di Reggio Emilia, Milan 1982; G. Ballarini, *Il prosciutto di Parma: prodotto tipico dell'industria e dell'artigianato alimentare. Storia delle origini, metodo di preparazione, il prosciutto di Parma nella gastronomia*, in *Lo scrigno di Crisopoli: piatti e prodotti tipici della gastronomia parmigiana: storia, origini, tradizione*, Tecnografica, Parma 1985; E. Dall'olio, *Prosciutto di Parma*, Agenzia 78, Parma 1989; N. Innocente, R. Mattioni (edited by), *Il Prosciutto: un alimento moderno di origine antica*, Editrice Universitaria Udinese, Udine 2007; G. Gubiani, *San Daniele, L'anima commerciale*, Stampa Tipografica Ogv, Palmanova (UD) 2009; A. Giusa (edited by), *Cinquant'anni per il San Daniele. Storia del Consorzio del prosciutto di San Daniele (1961-2011)*, Consorzio del prosciutto di San Daniele, San Daniele del Friuli (UD) 2011; www.museidelcibo.it/prosciutto.asp; www.prosciuttosandaniele.it.

→Prosciuttificio Friulano
in San Daniele del Friuli (UD).

→A poster with the trademark
of the Consorzio Prosciutto,
1972.

→Fire-branding the Prosciutto
di Parma (Museo del Prosciutto
e dei Salumi di Parma, Musei
del cibo della provincia
di Parma).

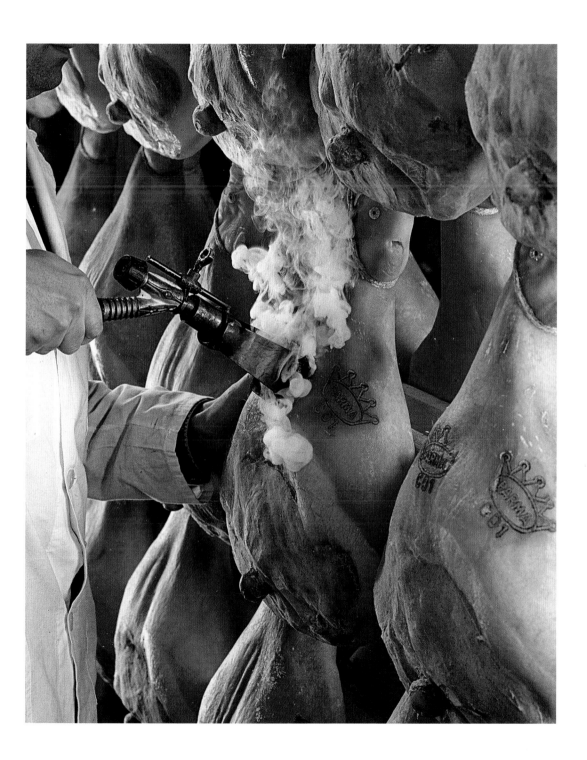

the industrialization of traditional food products
1850–1920

The Design of Food Products within the Industrial System

Within the context of the history of the food industry in Italy,[1] it is important to focus on the more significant aspects involved in the design of the product: from the identification of the contexts, constraints and characteristics underlying the design process that will lead to the development of the artefact-product-food commodity (from the organoleptic concept to the "engineering," within the parameters of the energy-production-logistics systems), to the design of the food-shape, the packaging and communication, and the distribution and retail channels. The age of the industrial revolution brought with it a radical transformation, carving out a new context for food products within the economy, society and culture, which began with the large-scale production of existing foods which until that time, had generally been home-made, or at most produced by hand by farmers and artisans.[2]

This transformation helped to progressively establish the conditions for a mass market, by developing a different organization for standardized mass production, a specific design process that involved a variety of professional figures (engineers, technicians, architects, product and graphic designers), forms of labour division and mechanical production systems powered by new energy sources (first steam, then electricity). And finally, it built a comprehensive system of communication-distribution-sales-consumption around the food product.

These systems, which began to develop around the turn of the century, concerned most typologies of artefacts, including food products. Food however required certain specific means, methods and innovations before it could be introduced into the mechanisms of industrial goods: first and foremost it had to address the congenital problem of spoilage, and create the physical and organoleptic premises for the preservation and transportation of the food product.

The packaging systems provided answers to some of these basic needs: function (to preserve and protect), aesthetics and form (to develop a configuration that represents/contains/distinguishes/signifies the product), information (explaining what the product contains or how to use it).

The earliest phases in the development of the food industry may be divided into two stages.

The initial stage mainly involved activities related to primary processing (mills, distilleries, olive presses, sugar refineries), followed by those concerned with secondary processing (for example, the production of preserves or pasta).

→**Packaging department for Barilla pasta, 1927 (Barilla Historic Archives, Parma).**

[1] See, among others, L. Sicca, *L'industria alimentare in Italia*, Il Mulino, Bologna 1977; G. Gallo, R. Covino, R. Monicchia, "Crescita, crisi, riorganizzazione. L'industria alimentare dal dopoguerra ad oggi," A. Capatti, A. De Bernardi, A. Varni (edited by), *Storia d'Italia, Annali 13. L'alimentazione*, Einaudi, Turin 1998, pp. 269–343; A. Bagnato, *L'industria agro-alimentare italiana. Impresa familiare, cooperative, multinazionali*, L'Albatros, Rome 2004.

[2] This happened at different times depending on the towns and regions. See M. Montanari, F. Sabban (edited by), *Storia e geografia dell'alimentazione*, Utet, Turin 2006, pp. 439 and ff.

The first companies to become mechanized were those that relied on chemical processes (distilleries, beer breweries, etc.) or mills that ground grain (to produce flour, for example)—sectors in which the raw materials were homogeneous and could sustain mechanized processing without damage. This meant, for example, automating the conveying process from one phase of production to the next (on conveyor belts or moving walkways) or instituting procedures for uninterrupted production processes that did not require manual intervention. These changes took place at different speeds: they came earlier in the more advanced *capital-using* food industries, and later in those that relied on manual labour.[3]

In this phase, which led to the vigorous development that took place between the two world wars (which involved much of the production system in Italy), it is important to highlight the origins of a divergence that was later to become characteristic (and again, not just in the food industry).

On one side, the evolution of domestic-based or artisanal activities into small-scale enterprises, a frequent occurrence in traditional food clusters; on the other, and rather early for Italy, the growth of industries with large-scale production and organization structures (in the food preservation industry, for example Cirio, Bertolli or Buitoni; in the pasta industry, Voiello or Agnesi; or the winemaking industry, Florio, Carpano or Cinzano), driven by the necessities of food preservation which required a rational modern and comprehensive planning approach. The process of designing traditionally handmade wares to turn them into industrial products (an undertaking often led by the many expert professionals working within the companies themselves) was motivated by the difficulty of the necessary transition towards processes of "artificialization" (in the phase of production and in the development of the product) intrinsic to the very nature of food itself (perishability and physical and structural instability).

This endeavour took three different needs into account: the need to preserve the identity and the association with the original archetype; the need to introduce judicious variations to the content and form in response to the requirements of production and preservation; the need to enhance the components, which sometimes existed at an embryonic stage but not always, that could help engage a wide range of users and a market, and in particular the development of attractive aesthetics and communication features, in the design of the product, the packaging, the trademark and the graphic design.

From the very beginning, certain components coexisted in the outcome of these entrepreneurial and design processes that might appear antithetical—such as tradition, handcrafting and/or industry; natural and/or artificial; local and/or national. But a founding element in the success of Italian food products is the ability to harmoniously recon-

[3] Ibidem, p. 468.

→Worker at the press, early twentieth century (Barilla Historic Archives, Parma).

→Cutting and bending machine, Officine Zamboni & Troncon, Bologna, catalogue page, 1911 (Barilla Historic Archives, Parma).

→"Doseuse automatique Simplex," manufactured by Tito Manzini e Figli, Parma, double catalogue page, 1931.

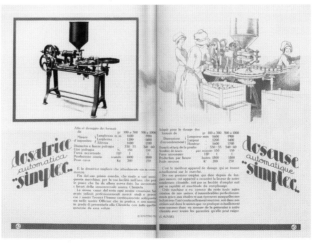

→Bell pepper market at
Carmagnola (TO), 1970s
(Saclà Historic Archives, Asti).

cile elements that appear to be discordant or mutually exclusive. An artefact built with this in mind provides reassurance, because it comes down from the past (real, reconstructed or imaginary), but it also communicates and calls attention to itself by means of the design process and the specific conditions of the industrial system, which are essential to its success and continuity in time. The early phases of modernization therefore demonstrated a certain continuity, but at the same time they broke with the past. Divergence, because the manipulation of nature and know-how builds conditions that no longer depend on the sedimentation of a historical past;[4] persistence, because different techniques and methods end up coexisting. One example is the case of systems for food preservation, where the traditional curing of cheeses and charcuterie coexisted with the technology that not only replaced the handcrafting processes, but optimized them from an economic and hygienic standpoint.

This "formula" may help to explain the longevity of certain traditional products, even when contrary eating philosophies seemed to prevail, yet it seems to be particularly relevant today, in the light of the "pluralistic" approach to food that distinguishes our contemporary society.

The development of industrial foods led to an evolution in the systems of intermediation between agricultural production and consumers, including a different consideration of farm-grown foods, which paradoxically, as a result of industrial processing, are now perceived as safer, being handled to ensure better quality and freshness.

Better transportation conditions also improved the preservation of the food, which received further protection from its packaging, leading to the consolidation of new models of consumption for "industrial" agricultural products that coexisted side by side with the traditional models, which in fact had never been abandoned.[5] The concept of organoleptic stability in the industrial product was gaining acceptance, and the idea of safety began to be associated with the idea of quality. This marked the beginning of an evolution—which continues to the present day—in which the original typical characteristics of a product are increasingly determined "by production techniques rather than by the geographical provenance of the raw materials";[6] the place of origin becomes less of a guarantee and greater faith is placed on the reliability of a manufacturer, on a trademark that protects the identity and certifies the process, production and product.

As for society, the turn of the twentieth century in Italy witnessed a marked improvement in eating habits, though considerable differences remained between the city and the country, and between one city and another. For example, cornbread was gradually replaced by

→**Washing and selection of tomatoes under running water (from** La cucina italiana, **September 1958, p. 801).**

[4] A. Capatti, M. Montanari, La cucina italiana, storia di una cultura, Laterza, Rome – Bari 2005, p. 95.
[5] M. Montanari, F. Sabban (edited by), Storia e geografia dell'alimentazione, cit., p. 440.
[6] A. Capatti, M. Montanari, La cucina italiana…, cit., p. 97.

→Gino Francioli, "La cloche,"
Conti Calda & C., advertising
poster, 1925 (Museo del
Pomodoro, Parma Musei
del Cibo).

→R.F. Quillio (Carlo Pandolfi),
Bel Paese Galbani, advertising
poster, c. 1930 (Galbani Historic
Archives).

wheat bread, pasta and soups become food staples, while potatoes and tomatoes were the new inexpensive produce, available year round.[7] While over the centuries, taste in food had favoured more elite models based on rare ingredients and sophisticated combinations of flavours, with the rise of the middle class, tastes veered towards greater simplicity with less creativity, sustained by a process of standardization in the choice of foods and recipes that is typical of industrial and commercial systems. Yet this tendency did safeguard variations: the products were standard, or started with a bland insipid base, but could be varied and enriched by adding other ingredients. Pasta was a perfect case in point: the base element was always the same or similar (in a variety of formats; fresh or dried) but it could be flavoured with an infinite variety of ingredients.[8]

As for the general organization of a meal, middle-class (and country) cuisine, at the domestic level in particular, limited the role of appetizers (which were reminiscent of the variety available to aristocratic tables) and added cheese to the menu (which had a precise agricultural and traditional connotation) in industrial versions that were easier to deal with because of their form and packaging.[9] As food habits and products changed, so did the organization of the household. Once again, it is worth remembering that these changes occurred in ways that were not necessarily univocal—as confirmed by Capatti and Montanari, who once again underscore the coexistence of different concerns: "The rise in the level of wellbeing led the rural populations to adapt to the lifestyles of the city, though this did not result in uniform consumer spending across the nation. Instead of leading to a predominance of ready-to-eat industrial products made at a distance, even hundreds of miles away from the place of purchase, in Italy wealth brought with it an increased appreciation of the value of traditional foods and recipes (which needed to be protected) and of small-scale productions, and the cult of rare foods and wines."[10]

Preservation Systems and Foods for Collective Populations
A food product becomes part of the industrial system when it can be transported onto the market, and to this end, it must be adequately preserved.

[7] A. Capatti, M. Montanari, La cucina italiana..., cit., pp. 140–43.
[8] A. Capatti, M. Montanari, La cucina italiana..., cit., pp. 140–43.
[9] Ibidem, p. 180.
[10] Ibidem, p. IX.
[11] "Industrial food preservation boasts an important bloodline, with ancestors who were doctors, pharmacists or grocers" (A. Capatti, "Il gusto della conserva," J.L. Flandrin, M. Montanari (edited by), Storia dell'alimentazione, Laterza, Rome – Bari 1997 p.625). See also G. Pedrocco, "Industria del cibo e nuove tecniche di conservazione," ibidem cit.,

pp. 610–22; G. Pedrocco, "La conservazione del cibo: dal sale all'industria agroalimentare," A. Capatti, A. De Bernardi, A. Varni (edited by), Storia d'Italia, Annali 13. L'alimentazione, cit., pp. 379–450.
[12] In 1810, this invention won Appert the prize of twelve thousand franks tendered by Napoleon Bonaparte for the discovery of a method for preserving foods, with the purpose of providing better rations for his armies.
[13] Valeria Bucchetti provides a summary of other significant steps in the development of containers for food, such as the

Two different directions emerged in the research undertaken to address the basic need for "artificial" preservation: one was "technological," leading to the development of industrial refrigeration based on the experiments conducted on procedures and machinery in various locations around the world in the mid-nineteenth century; the other was "chemical," with the goal of ensuring controlled hygienic conditions for foods by means of procedures such as vacuum-packing.[11] French-born Nicolas Appert began to work on sterilization procedures in sealed containers around 1783. He developed a method for vacuum-packing foods known as "appertisation," which consisted in preserving foods in hermetically sealed containers, boiled in water for a certain length of time.[12] This system had several drawbacks, because the glass jars were fragile and could not always be sealed perfectly; they were expensive, and were more appropriate for use in the home and in artisans' workshops than on the industrial scale.

In 1810, Peter Durand patented his version of "appertisation" in England, using a can instead of glass, which he made by hand by bending the tinplate and welding the bottom and top onto it. Durand sold his method to Bryan Donkin and John Hall, who began an industrial-scale production of canned foods the following year, becoming official suppliers to the English Army and Navy. After that, there was a steady stream of innovations in the technology and production processes: in 1847, American-born Allen Taylor patented a machine that produced tinplate cans with rounded, welded edges; that same year, Justus von Liebig canned meat extracts; in 1859, the twist-on cap for glass jars was invented by John Landis Mason; in 1860, the first canned meat industry opened in Chicago, followed in 1875 by the first canned meat manufacturer in Italy, Cirio in Turin.[13]

In the second half of the nineteenth century, these new methods of food preservation and production, and the products they generated, would initially be earmarked for "collective" populations: barracks, schools, hospitals.[14] The military in particular, which became one of the first to adopt these foods at a larger scale, was one of the sectors that drove the creation of food products that would not spoil and would be easy to transport in appropriate containers.[15]

In this sense, an important international precedent, later imported,

airproof tin can with a rubber gasket, the machine for gluing on labels, the metal can with a sliding or hinged lid, the pull-tab, the bottle cap, the folding tube, combined with chromolithographic technology, which makes it possible to print directly on the metal surface (V. Bucchetti, "Packaging," E. Castelnuovo, *Storia del disegno industrial, 1815-1918. Il grande emporio del mondo*, Electa, Milan 1990, pp. 377–80). See, more in general, K.L. Yam, *The Wiley Encyclopedia of Packaging Technology*, John Wiley & Sons, Hoboken, NJ 2010.
[14] M. Montanari, F. Sabban (edited by),

Storia e geografia dell'alimentazione, cit., pp. 449–50.
[15] It is worth briefly recalling how historically significant the military research, experimentation and practices were (for their high level of innovation and criteria of necessity and efficiency) in the design of technical products and the development of the industrial model. See A. Trova, "L'approvvigionamento alimentare dell'esercito italiano dall'Unità alla seconda Guerra mondiale," A. Capatti, A. De Bernardi, A. Varni (edited by), *Storia d'Italia, Annali 13. L'alimentazione*, cit. pp. 497–530.

→Achille Luciano Mauzan,
Conserve alimentari Bertozzi,
advertising poster, 1925 (Museo
del Pomodoro, Musei del cibo
della provincia di Parma).

was the *hard tack* (also known as *sea bread* and then *crackers*) made with flour, water and sometimes salt. Cheap and long-lasting, it was commonly used for food during long journeys across the sea or on military campaigns. It was produced on a large scale, on automatic assembly lines, and may be considered as a mass consumer product ahead of its time.[16] This transformation in the production processes would later influence the sector of cookies, a product originally baked in the home or in artisanal pastry shops. The application of the industrial methods used for the production of hard tack would reduce its price and thereby increase its diffusion.[17]

In Italy, the military was also among the earliest customers and consumers of canned foods, as demonstrated, just to make one example, by the growth of the company founded by Monza-born Pietro Sada (known by its trademark Simmenthal after 1923), which was one of the Army's first suppliers.

After all, it is important to note that the Army (as well as schools and cafeterias) played a decisive role in the dissemination and standardization of the food culture, in a sort of project to unify taste on a national scale, working on two levels. The first focused on the preservation of the memory of the food tradition, of the land, of the local origins of the ingredients and the ways they were cooked; the second moved towards the development of industrial versions, the only practical solution for ensuring production quantities and a minimum guaranteed quality. The military standards introduced a daily diet that included dry pasta, canned meat, cheese and coffee, above the standard level of most of Italy's population at the time.

Italian taste was shaped "by this levelling process in which the middle-class model served as the "highest" benchmark, while its "lower" terms of reference were military rations, cafeterias in factories, schools and summer camps, and hospital kitchens." And again, "mass taste grew by imitation, but was consolidated by cafeterias and food rations."[18]

Packaging: an "Ingredient" of the Food Product
One of the requisites that make a food product compatible with the industrial system is therefore its potential for being effectively preserved, packaged and transported in boxes, bags or bottles.[19]

---

[16] In 1801 Josiah Bent began to produce "water crackers" in Massachusetts; made out of flour and water, they did not spoil during the long journeys across the sea. (He later sold the crackers to the military during the American Civil War.) The name cracker, by which they later came to be known, derives from the "crackling" sound they made as they baked.
[17] M. Montanari, F. Sabban (edited by), *Storia e geografia dell'alimentazione*, cit., p. 449. See B. Haber, *From Hardtack to Homefries: An Uncommon History of American Cooks and Meals*, Simon and Schuster, New York 2010.

[18] A. Capatti, M. Montanari, *La cucina italiana...*, cit., p. 141.
[19] As the most significant moments in the food industry up to the present day, Capatti selects, in order: Appert's vacuum-packing in glass jars; machine-welded sardine cans; condensed milk; instant coffee; pharmafoods, functional foods, bioregulators (A. Capatti, "Artefatti alimentari. Per un museo immaginario del cibo industriale," G. Bosoni, F. Picchi (edited by), *Food design. Il progetto del cibo industriale*, Domus, 823, 2000, pp. 68–71).

Ettore Sottsass sustains: "In my opinion the package is an integral part of the food product. Today most of the food we eat is canned, and we perceive it on the basis of its packaging."[20]

The history of packaging is a unique crossroads of innovation in technology and production, of new materials, new methods of preservation-containment-communication, in which we can read the evolution of design processes, visual languages, culture, society, lifestyles and the economy.[21]

It is interesting to note, in this initial phase, how over time the forms, materials and functional solutions (for storage or opening the packages) basically evolved in two distinct directions.

The first is that in which the packaging system was constrained by the needs of preservation and hygienic-sanitary considerations, as in the case of cylindrical metal cans or hermetically-sealed glass jars. The only way to make the product recognizable, to identify or communicate the contents, was the graphic design on the outside, such as the label, for example.

The second was to develop packaging that could serve more than its technical and functional role and go so far as to ensure the physical protection of the product, communicating by means of the form itself, and even using the surface as a physical support for elements that would define the identity of the food product.[22] Packaging was thus transformed from the mere container it was into a sophisticated artefact for communication, which borrowed the tools of visual rhetoric to promote the quick and easy consumption of goods.[23] Valeria Bucchetti defines it as "an ostensive prosthesis that illustrates the content while gratifying the taste and eye of the consumer."[24] The packaging was progressively viewed as the guarantee of the brand name, since the image of the products represented the entity with which each consumer, when addressing the market, establishes a dialogue and a relationship based on interest, involvement, rejection or total affective and symbolic symbiosis.[25] As Mauro Ferraresi writes: "The packaging is a semantic threshold that brings together an object and a subject."[26]

Certain elements are constant in packaging. First of all, packaging helps to ensure safe consumption of the food inside: a container may be closed after use to extend the life of the product, so that it does

→Vegetables-canning department in the Saclà factory, 1950s (Saclà Historic Archives, Asti).

→Honey packing department in the Ambrosoli factory, 1950s (G.B. Ambrosoli Historic Archives, Ronago).

[20] E. Sottsass, "La simbologia dell'oggetto," F. Burkhardt (edited by), Cibi e Riti, atti del seminario di progettazione svoltosi all'IDZ di Berlino gennaio 1981, printed by A.F. Lucini, Milan 1988, p. 60.
[21] See V. Bucchetti, Packaging, design, storia, linguaggi e progetto, Franco Angeli, Milan 2005. In particular, in the final decades of the twentieth century, this field emerged as an interesting opportunity for debate, research and design on the theme of environmental sustainability.
[22] "The new products shaped their own packages" (A. Capatti, Il gusto della conserva, cit., p. 626).
[23] V. Bucchetti, "Packaging," E. Castelnuovo, Storia del disegno industriale, 1815-1918…, cit., pp. 377–80.
[24] Ibidem, p. 377.
[25] A. Colonetti, "Packaging come sistema," Linea grafica, 5, September 1989, p. 28.
[26] M. Ferraresi, Il packaging oggetto e comunicazione, Franco Angeli, Milan 2003.

→Specialità Agricole Calabresi
e Affini, Reggio Calabria,
price list (from *Le vie d'Italia*,
12, 1948, inside front cover).

not necessarily have to be eaten all at once. It is also subject to rapid obsolescence, both physically (during and after use) and from a visual-formal, technical-functional and informative point of view, due to the evolution of expressive languages, dimensional and technological standards, and communicative contents. But to be recognizable (and attractive) packaging and products must nevertheless maintain certain characteristics that give them continuity over time, to serve as a visual signal, or to reassure the consumer at an emotional level.

And in relation to systems for packing and containing goods, it is worth recording the tight relationship that developed in Italy between the food industries and the companies that produced packaging. Like the industries in the regions of Liguria and Lombardia that produced tinplate cans, the packaging-machine manufacturing cluster around Bologna achieved a level of excellence thanks its capacity for innovating technology and processes, and its ability to respond to the need for flexible production and specialization, as an alternative to or integration of systems of mass production.[27]

This was another specific aspect of Italian entrepreneurship within a global economic system that was far ahead of its time, and characteristic not only of the food industry, but of the fashion and design industry as well.

Canned, Wrapped and Bagged, or Bottled

In this historical phase, an ample range of commodities and typologies for food product design were developed in Italy. The selection in the Inventory seeks to identify archetypal products (the first in a Kublerian "series") from the point of view of typology or for their innovative contribution to technology or design, understood in the wider sense, from the "form" to the packaging to the communication and/or advertising, and the systems of publicity and distribution. In some cases the authorship is clear, in others it may be more controversial, but will nevertheless provide a solid basis for an initial historical and critical approach.

Another preliminary observation regards the fate of "fresh" food products, which is important in relation to the particular tendency towards the standardization of taste and typology that is typical of the industrial model, which considers it as a means to intercept the tastes of a mass consumer base. It might well be sustained that this has had a stronger impact on fresh food, and less on preserved foods.[28] Basically, products that have been preserved either traditionally or industrially, have maintained an identity that is intrinsic to the characteristics of the food or to those that were designed on the basis of the production processes; it is the fresh foods, which require

[27] See R. Curti e M. Grandi (edited by), *Per niente fragile Bologna capitale del packaging*, Editrice Compositori, Bologna 1997.
[28] A. Capatti, M. Montanari, *La cucina italiana...*, cit., p. 95.

SPECIALITÀ AGRICOLE CALABRESI E AFFINI - REGGIO CALABRIA

La più grande organizzazione di rifornimento familiare dei prodotti del suolo

OLIO D'OLIVA EXTRA GENUINO

(non raffinato)

				Prezzo al litro
Lattina da litri 2	. .	**L. 1300**	.	L. 650
Lattina da litri 4	. . .	**L. 2500**	.	L. 625
Lattina da litri 8	.	**L. 4800**	.	L. 600
Lattina da litri 12	.	**L. 7080**	.	L. 590

(Spedizione a mezzo pacco postale assicurato)

Damigiana litri 15	.	**L. 8850**	.	L. 590
Damigiana litri 25	.	**L. 14500**	.	L. 580
Damigiana litri 35	.	**L. 20125**	.	L. 575
Damigiana litri 50	.	**L. 28500**	.	L. 570
Cass. da 24 lattine da litri 1		**L. 15120**	.	L. 630

(Spedizione a mezzo ferrovia)

Il nostro olio è squisito ed a bassissima acidità naturale.

PACCHI AGRUMI

ARANCE (frutto incartato)

Cassetta Extra	Tarocchi	Kg. 20	**L. 2600**	70-80	frutti
»	»	» 10	**L. 1400**	35-40	»
Cassetta tipo **C**		» 20	**L. 1800**	80-90	»
»		» 10	**L. 1000**	40-45	»
Cassetta tipo **B**		» 20	**L. 1700**	100	»
»		» 10	**L. 950**	50	»

MANDARINI (frutto incartato)

Cassetta Extra		Kg. 20	**L. 2200**	160-180	frutti
»	»	» 10	**L. 1200**	60-90	»
»	Lusso	» 20	**L. 2000**	200	»
»	»	» 10	**L. 1100**	100	»

(Spedizione a mezzo ferrovia)

SPECIALITÀ CALABRESI

PACCO SC/10 L. 3900

Fichi imbottiti sciroppati	Kg.	2
Fichi bianchi extra	»	1
Miele di fiori d'arancio	»	1
Marmellata candita d'arance	»	1
Torrone 5 fiori	»	1
Torrone candito	»	0,500
Uva al forno 8 Pacchetti	»	0,640
Mandorle dolci sgusciate	»	0,500
Uva malaga passita	»	0,500

Lordo Kg. 10   Netto Kg. 8.140

PACCO SC/5 L. 1640

Fichi imbottiti sciroppati	Kg.	1
Fichi bianchi extra	»	1
Miele di fiori d'arancio	»	0,500
Marmellata candita d'arance	»	0,500
Torrone 5 fiori	»	0,500
Uva al forno 6 pacchetti	»	0,480

Lordo Kg. 5   Netto Kg. 3,980

PACCO SC/3 L. 990

Fichi imbottiti sciroppati	Kg.	1
Miele di fiori d'arancio	»	0,250
Marmellata candita d'arance	»	0,500
Torrone 5 fiori	»	0,250
Uva al forno 3 pacchetti	»	0,240

Lordo Kg. 3   Netto Kg. 2,240

(Spedizione a mezzo pacchi postali assicurati)

Desiderando ricevere le Specialità Calabresi in pacchi diversamente assortiti conteggiarle come appresso:

Miele di fiori d'arancio	.	al Kg.	**L. 450**	Torrone 5 fiori (alla vaniglia)	al Kg.	**L. 900**
Marmellata candita d'arance		» »	**L. 500**	Torrone candito	» »	**L. 1000**
Fichi imbottiti sciroppati	.	» »	**L. 275**	Mandorle sgusciate	» »	**L. 500**
Uva al forno (pacchetti da gr. 80 cad.)	»	» »	**L. 40**	Uva Malaga passita	. » »	**L. 500**
Fichi bianchi extra		» »	**L. 200**	Mandorlato di fichi	» »	**L. 500**

Nelle ordinazioni attenersi ai seguenti pesi netti: kg. 2.250 4 - 8 12
Per quantitativi inferiori ai 2 kg. netti aggiungere L. 100, per pacco, per maggiori spese.

ESSENZA DI BERGAMOTTO

Flacone da gr.	30	50	75	100	200
	L. 250	**325**	**475**	**600**	**1150**

ESSENZA NATURALE DI AGRUMI

Dose per un litro di acqua di colonia	**L. 550**

LISTINO DI NOVEMBRE (per quanto in tempo) CHIEDERE LISTINO PACCHI AGRUMI

Imballi e recipienti gratis. — Trasporto ferroviario o postale fino al domicilio del cliente a nostro carico. — Dove non esiste servizio la consegna è franco stazione. — Eventuali aumenti delle tariffe ferroviarie saranno gravate sulle spedizioni. — Per la Sordegna solo le spedizioni a mezzo ferrovia vanno soggette a forte maggiorazione. — Pagamento anticipato (oppure 1/3 anticipato ed il resto contro assegno) a mezzo vaglia bancario o postale oppure con versamento sul conto corrente postale 6/15233 intestato a SACARC Catona (Reggio Calabria).

ALCUNI GIUDIZI

Invio prezzo cassetta arance. Ringraziamenti e doverosa attestazione della bontà superlativa dei frutti spediti. Felicitazioni.
Dott. ANDREA FERRARA
Primo Presidente Corte Cassazione
Via Donizzetti, 1
Roma, 7 Giugno 1948

Vi prego spedirmi subito una lattina del Vostro insuperabile olio. da otto litri. A distanza di venti giorni da tale spedizione, vogliate spedirmene un'altra.
Avv. PASQUINI DANTE
Piazza S. Pietro e Lino, 4
Milano, 29 Ottobre 1948

Voi agite colle solite onestà, precisione e sollecitudine: chi è stato servito da Voi una volta è difficile che vi abbandoni.
Comm. ALBERTO BONAZZI Notaio
Via Teodoli, 2
Forlì, 29 Ottobre 1948

Ho avuto qualche tempo fà il Vostro pacco SC/10 in perfetto ordine e ottimamente confezionato. Eccellente tutto il contenuto, sintesi squisita e genuina dei prodotti germinati nella terra calabrese e maturati sotto il sole mediterraneo.
Ing. LUIGI ANGELINI
Via S. Caterina, 15
Bergamo, 31 Gennaio 1948

Migliaia di tali giudizi disponibili.

little or no processing or design intervention, that have paradoxically been more significantly "transformed" by the new manufacturing conditions, and by changing lifestyles and consumer models.

Coherently with our approach, it seemed appropriate for the Inventory to select and organize the products based on the characteristics of their containment system: canned, wrapped or packaged, bottled. The first group encompasses the foods contained in rigid metal, ceramic or glass containers, that serve primarily to preserve the product. In Italy, like the rest of the world, the variety of natural agricultural or animal products found new ways to reach consumers in forms other than fresh. This was true for vegetables (from peeled plum tomatoes, tomato sauce or paste, to vegetables preserved in oil or vinegar), as well as fruit (black cherries, for example), meat and even coffee. For some of these examples, the fundamental innovation focused on the technical properties of the container (which were often protected by patents), such as the pressurization system conceived by Illy for public establishments, to preserve the aroma of the coffee. The terms bagged or wrapped only partially describe the variety of different solutions, but they were less constrained by the requirements of hygienic-sanitary-organoleptic protection. In some cases, we are talking about fresh products protected by adequate wrappers (like cheese, or certain bakery products); in others, the preparation, processing and/or cooking methods were sufficient to set and stabilize the forms and characteristics, so that the packaging was only necessary to wrap and contain the product.

Pasta[29] probably deserved a chapter of its own, because it was during this moment of transition that it became the product-symbol of Italy. Our concise case study attempts to explore the history of pasta in the light of the advances in the design and production processes of pasta itself, and through its forms of communication and advertising.

For cheeses, we focused on the solutions that marked a turning point in the development of a comprehensive system of industrial ideation-production-communication, not coincidentally led by companies from the Lombardia region, which was the engine of economic development and modernization in those years. As a food product, cheese was reconceived within a design process that sought to reconcile the original natural food with the need to develop a different formal configuration around which to build a recognizable identity that would stand out amidst a vast array of similar products. Going one step further than the partial fragmented artisan-based approach, the rectangular Mio cheese spread with its unmistakable box represents the fulfilment of a complementary-synthetic system for food artefacts,

→**Interior of a municipal grocery in Milan, 1920s (Civico Archivio Fotografico, Milan).**

[29] We chose not to include rice which—as a forced synthesis that did require a number of necessary advancements in the production processes—went from the plant to bags and boxes most of which looked the same (except for the label). A different story, in the contemporary era, is the advent of parboiled rice, a functional organoleptic project conceived to satisfy the new "fast" cooking and living styles.

→Galbani stand at the Fiera
campionaria internazionale
in Milan, c. 1927 (Galbani
Historic Archives).

→Interior of the Unione
Cooperativa di Consumo
in Novara, early twentieth
century (Branca Historic
Archives, Milano).

on the following pages
→La Rocca, double-page
advertisement (from *L'Italia
nel Mondo*, 3, March 1942,
pp. 164–65).

developed on the basis of an integral design approach: product, production machinery, packaging and communication are the result of an integral conception that is expressed in an immediate, unitary and comprehensive manner.

The chapter illustrating traditional pastry products is particularly rich, focusing on cakes, biscuits, chocolate and candy. Most of the specialties that existed on the territory were developed in a version that lifted them out of their local context, and in some cases brought them excellent levels of distribution throughout Italy: examples are the tall *panettone* from Milan, the low *panettone* from the Piemonte region, or the *pandoro* from Verona. For many companies, and many different product typologies, the process leading to significant national and international recognition began to take root at the close of the nineteenth century.[30]

The organization of the part on liquids in a container to drink or for seasoning foods (mostly in glass bottles) presented several problematic aspects. This was such a broad area that it became necessary to establish a set of criteria. It is important once again to assert that this study is not focused on the assessment of the project for the food's distinguishing qualities, its properties so to speak, such as taste and so on. So how do we approach wine or oil, for example, which are absolutely characteristic of our country and its diet, when the contents are all bottled in similar containers (for example the standard for wine is the Bordeaux-style bottle) and the communication is limited to the label alone (though it is often quite interesting)? The study and the selection therefore concentrated on the morphological archetypes of the packaging (from the Chianti flask to the oil can, to the triangular bottle of Vecchia Romagna brandy) or on typological innovations of the product (from the "ritual of the aperitif" based on *vermouth* or *premixed* single servings, to the bottling of mineral water, which descended from the tradition of thermal spas).[31]

[30] Of course there are many products that do not fit this analysis. One example is *torrone*, a traditional product dating back at least to the nineteenth century, whose interest lies not only in the manufacturers, but also in the variety of versions developed by many Italian cities. A quick list might include Caltanisetta (Michele Geraci, 1870), Cremona (Sperlari, 1836–83), Asti (Mombercelli di Asti, Melchiorre Barbero, 1883) Grinzane Cavour, Cuneo (Giuseppe Sebaste, 1885), Benevento (San Marco dei Cavoli, Innocenzo Borrillo, 1891), L'Aquila (fratelli Nurzia, 1901). Without forgetting how a specific type, the *mandorlato*, is identified exclusively with the city of Cologna Veneta.
[31] A typology that is difficult to handle is the *amaro*, the bitter digestive. There are many examples, varieties, blends and tastes, but their design is not particularly distinguishable. Many of them boast important entrepreneurial and industrial histories, and significant communication and advertisement projects: they include Fernet Branca (Bernardino Branca and Maria Scala, Milan, 1845); Amaro Averna (Salvatore Averna, Caltanisetta, 1868); Amaro Ramazzotti (Fratelli Ramazzotti, 1877); Amaro Barulio (Francesco Peloni, Bormio, 1875); Amaro Montenegro (Stanislao Cobianchi, Zola Pedrosa, Bologna, 1885). For a useful and well-informed survey of Italian food products see C. and G. Padovani, *Italia Buonpaese. Gusti, cibi e bevande in centocinquant'anni di storia*, Blu Edizioni, Turin 2011.

CONSERVE DI PESCI

Tonno all'olio - Tonno bianco - Tonnetto all'olio - Tonnetto al naturale uso Salmone - Sardine all'olio - Aringhe fresche in salsa - Tonno bianco con verdura - Merluzzo fresco - Aringhe fresche affumicate Filetti di acciughe sott'olio - Filetti di merluzzo - Condimento di magro: « Venerdì » - Bel sugo - Budino con pesce - antipasti.

LA ROCCA
(Italien) BARI

FRUTTA e VERDURA IN CONSERVA

Conserve di pomodoro - Estratti e concentrati di pomodoro - Confettura di frutta - Marmellata di frutta Frutta sciroppata - Gelatina di frutta Ortaggi al naturale - Frutta congelata - Giardiniera all' aceto.

LA ROCCA

(Italien)   BARI

Cirio Peeled Tomatoes

Cirio, Turin, later San Giovanni a Teduccio, Naples,
now Conserve Italia, San Lazzaro di Savena (Bologna)
1875

One of the founders of the food preservation industry in Italy, Francesco Cirio (1836–1900) initially exported agricultural products to France, before founding his own business in Turin in 1856, when he opened the first factory for canning peas. To prevent spoilage, he relied on the new "appertisation" technique developed by French inventor Nicolas Appert in 1810, which consisted in sterilizing fresh foods, boiled and sealed in glass jars, by boiling the jars they were contained in. This "pasteurization" technique was developed in 1812 by Bryan Donkin and John Hall in England, associating Appert's technique with the use of tin cans to contain the food, applying a method patented by Peter Durand.

In Italy, points out Vittorio Gregotti, the tin can was one of the first examples of a mass-produced industrial product that brought together many different aspects of the design culture: on the one hand the artisan tinsmith, who cut the sheets of tin to predetermined sizes and thereby supervised the construction of the object, on the other the artist-designer who created the label made to encourage consumption.
If the synthesis between these two events may be conceived as a form of design, the proliferation of canned foods led not only to the dawn of the food industry but also, in the encounter with the Modernist culture, to the rise of a new idea of "home economics."
After winning a series of acknowledgments

at the Universal Exposition in Paris in 1867, among others, Cirio established his first factory in Turin in 1875, followed by others in the Campania region after the unification of Italy, at Castellamare di Stabia, San Giovanni a Teduccio (Naples) and in the provinces of Caserta and Salerno. The original peas were soon followed by meat broth, green beans, asparagus and various types of fruit; but the real success came with the tomato, the San Marzano variety in particular, a produce that would forever link its name to the company, and even become synonymous with it: the Cirio plum tomato.
After reaching an agreement with the railways to ensure transportation at advantageous prices and a rapid

Come il Pomodoro fresco...

POMIDORO PELATI
CIRIO

Fino al 30 Giugno 1965, ogni etichetta di "POMIDORO PELATI CIRIO", di "PI-SELLI CIRIO", di "SUPER-CIRIO" da 1/5 e di "CONDI-CIRIO", vale per DUE!

78   **the industrialization**   / **conserved**
      of traditional food products
      1850–1920

solo 4 pomidoro
su 10 diventano
Pelati Cirio

i più ricchi di sole, i più ricchi di sapore

CIRIO

I pomidoro contenuti in
questa scatola sono del-
la rinomata qualità San
Marzano che la CIRIO
coltiva nella famosa zo-
na agricola vesuviana.
Maturati sulla pianta al
sole, sono scelti con cu-
ra, uno per uno: i più
polposi, i più ricchi di
colore e di sapore di-
ventano pelati Cirio.
Per aumentare la loro
resa come condimento,
è stata aggiunta una
giusta dose di fragran-
te succo di pomodoro
condensato.

...midoro Pelati

Magnifici regali con le etichette Cirio! Per sceglierli richiedete a Cirio - 80146 Napoli-il giornale "Cirio Regala" (Aut. Min. Conc.)

CIRIO
IL SAPORE DEL SOLE

→Advertisement, 1965
(Cirio – Conserve Italia Historic
Archives, San Lazzaro
di Savena).

→Advertisement, 1970
(Cirio – Conserve Italia Historic
Archives, San Lazzaro
di Savena).

dispatch for the time, he stocked up on raw materials in southern Italy, transporting the food products in the first refrigerated freight cars to various parts of Europe, from France to Russia. At the same time, he expanded his fields of activity, dealing in eggs, milk products, poultry, wine and more, going into joint ventures with many companies, which led him to transform his own company into a public company (*Società anonima di esportazione Agricola Cirio*) in 1885, in partnership with various banks and personalities from the Swiss and Italian banking worlds, including the brothers Pietro and Paolo Signorini. It remained based in Turin, with affiliated production facilities and retail emporiums in Castellamare di Stabia and in Milan, Paris, Vienna, Brussels and Berlin. Upon the death of the founder, and with the help of the brothers Pietro and Clemente Cirio, the *Società generale delle conserve alimentari Cirio* was constituted in San Giovanni a Teduccio, with the majority share of the stock held by the Signorini family. Though it was a major supplier of canned meat to the army during the two world wars, the company made tomatoes one of its leading products, which it processed in several different versions, for example the condensed Super-Cirio, marketed during wartime to make up for the scarcity of tin cans, or the spicy Cirio Tomato Ketchup, which was publicized in the twenties

by association with elegant restaurants featuring an American iconography, "where they dance the shimmy." At the end of the nineteenth century, the Cirio company built a capillary distribution network, thanks to its use of advertising and promotional tools. The label registered in 1889 (no. 1757) introduces the radiating red star with the rearing horse in the middle. These elements progressively disappeared— first the horse and then the star—, and in the fifties the logotype alone remained as the trademark, in a serif typeface. The subsequent trademark, which featured the name in a sans-serif typeface inside a green contoured frame, was designed in 1970 by Gio Rossi, who later revised it in 1985 to add the slogan "*come natura crea*," "just as Nature made it," which the company had used before. Promotions such as free books for the home—written by Lidia Morelli— and labels to be collected and redeemed for prizes, accompanied the posters and advertisements designed in the thirties and forties by famous illustrators and graphic designers such as Leonetto Cappiello (1875–1942), Achille Luciano Mauzan (1883–1952), Sepo (Severo Pozzati, 1895–1983), Fortunato Depero (1892–1960) and Luigi Veronesi (1908–1998), working with agencies such as Acme-Dalmonte. Of all the television commercials broadcast on *Carosello*

since the programme began, the most unusual were those created by artist Pino Pascali in the mid-sixties. The company was a subsidiary of the Cragnotti & Partners Group in the early nineties, after gravitating in the sphere of Iri-Sme for several decades following a period of alternating fortunes. In 2004, Cirio became a part of the Gruppo Cooperativo Conserve Italia. (fb)

L. Agnello, *Francesco Cirio*, in *Dizionario Biografico degli Italiani*, vol. 25, Enciclopedia Italiana Treccani, Rome 1981 (available online at www.treccani.it/enciclopedia/francesco-cirio (Dizionario-Biografico)/Cirio); V. Gregotti, *Il disegno del prodotto industriale: Italia 1860-1980*, edited by M. De Giorgi, A. Nulli, G. Bosoni, Electa, Milan 1986, p. 49; F. Fontanella, M. Di Somma, M. Cesar, *Come cambiano i marchi*, Ikon, Milan 2003, pp. 96–98; N.D. Basile, *All'origine del "Made in Italy." I primi 150 anni della Cirio*, FG, Modena, 2006; Archivio centrale dello Stato, Italian Patent and Trademark Office, n. 1757, filed 21.02.1889, reg. 6.05.1889.

→Advertisement, 1937 (Cirio – Conserve Italia Historic Archives, San Lazzaro di Savena).

→Leonetto Cappiello, advertising poster, 1921 (Cirio – Conserve Italia Historic Archives, San Lazzaro di Savena).

CIRIO

Simmenthal Canned Beef

Simmenthal, Monza; now the Bolton Group, Milan

1923

SIMMENTHAL
...talmente buona!

In 1881 Pietro Sada (1855–1935), who ran a restaurant in Milan, studied new food preservation methods and founded a small company so that he could can the boiled meats in jelly that he produced in his shop in Crescenzago (Milan). At the turn of the century, Frenchman Nicolas Appert had invented a method for preserving fresh foods in airtight containers, a process known as *appertisation,* which Francesco Cirio also experimented with. When Sada began to receive substantial orders from the army for "canned beef," in 1915 he opened a second production facility in Crescenzago, expanding his business. His sons took over the company, but soon parted ways, and in 1923 Alfonso, known as Gino (1888–1964), founded the Alfonso Sada company in Monza—the trademark was registered in 1924 (no. 27726)—also dedicated to the production of beef in jelly, which Alfonso called Simmenthal (no. 39499, 1928). His ready-to-eat food product soon began to change the eating habits of Italians, sustained by company communication, starting with the choice of the name, which he borrowed from the Simmenthal breed of cattle raised in the Simme valley in the Bernese Oberland of Switzerland, a breed distinguished by its typical red and white spotted coat, and portrayed on the trademark from the very start. Between the thirties and the forties the company produced as many

as twenty-five thousand cans a day. The advertising in that period highlighted how convenient and economical it was: "Here is a delicious food that stimulates the appetite. It is nutritious and economical. Simmenthal, exquisite canned beef, may be eaten at room temperature with fresh salad," or "At home, or everywhere, it is a nutritious ready-to-eat meal made of the finest boiled meat." To make it easier to use, a new system was patented in the mid-thirties for opening the can: it consisted in a key fastened to the top of the can, made to insert a tab on the end of the lid and roll it up to open the can (no. DE 633372). In the fifties the company's communication focused on the health benefits of their beef, with slogans such as "Food for sportsmen"; over the following decade, the advertising campaigns were created by Armando Testa: "Eat more meat eat more Simmenthal."

Though the Monza-based company was undoubtedly the first and most famous producer of canned meat in Italy, other brands were established after World War II in the area north of Milan. They included Montana, a name registered in 1948 by Acsal (*Azienda carni società aninoma lissonese*) founded in Milan in 1941 (no. 86679) and renowned for its commercials featuring a cowboy named Gringo, broadcast on the television show *Carosello* in the sixties and seventies, or Manzotin, which

in the mid-sixties also became the name of the company based in Cermenate (Como), founded by the Zerbi family. These companies and brands changed hands many times over the years, bearing witness to the hard times encountered by this typology of product, conceived as an artefact that embodied the modern lifestyle and food innovation, but was subsequently forced to contend with the evolution of consumer habits and tastes. (fb)

Archivio centrale dello Stato, Italian Patent and Trademark Office, no. 27726, filed 6.03.1924, reg. 11.11.1924; no. 39499, filed 29.06.1928, reg. 21.07.1930; no. 86679, filed 3.06.1948, reg. 27.02.1949; *Befestigung eines doppelarmigen hochschwenkbaren Öffnungshebels am Deckel einer Konservendose,* no. DE 633372, reg. 25.07.1936.

→Studio Testa, advertisement (from *Pubblicità in Italia, 1968-1969,* suppl. to "L'Ufficio Moderno – la pubblicità," 11, 1968, p. 52).

→Patent no. DE633372, 25 July 1936.

→Advertisement (from *La lettura,* 6, 1 June 1938, p. 569).

→Advertisement (from *La lettura,* 10, 1 October 1938, p. 957).

Fig. 1

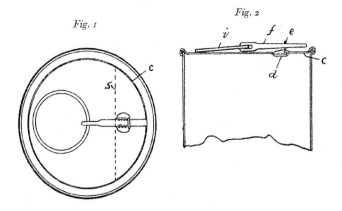

Fig. 2

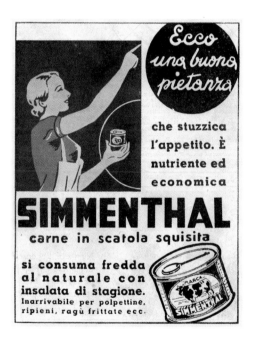

Amarena Fabbri Cherries in Syrup

Fabbri, Portomaggiore (Ferrara, later Bologna)

1920s

In 1905 Gennaro Fabbri (1860–1935) founded the *Premiata distilleria liquori G. Fabbri* inside a former grocery store with an attached fermenting cellar, and began to produce and sell liqueurs. When demand started to grow, in 1914 he transferred the company to the more ample spaces in Borgo Panigale, in Bologna, where it is still located today.

In the twenties, the production of liqueurs grew to include alcoholic and alcohol-free syrups, and a new product, "Marena con frutto," based on a recipe by Rachele Buriani, the owner's wife. Initially dispatched in demijohns, it grew immensely popular thanks to the idea of selling the product in ceramic jars, in other words of creating a container that looked valuable and refined, and could also in part be reused. The first jars were manufactured by the *Società cooperative ceramiche Minghetti* in Bologna; they were later replaced by the more famous white jar with blue ornamental motifs, with a contoured body on a circular base, created by ceramic artist Riccardo Gatti (1886–1972) in Faenza: inspired to a certain extent by the language of the Liberty style, it was also influenced by the forms and decors of Chinese art, and is still in production today in a version that is very similar to the original. In the twenties, Fabbri commissioned other jars from the Faenza-based *Fornace ceramica Bubani*, with black ornamental motifs on a white background, and from the *Cooperative Trerè*, with rust-red decors against a white background.

But it was the blue and white jar, crowned by a lid with a knob on top and substantially unchanged over time, though it is now slightly more rounded in the upper part, that has been the company's enduring signature element, featuring the name of the product written with a particularly recognizable type of lettering. The jar and product convey a soothing old-fashioned image and is the foundation on which Fabbri has built its continuity and success.

G.C. Bojani (edited by), *Riccardo Gatti (1886-1972): ceramiche*, exhibition catalogue, Comune di Faenza, Faenza (RA) 1987; R. Savini, *I faentini ceramisti*, Studio Grafico Publialfa, Faenza (RA) 1992, pp. 83, 85; G.C. Bojani, *Riccardo Gatti*, entry in *Dizionario biografico degli italiani*, vol. 52, Istituto dell'Enciclopedia Treccani, Roma 1999 (available online at http://www.treccani.it/enciclopedia/riccardo-gatti_%28Dizionario_Biografico%29/); *Cento anni Fabbri. 1905-2005*, Fabbri 1905-Editrice Compositori, Bologna 2004.

→Riccardo Gatti, drawing and prototype for a ceramic pot, 1929 (Fabbri Archives 1905).

→Blue and white ceramic pot, 1920s (Fabbri Archives 1905).

→Ceramic pot and production line of the Amarena in the factory at Anzola dell'Emilia, 2004 (Fabbri Archives 1905).

Illy Coffee
Illy, Trieste
1933

The port of Trieste—a transit hub for coffee destined for Central Europe which inaugurated a dedicated Stock Exchange in 1904—still handles over one third of Italian coffee imports. After World War I, Hungarian-born Francesco Illy (1892–1956) came to Trieste where, in 1933, he opened an industrial concern to process coffee and cocoa, in partnership with Hermann Hausbrandt who had been working in the field since 1892, and had invented roasted coffee and the roasting process itself.

The history of the company was from the very beginning driven by innovation and by design. In 1932, Illy patented a pressurization system, which it registered in 1934 (no. 322644), to preserve the coffee's aroma. By replacing the air contained in the cans with pressurized inert nitrogen gas, the aromas were stabilized, enhanced and preserved over time inside the structure of the coffee bean. This application made it possible for industrially-roasted coffee to travel without spoiling, as it used to in the coffee bags that offered no protection from atmospheric conditions. The company began to supply businesses all over Italy and later around the world.

The glass jar, which was both heavy and fragile, was replaced by a three-kilogram tinplate can—which is still manufactured in the company's industrial facilities—and which in the eighties was also produced in a 250-gram version for the consumer market, visually linking the quality of home-brewed coffee with that of coffee served at the bar. The surface of the can, which was originally black to highlight the red square of the logo—designed in 1966 by architect Carlo Mangani—was changed to a satin-finished silver in 2001, echoing the finish of the professional product, with the new red and white logo redesigned a few years earlier by artist James Rosenquist. The company's attention to the consumer is evident in the configuration and technical solutions adopted for the can. Such as the "easy open" system, which smoothly releases the pressurized gas with no need to perforate the can with a utensil; the hermetically sealed lid; the slightly raised centre of the lid, in correspondence with the indentation on the bottom, that makes it possible to stack the cans; the use of recyclable materials.

Demonstrating the company's emphasis on research, Illy, which has always been run by a member of the family, first Ernesto (1925–2008), then Riccardo (1955) and Andrea (1964), has filed many other patents over time: from the Illetta professional espresso machine in 1935 (no. US 2152410 A), to the pre-portioned paper espresso pods in 1974 (Ese – Easy Serving Espresso), which triggered the transformation in the way coffee is served today [**Illy Paper Coffee Pods** p. 268], to the system for the digital selection of coffee beans in 1988. The Illetta in particular, an automatic espresso machine with an open boiler, also intended for bars, is the forefather of today's professional espresso machine, replacing steam with air pressure that forced the water through the coffee without burning it.

Illy is clearly not the only Italian industry in the business of roasting coffee and developing solutions for production and design. For example, the oldest coffee-roasting industry is Caffè Vergnano, founded in Chieri (Turin) in 1882 by Domenico Vergnano, whereas credit must be given to Lavazza, founded in 1895 in Turin by Luigi Lavazza and a symbol of Italian coffee around the world, for the idea of packaging and selling coffee blends, rather than individual varieties, in 1910. (fb)

G. Muneratto, *Il visual design nelle organizzazioni*, Franco Angeli, Milan 2007, pp. 113–20; F. and R. Illy, *Dal caffè all'espresso*, Mondadori, Milan 1989; A.M. Sette, *Disegno e design. Brevetti e creatività*, exhibition catalogue, Fondazione Valore Italia, Rome 2010, pp. 239–40; Conversation between the author and Furio Suggi Liverani, director of research and innovation at Illy, 11 December 2014; Archivio centrale dello Stato, Italian Patent and Trademark Office, no. 322644, reg. 19.12.1934; United States Patent, *Apparatus for the preparation of coffee infusions*, no. US 2152410 A, priority 9.09.1935; reg. 28.08.1936, publ. 28.03.1939.

→Xanty Schawinsky/Studio Boggeri, advertising poster, 1934.

→Sealed can of coffee
preserved with the
pressurization system, 1930s,
and the can used today in public
establishments.

the industrialization / **conserved**
of traditional food products
1850–1920

Saclà Vegetables
Preserved in Oil or Vinegar

Saclà, Asti
1939

Sacla, the acronym for *Società anonima commercio lavorazioni alimentari*, was created in 1939 by Secondo Ercole, known as "Pinin," based on an intuition he had for the evolution of Salpa (*Stabilimento astese lavorazione prodotti alimentari*), the company he had founded in 1923 to sell fresh fruits and vegetables, an activity that had begun to take root in the region to supplant the cultivation of silk worms, in sharp decline for years. Ercole's idea for the new company, founded with his wife Piera Campanella and based in the centre of Asti, was to preserve the surplus of vegetables harvested locally during the warmer months, to make them available year-round. The preservation of vegetables in oil, vinegar or brine, traditionally a labour-intensive domestic process that provided exclusively for the family, now began to be applied at the industrial scale.

Hence a product derived from a domestic practice was introduced into the modern food distribution and marketing chains, making it possible to prepare hors-d'oeuvres and main courses much faster than before. Initially the company not only produced marmalades, tomato concentrate and brined vegetables, but also made dried vegetables for Arrigoni, a short-lived specialty for one of the most important companies in the preserved foods sector at the time. Thus in the fifties, thanks to the improved economic conditions of the country and the technological innovations that upgraded its production facilities, Sacla grew beyond the regional scale, spurred by the acquisition in 1956 of Sipa (*Società industriale prodotti alimentari*), which controlled a production plant in Rottofreno (Piacenza). The innovative decision to introduce family-size glass jars with a plastic lid increased the consumer base for its wide range of products, such as peas, lima beans and string beans.

Over the following decade, Sacla began to specialize its production, restricting it to pickled vegetables, vegetables preserved in oil and olives, since the canned vegetable industry had become too competitive, and adding the pasteurization of the vegetables to the production process. It adopted twist-off caps to make the jars easier to open and close, and at the same point in time inaugurated an original production of pitted olives—brined, whole or stuffed—which it packaged in plastic bags, supported by a successful advertising campaign launched in 1970 that read "Olivoli, Olivolà, Olivoli, Olive Saclà!," conceived by the Carlo Repetto advertising agency (Bozzetto Film production). The agency also suggested putting an accent on the final "a" of the name, adding yet another signature element to the company's corporate identity. In the decades that followed, still run by the founding family, Saclà continued to cultivate its innovative approach, seeking to respond to and/or anticipate the changes in consumer needs and tastes—introducing the Acetelli in 1977, pickled vegetables with a lower degree of acidity, and replacing the seed oil with olive oil—while developing new solutions for its production systems, packaging and communication. (fb)

C. and G. Padovani, *Italia Buonpaese*, Blu Edizioni, Turin 2011, p. 214; C. Rabaglino (edited by), *Saclà* in www.imprese.san.beniculturali.it/web/imprese/percorsi/dossier.

→Canning department, 1950s (Saclà Historic Archives, Asti).

the industrialization of traditional food products 1850–1920 / conserved

→Label for the Delizia peas, 1950 (Saclà Historic Archives, Asti).

→Agenzia Repetto, inside of an advertising brochure, late 1960s (Saclà Historic Archives, Asti).

Mutti Tomato Concentrate

Mutti, Basilicanova – Montechiarugolo (Parma)

1951

Of the many companies that produce tomato preserves, Mutti owes it fame primarily to its innovative packaging for food products.

The Fratelli Mutti factory, dedicated to processing tomatoes, was founded in 1899 by Marcellino (1862–1941) and Callisto Mutti (1870–1936) in Basilicanova, in the municipality of Montechiarugolo in the province of Parma, at a time when the food industry and the tomato-processing industry in particular were growing rapidly, hand in hand with the expansion of local agriculture which chose to invest in this particular crop because it was more profitable than the traditional corn. The increase in production was accompanied by the surge of exports, well-represented by Mutti, which distinguished itself among producers for the many official acknowledgments it won in international competitions, such as the I degree Gold Medal Diploma for the production of Double concentrate at the International Agricultural and Industrial Exposition in Rome and the Golden Palm at the Universal Exposition in Paris in 1925.

Until the forties, tomato preserves, a sector in which the company had been specialized since 1910 and for which it abandoned all its other activities in the fields of agriculture, animal husbandry, cheese and ham production, exploiting the methodologies developed as a result of Nicolas Appert's discovery in 1810, were canned in vacuum-packed tinplate cans sold to consumers.

Under the guidance of Ugo Mutti (1893–1980), who took over from his father Marcellino in 1941 as the executive director and head of research for production technologies and products, in 1951 the company developed an innovative idea: to package the tomato paste in an aluminium tube. The company thus won over consumers, guaranteeing hygiene, easier dosage, convenience and longer freshness than the traditional cans in use until then: at a time when refrigerators were few and far between, once opened, the can could no longer keep the product fresh, as the oxygen in the air drained the tomatoes of colour and flavour. Mutti borrowed the idea of the tube from toothpaste, and in collaboration with the *Tubettificio La Metallurgica* in Milan (which had produced the first aluminium tube with a rounded head the year before, for Binaca toothpaste), introduced it into the food industry for its Triple concentrate: no one, until then, had ever put "warm" products with some acid content into a receptacle of this kind. In the early phases of distribution, a certain wariness towards this new format was partly overcome thanks to a particular detail, which earned it the nickname "the tube with the thimble": instead of the traditional cap, the tube was closed with a screw-on cap made of Bakelite in the shape of a thimble, that could actually be reused for sewing when the tube was finished. The choice of a small package to contain the tomato paste made it much easier to use as an ingredient, and in the end, its favourable market reception led many other companies to adopt the same solution.

Over the years, Mutti has been able to maintain a recognizable identity as a product of the finest quality, with a graphic design inspired by traditional iconography and distinguished by the unmistakable trademark with the picture of the two lions, officially registered in 1918 (no. 17020).

The technological innovations developed for its entrepreneurial ventures contributed to the overall modernization of a sector that had made no substantial progress in decades.

G.L. Podestà, entry Ugo Mutti, in *Dizionario biografico degli italiani*, vol. 77, Istituto dell'enciclopedia Treccani, Rome 2012, available online at http://www.treccani.it/enciclopedia/ugo-mutti_%28Dizionario-Biografico%29/; F. Mutti, *Impresa agroalimentare e adattamento al cambiamento dei consumi*, in *Realismo e innovazione per costruire nell'incertezza. Lavoro e imprese nell'agroalimentare*, Maggioli, Santarcangelo di Romagna (Rimini) 2013; Archivio centrale dello Stato, Italian Patent and Trademark Office, no. 17020, filed 12.06.1918, reg. 29.10.1918.

→Mutti tube-filling department, 1956 (Mutti Archives).

**the industrialization
of traditional food products**
1850–1920

/ conserved

→Metallurgica Milanese (later
Tubettificio La Metallurgica),
advertisement, 1947
(Tubettificio La Metallurgica
Historic Archives, Albignano
d'Adda).

→Postcard, 1950s (Mutti
Archives).

Pasta

Various manufacturers
late eighteenth century

Known in Italy since the fourteenth century, pasta was made by hand for centuries in a process in which the dough was kneaded with a hand-operated "gramola," cut and extruded with a manual press, and sun-dried. The mechanized manufacturing methods appeared in the late eighteenth century in various parts of Italy, when the first "gramola a stanga" was introduced (a kneading machine consisting in a wooden board and a bar to press down the dough) and the pasta was shaped with wooden screw-presses. Exploiting a microclimate that was congenial to the manufacturing process, the most important centres for the production and exportation of pasta were therefore concentrated around Naples and the coast of Liguria; both of these locations were near the sea, which also gave them an advantage in terms of shipping. The sector was radically transformed as the entire production cycle gradually became automated between the end of the nineteenth century and the early twentieth century, producing larger quantities and, thanks to more modern systems of artificial drying, releasing the needs of production from the constraints of geographical position.

The number of pasta industries in Italy is considerable; this book will only mention a few that are notable for the innovation of their production processes, or the characteristics of their products. Filippo De Cecco, who founded the eponymous company at Fara San Martino (Chieti) in 1886, must be given credit for inventing a hot-air drying plant in 1889, making it possible to produce pasta in locations far from the coastal microclimates and to extend the lifetime of the product, creating the conditions for selling pasta in areas far from the manufacturing venues. This led the company, at the end of the nineteenth century, towards a process of internationalization: in 1904 it began to export its products regularly to the United States, ten years later to Argentina, where its main customers were mostly Italian immigrants.

The innovations of the time therefore redrew the map of pasta manufacturing plants, opening new possibilities for variations in the formats.

In the Liguria region, at Pontedassio (Imperia), the Pastificio Agnesi had been producing pasta since 1824 (in 1999 it was sold to the Colussi Group). It was, among other things, the first to package its pasta in 1920, instead of selling it in bulk in the traditional sacks. In the area between Gragnano and Torre Annunziata (Naples)—which was famous since the eighteenth century for its "white art"—the Antico Pastificio Giovanni Voiello, founded in 1879 (and sold to Barilla in 1973), was one of the first, early on, to adopt electricity-powered machinery and technology that could control moisture and temperature.

The widespread diffusion across the nation consequent to the industrialization process, is substantiated by the rise of the Pastificio Buitoni (a Nestlé brand since 1988), one of the precursors of mechanization, founded in 1827 by Giovanni Battista Buitoni (1769–1841) in Sansepolcro (Arezzo), a town located in the Grand Duchy of Tuscany near the borders of the Vatican State and the Umbria region, along the Tiber River. Buitoni began to diversify in 1884, when it introduced pasta with gluten, in response to the nutritional needs of an underfed population. The packages, sealed to guarantee freshness and quality, also became elements of communication for the product. This goes to show how, since the early decades of the century, advertising had become one of the cornerstones of the company's

→Pastificio Voiello, advertising poster, 1930s (Barilla Historic Archives, Parma).

→Renato Rovetta, *Industria del pastificio o dei maccheroni*, Hoepli, Milan 1921, II ed. Exp., cover and illustrations inside (Fondazione Isec, Sesto San Giovanni).

94   **the industrialization   / packaged**
      of traditional food products
      1850–1920

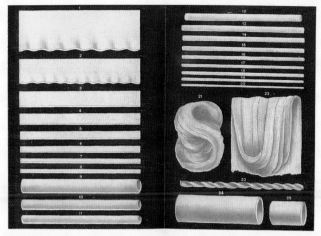

Fig. 131.

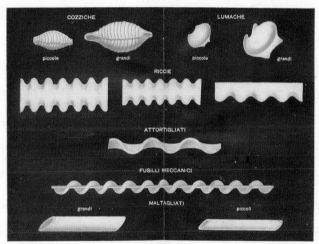

Fig. 135.

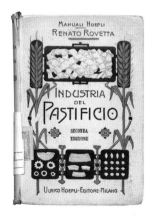

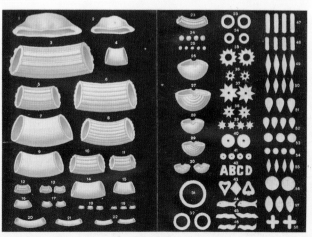

Fig. 132.

marketing strategy, thanks to the work of Federico Seneca, a painter and graphic designer who directed the Advertising Department for Buitoni (and for Perugina after it joined the Group) from 1925 to the mid-thirties, when he was succeeded by Giovanni Angelini. Barilla also played a prominent role, if anything for the fame it achieved at the international level. In 1877, Pietro Barilla Senior (1845–1912) began to produce pasta with a wooden press in Parma. In 1910, he introduced the first oven to make the baking process "continuous," initiating the transition towards a more industrial dimension. In a parallel process, the company began to define its identity: sculptor Emilio Trombara (1875–1934) designed the first trademark in 1910, the "Garzone Barilla" pouring the yolk from a gigantic egg into a chest full of flour. In the fifties, the Parma-based company was one of the first to construct a modern corporate image to support the decision to scale up its industrial dimension, in order to penetrate the mass distribution market. To lead this operation, the company hired Erberto

Carboni (1899–1984) who, from 1952 to 1960, redesigned all the communication artefacts, from the advertisements to the visuals on the company vehicles, from the stands at the trade fairs to the industrial films and television commercials; he also presented a new trademark—based on the memory of the egg—an oval with the name of the company in negative in a Bodoni-inspired typeface, instantly characterized by the white "beak." Just as important was the patent filed in 1955 for the signature classic rectangular box with the transparent window (no. 57571).

This typical Italian product has also stimulated the efforts of designers, from the controversial project for the Marille, designed in 1983 by Giorgio Giugiaro for Voiello, to the Campotti di Gragnano by Mauro Olivieri for Pastificio dei Campi, which won an honourable mention at the Compasso d'oro-Adi awards in 2014.

C. Rodanò, *Pasta alimentare*, in *Enciclopedia Italiana*, Istituto dell'Enciclopedia Italiana, Rome 1935 (it is available online at www.treccani.it/ enciclopedia/pasta-alimentare_ (Enciclopedia_Italiana)/); A. Ivardi Ganapini, G. Gonizzi (edited by) *Barilla. Cento anni di pubblicità e comunicazione*, Historic Archives Barilla, Parma 1994; VV. AA., *Brevetti del design italiano 1946-1965*, Electa, Milan 2000, p. 138; S. Serventi, F. Sabban, *La pasta storia e cultura di un cibo universale*, Laterza, Rome – Bari 2000; G. Gonizzi (edited by), *Barilla 125 anni di pubblicità e comunicazione*, Barilla Alimentare, Parma 2003; *Pasta De Cecco Una storia di qualità*, Cierre edizioni, Sommacampagna (VR) 2006; L. Masia, *Buitoni la famiglia, gli uomini, le imprese*, Silvana Editoriale, Cinisello Balsamo (MI) 2007; Archivio centrale dello Stato, Italian Patent and Trademark Office, no. 57571, 20.10.1955.

→Buitoni, Buitoni Restaurant, Times Square, New York, advertising billboard, 1942.

→Studio Testa, Agnesi, advertising poster (from *Pubblicità in Italia, 1968-1969*, suppl. to *L'Ufficio Moderno – la pubblicità*, 11, 1968, p. 49).

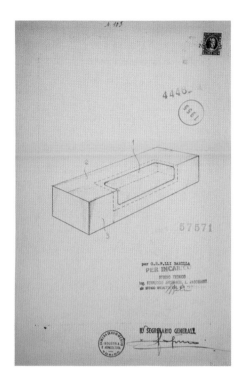

→Patent (no. 57571, 20 October 1955) and box for Barilla egg noodles designed by Erberto Carboni (Barilla Historic Archives, Parma).

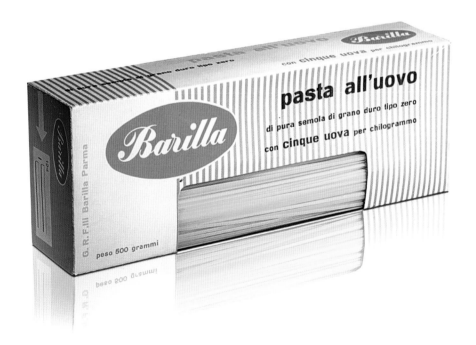

Bel Paese Cheese

Galbani, Ballabio (Como);
now Lactalis Italia, Milan
1906

Bel Paese, a cheese made from uncooked curd, was invented in 1906 by Egidio Galbani (1859–1950), who founded the eponymous cheese factory based in Ballabio (Como), in 1882. The name comes from a book dedicated to the natural wonders of Italy, published by Antonio Stoppani, a geologist and geographer from Lecco, and entitled *Il Bel Paese. Conversations on the natural beauty, the geology and the physical geography of Italy.*

The new production concept—the round Bel Paese Cheese was not inspired by any existing traditional artisanal product, as other Galbani products had been before it—went hand in hand with a new idea of packaging that introduced yet another distinguishing feature at a time when the tradition of selling bulk products by weight was still widespread. Galbani, like other entrepreneurs of his time, understood that unpackaged products, which had heretofore been the mainstay of Italian grocery stores, were on the way out; yet he also used the paper the cheese was wrapped in, which both preserved it and made it easier to store and transport, as a communication tool. Not only was it printed with the image of Stoppani and the Italian peninsula, it also highlighted the most important geographical locations of the company: from Ballabio to Maggianico, from Melzo to the sites of its various production plants.

It should be emphasized that this product, along with others by companies in the Lombardia region, first and foremost Invernizzi and Locatelli, represented a fundamental step forward in the history of cheese production, not only because it invented a new typology, but also because it marked the beginning of an all-encompassing method of industrial organization, from ideation to packaging, from production systems to corporate communication. And it is no coincidence that

it originated in the Lombardia region, the most industrialized in Italy, where there was greater opportunity for contact with the productive, operational and organizational methods of the most advanced and progressive entrepreneurs.

The new cheese soon spread across Europe, partly in the wake of its appeal to the sentiments of Italians living abroad. Thanks to the success of Bel Paese in the first decade of the twentieth century, Galbani erected a new production unit in Melzo (Milan), expanding the facilities that had been built in the 1890s to satisfy the company's increasing need for provisions, as it began to grow beyond the regional scale. It thus solved the problem of the seasonal nature of production in Valsassina, by settling in an area with better transportation systems and road networks, as well as an abundance of raw material available in consistent quantities. The new plant truly represented the transition to an industrial dimension: it featured avant-garde technology that ensured refrigeration and a constant flow of the raw material required for production. It therefore became more competitive with the French manufacturers, who had heretofore enjoyed the benefits of rapid transportation, which brought the French cheeses to the markets of major Italian cities at competitive prices. An equally important factor was Galbani's sales structure, based on a network of warehouses and representatives who were responsible for the widespread distribution of the products across the entire territory of Italy and abroad.

From the very beginning, the diffusion of the product was supported by an excellent corporate communication plan, which included participation in the major international trade fairs, publicity in newspapers and magazines, and advertising posters,

illustrated by the likes of R.F. Quillio or Piquillo (pseudonyms for the *affichiste* Carlo Pandolfi) in the thirties or Raymond Savignac, Germano Lombardi e Carlo Dradi in the fifties. Equally significant were the catchphrases they used: in a 1953 advertisement Bel Paese "over time remains the most rational, the most delicious and most aristocratic of cheeses," while in 1956 the company coined the enduring motto "Galbani means trust," broadcast on the *Carosello* television show. Purchased in the thirties by a branch of the Invernizzi family from Melzo, related to the Galbani family, the company was sold in 1974 to investment companies and in 1989 it became part of the Bns-Danone Group. In 2006, it joined the French group Lactalis (since 2008 Lactalis Italia), which also owns other historic Italian dairy industries such as Locatelli, Invernizzi, Cademartori and Président. (fb)

A. Colli, "Egidio Galbani," *Dizionario biografico degli Italiani*, vol. 51, Istituto dell'enciclopedia Treccani, Rome 1998 (available online at http://www.treccani.it/enciclopedia/galbani/); G. Pizzorni, *Egidio Galbani spa*, in www.lombardiabeniculturali.it/archivi/soggetti-produttori/ente/MIDB0018B3/, 2000; F. Fontanella, M. Di Somma, M. Cesar, *Come cambiano i marchi*, Ikon, Milan 2003, pp. 126–29.

→Advertising totem, Milan trade fair, 1930 (Fondazione Fiera Milano Historic Archives, Milan).

→Advertisement, c. 1930 (Galbani Historic Archives).

→Raymond Savignac, advertising poster (from *Pubblicità in Italia, 1958-1959*, suppl. to *L'Ufficio Moderno – la pubblicità*, 11, 1958).

98   **the industrialization**   / **packaged**
      of traditional food products
      1850–1920

Invernizzina Cheese

Invernizzi, Melzo (Milano);
now Lactalis Italia, Milan
1928

Crescenza is a traditional soft creamy cheese from the family of *stracchino* cheeses, native to the foothills of the mountains in Lombardia; the term derives from the Latin *crescentia*, meaning "to grow, to expand, to form" or from the Lombard *carsenza* (a type of bread), because during the production of the curd, the cheese increases in volume and rises like bread.

The most famous Italian *crescenza* is undoubtedly Invernizzina, which owes its name to the Invernizzi family of industrialists. In 1908 Giovanni Invernizzi founded a creamery in Pozzuolo Martesana (Milan), a town located in a region traditionally associated with breeding milk cows and producing cheese, *stracchino* in particular. In 1914, he moved it to Melzo (Milan), just a few blocks away from the Galbani factory. When in 1928 the production facilities were relocated to Caravaggio (Bergamo), where production included *stracchino*, *gorgonzola*, *taleggio* and processed cheeses, the company began to consolidate its standing as one of the major dairy industries in Italy.

The concept developed in the twenties by Invernizzi, who would later be joined by his son Romeo (1906–2004) and his nephew Remo (1918–2013), was to package a traditional local product and to identify it with the name of the company, deriving a pet name from it for the product as an expedient to help establish brand recognition. The name Invernizzi was first registered in 1925, in association with its Savoia cheese (no. 30877), but the number of trademarks registered after that for *stracchino*, *robiola*, *robiolina*, *taleggio* and other cheeses corroborate the company's recourse to this practice. After World War II, the names of the Invernizzi cheeses, packaged and appropriately publicized with reassuring references to simplicity and trustworthiness, in many cases replaced the name of the cheese typology itself, maintaining a traditional approach to communication with an accent on nature, despite the industrial scale of the company, such as the figure of the grocer or that of a child licking his fingers, the stars of many advertising campaigns conceived by the company's in-house advertising department. This was true of Invernizzina, which became a synonym for *crescenza*, or the Milione, a processed cheese introduced in 1951 (no. 111072) that owes its fame to Signor Bonaventura, a famous cartoon figure created by Sto (Sergio Tofano, 1886–1973) chosen to endorse the product, whose every misadventure ended with his winning a million lire.

The company's fame continued to spread in the mid-sixties thanks to the introduction of a new means of corporate and product communication. The characters identified with the company's promotion and advertising, such as Carolina the Cow and the "Susanna tutta panna" doll, originally conceived as cartoon figures by Francesco Misseri of Studio K in Florence, became inflatable toys that could be won by collecting points, a device used to promote customer loyalty ("Susanna" would later become the name of a pre-portioned processed cheese). This scheme was a new approach to the idea of trading cards, which the company, like many others, had already made use of in the thirties, with illustrations by Umberto Onorato (1898–1967) and Giuseppe Zanini (1906–1996).

The successful television campaigns, in particular the ones broadcast on Carosello which launched jingles and slogans such as "tolon tolon," "Pitupitumpa" or "Invernizzi Invernizzina che bontà!" that became very popular, were animated with the contribution of illustrators such as Osvaldo Cavandoli (1920–2007). Curiously, the inflatable armchair Blow, designed by DDL (De Pas, D'Urbino, Lomazzi) in 1967 for Zanotta, an icon of Italian furniture design in the seventies, was manufactured by the same company that produced Carolina the Cow.

In 1985 Invernizzi was purchased by Kraft Foods, which sold it in 2003 to the Franch group Lactalis (since 2008 Lactalis Italia).

C. and G. Padovani, *Italia Buonpaese*, Blu Edizioni, Turin 2011, p. 183; F. Fubini, "Morto Invernizzi, inventò il formaggio di massa," *Corriere della Sera*, 19 July 2004; Archivio centrale dello Stato, Italian Patent and Trademark Office, no. 30877, filed 2.04.1925, reg. 17.05.1926; no. 111072, filed 5.12.1951, reg. 7.04.1953.

→Advertisement (from *Album per la raccolta delle figurine – Caricatura*, Invernizzi, 1937, p. 2).

→Wrapper for Robiolina Invernizzi, 1933 (Invernizzi Historic Archives).

→Franco Mosca, advertisement, 1952 (Invernizzi Historic Archives).

Formaggino Mio Cheese Spread

Locatelli, Ballabio (Lecco);
now Nestlé Italiana, Assago (Milan)

1936

The first processed cheese to be specifically conceived and designed for children in terms of shape and nutritional content, the Formaggino Mio was sold nationwide starting in the thirties by Locatelli, a company founded by Mattia Locatelli in 1860 in Ballabio, Valsassina (Lecco), one of the Alpine regions specialized in making and aging certain varieties of traditional soft cheeses, such as *taleggio*, *quartirolo* and *gorgonzola*. The company, headed by Giovanni Locatelli in 1874 and then by his five children, distinguished itself from its competitors, Invernizzi and Galbani, in that it was not only concerned with production but also acted as a commercial intermediary towards wholesalers and organized large-scale exportations abroad of both its own products and those of other food industries, thanks to the creation of branch offices in France, England, Germany, the United States and Argentina.

The urgent need to give the brand a more specific connotation, an operation which in the mid-thirties was becoming a sign of quality that soon began to overshadow the idea of quality that only traditional products could guarantee, convinced Locatelli to buy back the factory in Robbio (Pavia) from Galbani in 1935—with a company called Lir (Latterie industriali reunite)—and to structure it as required to produce and distribute an innovative product, packaged and intended for mass consumption: the Formaggino Mio, launched on the market in 1936 (no. 54067). With the extra-creamy consistency that came from submitting the product to one final process after it had finished aging, it stood out, at a time when cheese was still sold primarily in bulk,

for its unmistakable square packaging, containing small individual portions wrapped in paper that made it possible to hold and eat the cheese no matter how creamy. The small size of the serving, determined on the basis of the child's nutritional needs and the way he might eat it, anticipated and opened the door to the idea of individual servings, which would later become a staple in the food industry.

What was truly innovative for those years was the idea of a food product conceived especially for children—a target that would later, especially in the fifties, become a key segment for this market—and the design of both the formal configuration and the way the product would be used. As a demonstration of the groundbreaking challenge that the company had chosen to take on, Ercole Locatelli (1910–1985)—who ran the company after World War II—patented a device for the production of individual cheese servings in 1953 (no. US 2777124 A). The widespread distribution was sustained by intensive advertising campaigns featuring special offers: from the trading cards that were first included in the packages in the thirties, to the square cards in the blue box that became consolidated in the collective imaginary of the fifties and sixties: shimmering flickering images, that through 1965 were made with a technology patented in the United States ("Children!—read the ad—look for these amazing moving trading cards... like having a movie in your pocket!").

The commercials illustrated the product, describing how it was packaged, manufactured and eaten, and pointed out its nutritional qualities (a "super-nutritious vitamin-packed

food"). Another strong point consisted in its health benefits, which included the vitamin supplements added in collaboration with Roche pharmaceuticals. Renowned graphic designers and illustrators were commissioned to reinforce the image of the brand, such as Gino Boccasile (1901–1951), Raymond Savignac (1907–2002) or, for the television cartoon versions starring the famous Huckleberry Hound, the brothers Toni and Nino Pagot.

Over the years the packaging became flat and rectangular, but the distinctive square shape of the cheese portions remained unchanged.

In 1962 the company was sold to the Swiss corporation Nestlé, which has owned the Mio brand ever since. (fb)

C. and G. Padovani, *Italia Buonpaese*, Blu Edizioni, Turin 2011, p. 212; A. Mantegazza, *Locatelli*, in *Dizionario Biografico degli Italiani*, vol. 65, Istituto dell'enciclopedia Treccani, Rome 2005, available online at http://www.treccani. it/enciclopedia/locatelli_(Dizionario-Biografico)/; Archivio centrale dello Stato, Italian Patent and Trademark Office, no. 54067, filed 19.07.1936, reg. 6.10.1936; United States Patent, *Apparatus for processing individual cheese rations*, no. US 2777124 A, priority 28.02.1953; reg. 10.11.1953, publ. 8.01.1957.

→Advertisement, c. 1952.

→Gino Boccasile, advertisement (from *Le Vie d'Italia*, 4, April 1950, p. 371).

→Advertisement to promote the moving trading cards, 1960s.

... e fa che la mamma mi dia anche oggi il formaggino

MIO FORMAGGINO Locatelli

MIO

un MIO al giorno

MAMME: *ai vostri bimbi ....*

Locatelli

MIO formaggino vitaminizzato Locatelli

Pandoro Melegatti
Melegatti, Verona
1894

Pandoro, a cake with a soft golden colour from which it borrows its name, was officially created on October 14th 1894 when Domenico Melegatti (1844–1914), the owner of a pastry shop in Verona, won a Certificate of industrial property rights from the Ministry of Agriculture, Industry and Trade of the Kingdom of Italy for having invented the name, shape and recipe (General Register, vol. XXIX, no. 36964; Register of certificates, vol. LXXV, no. 89). It was inspired by the "levà," a traditional cake from Verona consisting in a dough made of flour, milk and yeast, and baked on Christmas Eve by the women gathered in the kitchens of the Venetian courts. With the same motivation that had driven him to experiment with other original products, such as the "pebbles of the Adige" candy, or "meat candies," the forerunners of bouillon cubes, Melegatti sought to invent a new cake. To bake a product that would rise significantly, making it light and fluffy, but more importantly to give it a recognizable shape that could be accurately duplicated, with the help of Verona-born artist Angelo dall'Oca Bianca (1858–1941), Melegatti conceived a truncated pyramid-shaped mould with eight pointed ends—which he first made out of metal, then stainless steel and finally aluminium—that would mould the dough into shape as it was baking. In addition to this characteristic star shape, the formal identity of the product was finalized by a dusting of confectioner's sugar over the top, which made it sweeter and more delicious, evoking Christmas cheer and the winter snow. To make it, Melegatti procured a specialized staff and the spaces required for the various phases of the production process, especially the long natural leavening, and purchased machinery that could ensure an even baking process for the dough, including a special "constant heat oven" which he himself invented. However, the production

process for the *pandoro* did not become fully automated until 1951, when the first industrial manufacturing plant was inaugurated in Verona, at a time when technological advancements could guarantee the products a longer shelf life. Other companies in this area followed the same innovative approach to design and production, including Bauli, which filed a patent in 1964 for an eight-pointed mould (no. 89275). The development of the *pandoro* in Verona and the *panettone* in Milan [**Panettone Motta** p. 106], the traditional confectioners' "holiday cakes" which had grown into industrial products available year-round, initially moved in two directions: on the one hand, they became part of a system of production, distribution and sales befitting to the age of mass consumption; on the other, they reflected the intent to extend the boundaries of seasonal demand. To achieve this goal, both adopted a strategy that included the design of a unique and inimitable food product, and the development of an equally iconic form—the dome of the *panettone* and the eight-pointed star of the *pandoro*—, supported by a corporate image and communication strategy that firmly established their identity.

Melegatti 1894-1994. I cento anni del pandoro, Cortella, Verona c. 1994; G. Roverato, *Melegatti*, in *idem*, *L'industria nel Veneto: storia economica di un "caso" regionale*, Esedra, Padua, 1996, pp. 351–53; VV.AA., *Brevetti del design italiano 1946-1965*, Electa, Milan 2000, pp. 132–33; Archivio centrale dello Stato, Italian Patent and Trademark Office, no. 89275, 23.03.1964.

→Certificate of industrial property rights, 14 October 1894 (Melegatti Archives, Verona).

→Leavening the dough, packaging and product (Melegatti Archives, Verona).

Panettone Motta

Motta, Milan; now Bauli,
Castel d'Azzano (Verona)

1919

The *panettone* is one of the traditional confectionery products that, at the turn of the twentieth century, grew to an industrial scale in terms of production, distribution and communication systems. This meant that the cake was no longer viewed as a local speciality confined to the area of Milan; nor was it to be just a seasonal, holiday cake. Production originally began with the handmade then industrial versions of the original Motta and its main competitor Alemagna, then spread to many other cities that developed their own local versions, such as the short *panettone* in Turin (such as the one produced by Galup in Pinerolo by Pietro Ferrua, who registered it in 1928, no.37173) or the *mandorlato* (like the one produced by Balocco in Fossano, province of Cuneo, created by Francesco Balocco).

Angelo Motta (1890–1957) founded the Motta company in Via della Chiusa in Milan in 1919. It was a small confectioner's shop dedicated to the production of the *panettone,* the typical Milanese Christmas cake. He was successful in diversifying the product, which came out light and fluffy thanks to the brewer's yeast he used to make it rise, from those of his competitors, thanks to its natural leavening process and the "exaggerated height of the cake which traditionally was shaped like a pagoda," writes historian Guido Vergani. The transformation from a small artisan's shop, typical of the food sector of the time, to the industrial dimension began in the mid-twenties when Motta bought the machinery and equipment he needed to increase the volume of production and, in 1924, registered the factory trademark which he anchored to the image of the *panettone* (no. 29974). In a short time, he was able to enhance his distribution system by opening several new retail stores in the city in 1929, and at the same time launched a number of publicity campaigns conceived to distinguish his production from that of other local artisans. Specifically, Motta began to collaborate with artists and graphic

designers, directed by Dino Villani who was commissioned, in 1934, to develop the corporate image. It was in this context that the first big "M" appeared, the first logo designed by poster artist Sepo (Severo Pozzati, 1895–1983), portrayed behind a sliced *panettone*, and repeated lower down within a circle where its shape is echoed by a smaller "M" with the spires of the Duomo. Ever since, it has been an element of brand recognition for the company, referring to both the name of the confectioner and the city of Milan. During that period, the company also worked with Erberto Carboni (1899–1984), who created posters, advertising campaigns and shop window installations, as well as Studio Boggeri and Fulvio Bianconi, among others.

In the meantime, the Alemagna bar and pastry shop in Milan, a company founded by Gioachino Alemagna (1892–1974) in 1921, responded to Motta's "M" with his own "A," a signature element of the graphic and packaging design which circulated, for example, on round cardboard boxes, inspired by the hatboxes of the time, which were shipped all over the world with their own version of the Milanese *panettone*. Relying on advertising campaigns, Motta and Alemagna transformed the *panettone* into a consumer product. They designed packages and wrappers for sales and distribution, often protected by patents. Motta filed patents, respectively in 1952 and in 1955, for a "Device to wrap *panettoni* and similar products..." (no. 40930) and a "Bag to package *panettoni* with coloured figures and friezes shaped like a carrying case..." (no. 52522), while in 1955 Alemagna patented the "Package made out of a paper-based material, preferably cardboard... to contain confectioners' products in a single piece..." (no. 55625).

In 1945 Motta became the second largest confectionery industry in Italy (following Venchi-Unica and ahead of Perugina, Caffarel and Ambrosoli); by the fifties, it could count on at least

ten production lines (from *panettoni* to crackers, from ice cream to *torrone*, from marrons glacés to *confetti*), and about three thousand six hundred employees, with a sales volume equivalent to a 10% share of the entire sector and contributing with over 7% to all the advertising expenses in Italy. Between 1968 and 1970, Motta and Alemagna became part of the Iri-Sme Group, and after changing hands several times, in 2009 Bauli purchased the baked goods divisions of the two brands. (fb)

G. Vergani, "Il panettone trasloca Milano perde un mito," *La Repubblica*, 20 November 1984; L. Segreto, "Gioachino Alemagna," *Dizionario Biografico degli Italiani*, vol. 34, Enciclopedia italiana Treccani, Rome 1988 (available online at www.treccani.it/enciclopedia/ gioachino-alemagna_(Dizionario-Biografico)/); VV.AA., *I Pozzati: Mario, Sepo, Concetto*, exhibition catalogue, Electa, Milan 1990; G. Bianchino (edited by), *Erberto Carboni, dal futurismo al Bauhaus*, exhibition catalogue, Mazzotta, Milan 1998, passim; VV.AA., *Brevetti del design italiano 1946-1965*, Electa, Milan 2000, pp. 132–33; L. Masia, *Alemagna. Storia italiana di vite e impresa*, Silvana Editoriale, Cinisello Balsamo (MI) 2008; A.M. Sette, *Disegno e design. Brevetti e creatività*, exhibition catalogue, Fondazione Valore Italia, Rome 2010, pp. 354–55; A. Colli, "Angelo Motta," *Dizionario Biografico degli Italiani*, vol. 77, Enciclopedia italiana Treccani, Rome 2012 (available online at www.treccani.it/enciclopedia/ angelo-motta/); Archivio centrale dello Stato, Italian Patent and Trademark Office, no. 29974, filed 6.11.1924, reg. 19.03.1925; no. 37173, filed 20.11.1928, reg. 29.04.1929; no. 40930, 4.04.1952; no. 52522, 4.02.1955; no. 55625, 30.09.1955.

→Leo Lionni, Advertisement (from E. Persico (edited by), *Arte Romana*, suppl. to *Domus*, 96, December 1935, p. XLI).

L'ARTE DI FAR DOLCI È ANTICHISSIMA ED IN TUTTI I TEMPI È STATA TENUTA IN GRANDE RISPETTO ● IL SECOLO XX HA OFFERTO AL PASTIC-CERE L'AUSILIO DELLA SCIENZA, MACCHINE ED IMPIANTI PERFETTI ● IL PANETTONE **Motta** È PRODOTTO DALLA PIÙ GRANDE ORGA-NIZZAZIONE SPECIALIZZATA NELLA FABBRICAZIONE DI UN DOLCE ● LEGGERO, FRAGRANTE, GUSTOSISSIMO, PERFETTO: UN CAPOLAVORO.

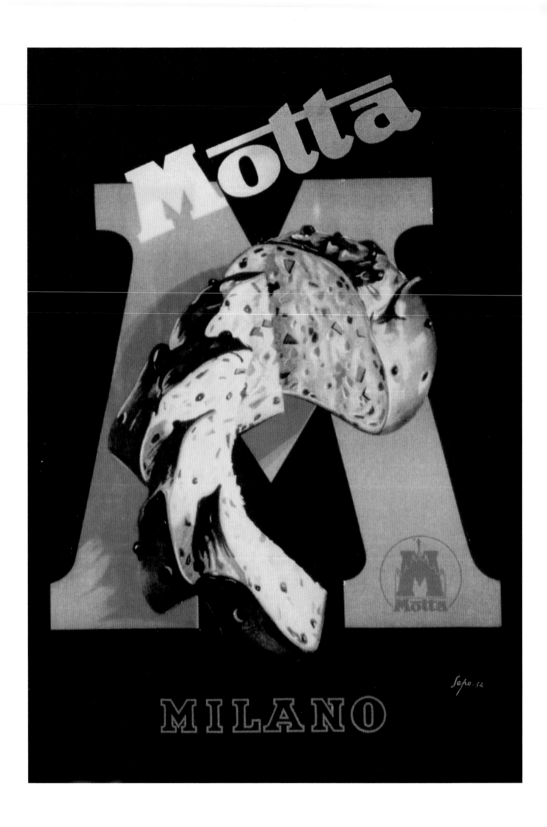

**the industrialization
of traditional food products**
1850–1920   / **packaged**

→Sepo (Severo Pozzati), Motta,
Advertising poster, 1934.

→Motta, advertisement
(from *Le Vie d'Italia*, 12, 1950,
p. 1351).

→Cesare Aliverti, Motta,
advertisement, mid-1950s
(from VV.AA. (edited by),
Due dimensioni, Editype, Milan
1964, n.pag.).

→San Babila pastry shop,
brochure, 1930s (Private
archives, Milan).

Mattei "Cantucci" Biscuits

Mattei, Prato

1858

A legacy of the eighteenth-century traditional "biscotti di Prato," credit must be given for the version of *cantucci* with unpeeled almonds and the characteristic blue paper bag they come in, known as the *Mattonella*, to Antonio Mattei, the owner of a biscuit shop which opened on September 29, 1858 in Via Ricasoli 22 in Prato. He immediately began to publicize his biscuits by participating in various expositions in Italy and in Europe, winning awards and many acknowledgments. "Biscuits flavoured with anise, with a dry dough that keeps them fresh, porous, brittle, permeable, these are the *cantucci* from Prato in Tuscany," reads the report of the jury at the Italian Exposition in Florence in 1865 in the Pastry section, "exhibited by Mister Mattei Antonio, who every year makes 40 thousand dozens, and at 48 cents a dozen they are sold in Florence, Livorno, Pisa and other cities in Italy, and abroad in Egypt." Pellegrino Artusi, a friend of Mattei's, sang his praise as a man and a confectioner in 1891, in the first Italian recipe book to be distributed on a massive scale. In 1885, upon the death of the father, the business passed down to his sons and then to Alberto and Ernesto Pandolfini, whose family has now run

the biscuit company for three generations. Among the many biscuit manufacturers in Prato, Mattei has maintained the specific identity of its production and corporate image over time, which even after the introduction of more advanced production processes, continues to convey the idea of an exquisite artisanal product, a notion supported by the scrupulous packaging, reminiscent of traditional pastry-shop packaging, and distinguished by the unmistakable colour blue.

P. Artusi, *La scienza in cucina e l'arte di mangiare bene*, 1st ed., L'Arte della Stampa di Salvatore Landi, Florence 1891, p. 423; "I biscottini di Prato e altre specialità," *La cucina italiana*, December 1969, pp. 1504–05; U. Mannucci, *Bisenzio tradizioni e cucina*, Edizioni Libreria del Palazzo, Prato 2003, pp. 63–66; AA.VV., *Dolcezze d'Italia, Storie di arte pasticcera e confettiera*, Maria Cristina de Montemayor Editore, Florence 2004, pp. 139–45; P. Becarelli, "Prodotto Tipico. Il biscotto," *La cucina italiana*, October 2007, p. 43.

→Product, package and production system with cookie-cutting process (Biscottificio Antonio Mattei Archives, Prato).

Rossi "Krumiri" Biscuits

Rossi, Casale Monferrato (Alessandria)
1878

The official date of birth of the curved *krumiro* biscuit was 1878 in Casale Monferrato, conceived by confectioner Domenico Rossi who from then on, enacted a series of measures to expand his market and protect his product from the competition. In 1884, for example, he took his biscuits to the Universal Exposition in Turin, winning, between 1886 and 1891, the Royal Warrant of Purveyor to the Houses of the Princes of Aosta, Genoa and the Italian Royal House of Savoy, as documented by the emblems that are still printed on the cookie boxes today. Imitated by many, it was recognized as the original in 1890 by the Mayor of the city who granted it a special "licence," filed as "patent 7436."

The *krumiri* are shortbread biscuits, made of wheat flour, butter, fresh eggs, sugar and vanilla with no water added to the dough. The company, which had been owned since the twenties by Angelo Ariotti, was purchased in 1953 by Ercole Portinaro, a member of the family that still runs it today. The biscuits are still made by hand, using an extruder that pushes the dough through serrated holes, producing long "ropes" of dough with the ridges that have remained the unmistakable signature feature of this type of biscuit.

Cut and curved by hand, they are then packed into red tin boxes which have basically remained unchanged since the earliest years of production, demonstrating the company's consistent attention to the aspects of preservation, distribution and communication of the product. After becoming the typical biscuit of Casale Monferrato, the *krumiri* quickly became popular after World War II thanks to other methods of production, such as those of the Bistefani company (since 2013 part of the Bauli group), also based in the city of Casale Monferrato.

P. Bonzanino, *Krumiri Rossi srl*, available online at http://siusa.archivi.beniculturali.it/cgi-bin/pagina.pl?TipoPag=prodente&Chiave=55701.

→Lithographed tin can and production system, 1950s (Krumiri Rossi Archives, Casale Monferrato).

Amaretti di Saronno Biscuits

D. Lazzaroni, Saronno (Varese)
1890

"A round and spongy macaroon, made of bitter almonds or ground peach seeds, mixed with sugar and egg whites and baked in the oven": this is how in 1839 Francesco Cherubini, in his *Vocabolario Milanese-italiano,* defined the *Amarètt,* a recipe that dated back at least one century before. Saronno's speciality was a mixture that contained apricot kernels. This was therefore a traditional pastry that became very popular at the end of the nineteenth century, and grew to be identified in particular with the Lazzaroni company.

The company was founded officially in 1888, when the brothers Giacinto (1840–1894), Ernesto (1844–1909) and Pietro (1851–1904) Lazzaroni established the *Stabilimento anglo-italiano D.Lazzaroni & C. Saronno* in the name of their father Davide (1808–1879), who owned a confectioner's shop which produced *amaretti* and other types of traditional Italian confectionery products. Determined to exploit the popularity of English biscuits in Italy, they equipped a new production plant with modern English ovens in Via Carcano in Saronno, for which they also hired specialized personnel from across the English channel, to train the local staff. The production, which included *amaretti* and English tea biscuits, crackers, cream wafers, shortbread cookies, *panettoni* and chocolate, began in 1890 and within a few years, Lazzaroni had become one of the largest and most important companies in the confectionary industry of the Lombard region, with an avant-garde production. It soon began

to export in large quantities, prevalently towards South America, and based its entire communication strategy on this decision. The trademark, registered in 1895, represents a Rubattino company steamship as it carries the first load of Lazzaroni products overseas with the word "Esportazioni" printed across it (no.2957), repeated in several languages on the label of the Amaretti di Saronno, registered in 1908 (no. 8686). The need to protect the macaroons, which are hygroscopic and sensitive to variations in moisture levels, led to the decision to contain them in sealed metal boxes that became one of the company's most effective advertising tools. Under the guidance of Luigi (1847–1933) and in particular, after 1920, of Mario Lazzaroni (1895–1982), the boxes were decorated by renowned illustrators—who celebrated the glories of Art Nouveau and Déco, depicting current events or re-evocations of historical themes; furthermore, new types of packaging were developed to extend the life of the product during distribution, and to work out more economical solutions. For example, sheets of aluminium were used to make smaller boxes, and a new type of "returnable" biscuit tin was created. The tin boxes were supplied to Lazzaroni by the company *Ebi Butti,* located in the vicinity, while the ones with more complex silk-screening procedures were commissioned to specialized companies that generally operated out of Genova Sampierdarena, such as the *Società ligure lavorazione latta* or *Società anonima De Andreis.*

Conceived as an élite product, after World War II it became a key element in the expansion strategy of the company which was now becoming fully industrialized, like many of its competitors in the confectionery industry. In 1980 it introduced a new totally automatic production line for the *amaretti,* from the kneading to the packaging. Purchased in the mid-eighties by the American company Campbell's, Lazzaroni was later sold to Enrico Citterio (Salumi Citterio), then to the Ferax Merchant financial fund and finally, in 2013, to the Casalini group. (fb)

F. Cherubini, *Vocabolario milanese-italiano,* vol. I, Milano 1839, p. 16; *Biscotti & C. La tradizione verso il futuro,* D. Lazzaroni & C., catalogue of the travelling exhibition on the history of biscuits, La Editoriale Libraria, Trieste 1986; D. Pozzi, "Lazzaroni," *Dizionario Biografico degli Italiani,* vol. 64, Enciclopedia italiana Treccani, Rome 2005 (available online at www.treccani.it/enciclopedia/lazzaroni_(Dizionario-Biografico)/); Archivio centrale dello Stato, Italian Patent and Trademark Office, no. 2957, filed 14.02.1895, reg. 13.03.1895; no. 8686, filed 28.02.1908, reg. 11.08.1908.

→Trademark, no. 8686, 28 February 1908.

→Wrapping machine, Saronno, 1933 (Lazzaroni Archives, Saronno).

→Advertisement, 1910s (Lazzaroni Archives, Saronno).

Amarelli Liquorice

Amarelli, Rossano Calabro (Cosenza)
mid-eighteenth century

Liquorice syrup has been extracted in Calabria since the sixteenth century, and the family of the Amarelli Barons has been active in this business since then, founding their current factory in Rossano Calabro (Cosenza) in 1731. The production of foods based on liquorice syrup grew considerably through the nineteenth century, thanks to the development of maritime transport and to the privileges and tax breaks granted by the Borbonic government to traditional industries, and so by the mid-century, the product was known as far as Naples, the capital of the Kingdom. Nicola Amarelli registered the trademark in 1900 with the words "Liquirizia di Calabria pura garantita Barone Amarelli" (no. 4858), and in 1907 modernized the production facilities by introducing steam boilers, used to prepare the root paste and extract the syrup, and a powerful motor-driven pump that would trigger the hydraulic presses to crush the paste again and squeeze out more liquid. Following the crisis in 1929, Amarelli introduced further technological innovations, expanding the business and perpetuating

a tradition typical of the area with a modern entrepreneurial approach, concerned with production systems but also with cultivating and upholding a specific identity inspired by its own history.
The range of products which was inaugurated at the time, now includes everything that can possibly be derived from liquorice root: from the stick of liquorice wood to pure liquorice, natural or flavoured with anise or mint aromas, from chewy orange or violet-flavoured liquorice to sugar-coated liquorice products. The manufacturing process, which begins by mincing the roots and goes through various phases controlled by computer systems, requires artisan-like attention in the final steps, with a "liquorice master" who must monitor the exact solidification point for the product. Along with its technological innovation, Amarelli based its communication on the choice of the illustrations and lettering that have made its packaging so characteristic. A patent was filed in 1946 for the trademark on the label, decorated with a design showing three children dressed in winter clothes,

a scarf and hat: "Pasticche di liquirizia extra "Amarelline" Specialità della Casa "Amarelli" Rossano (Calabria)" (no. 71868).
In 2001, the company opened the Giorgio Amarelli Liquorice Museum on the grounds of their headquarters, which houses the Amarelli Archives.

P. Amarelli Mengàno, *Azienda famiglia e passione per il futuro*, in E. De Simone, V. Ferrandino (edited by), *L'impresa familiare nel Mezzogiorno continentale fra passato e presente*, Conference proceedings, Benevento, 30 November – 1 December 2007, Franco Angeli, Milan 2009, pp. 185–90; Archivio centrale dello Stato, Italian Patent and Trademark Office, no. 4858, filed 22.10.1900, reg. 3.03.1901; no. 71868, filed 26.04.1946, reg. 13.12.1946.

→Liquorice boxes (Amarelli Archives, Rossano Calabro).

"Confetto" Sugared Almond

Various producers
late eighteenth century

The *confetto* (from *confectum*, the past participle of the Latin *conficere*, which means *prepared, produced*) is a confectionery product consisting in a shelled and peeled almond finely coated in sugar, though many variations on the theme have evolved over time using pistachios, hazelnuts or chocolate. Italy boasts an important tradition in the production of fine *confetti*. This speciality, which existed in Roman Antiquity and has always been a symbol of good luck and prosperity, was significantly transformed when instead of honey it was made with sugar, imported by the Arabs into Europe around the sixth century though for economic reasons, it did not become available for more widespread usage until the fifteenth century. It was then that Sulmona, a small town in the province of L'Aquila in the Abruzzo region, invented the modern fabrication of *confetti* and became known as the "city of confetti." Sulmona was the hometown of Pelino, Italy's oldest manufacturer of *confetti*, founded in 1783 by Bernardino Pelino (1750–1821), which brought significant innovation to the production processes

over time, filing a series of patents in the 1920s. Today the factory is still run by members of the original family, who also founded a museum, the *Museo dell'arte e della tecnologia confettiera Pelino.*
The main ingredient of *confetti* from Sulmona, and of most *confetti* from Italy and abroad, are the almonds that come not only from local farmers, but also from the Sicilian provinces of Siracusa and Ragusa. The finest among them are said to be the almonds from Avola, and the Pizzuta variety in particular. Selected to produce classic *confetti* with their characteristic flavour, this variety is distinguished by the flattened oval shape that allows the sugar to form a perfect coating, one layer at a time, providing remarkable results in terms of the product's form and fragrance. Another important centre for the *confetti* industry is the city of Andria in the Puglia region, which owes its fame in this case to the Fabbrica Mucci. Founded in 1894 in the historic city centre by Nicola Mucci, who had been an apprentice for many years at the Caflisch chocolate confectionery in Naples, the company produced

confetti, chocolate and candy. In the twenties, Mucci developed a new type of *confetti*, made with almonds from Bari covered in a layer of white chocolate and lightly coated with sugar, a forerunner of the famous Tenerello, a much softer version. Created ten years later, it was made with almonds from Toritto in Puglia and hazelnuts from the Piemonte region, covered in a double layer of chocolate and lightly coated with a pastel-coloured sugar coating.
Today Mucci is still owned by the original family, which also founded, inside the company facilities, the *Museo del Confetto Giovanni Mucci.*

S. Gaetano, *Il casato Pelino e la storia dei confetti di Sulmona*, Stampa D'Amato, Sulmona 1962; *1783-1983: primaria e premiata fabbrica Confetti Mario Pelino*, Tipografia la Moderna, Sulmona (AQ) 1991; A. Musaico Guglielmi, *Antica Fabbrica di confetti Mucci Giovanni Andria: 1894-1994*, Grafischena, Fasano di Puglia (BR) 1994; F. Cercone, *I confetti di Sulmona: fra storia e folklore*, printed by Qualevita, Torre dei Nolfi (AQ) 1999.

→Mucci Tenerelli and classic *confetti* made with Pizzuta di Avola almonds (Giovanni Mucci Archives, Trani).

Baratti & Milano Candy

Baratti & Milano, Turin;
now Novi-Elah-Dufour, Novi Ligure
(Alessandria)

1858

Baratti & Milano, one of the most prestigious brands in the Italian confectionery industry, known primarily for its "barattine" candies, was founded in 1858 by two confectioners born in the Canavese area, who had recently moved to Turin: Ferdinando Baratti, a native of Piverone, and Edoardo Milano, from Bollengo.

The fruit-flavoured hard candies, which were long the company's core product and praised for their therapeutic properties, have maintained a distinct identity over time, thanks to their special alimentary quality on the one hand, and the enduring nature of many key elements in their communication: from the trademark, which has remained rather recognizable, to the distinctive paper wrapping around each individual piece of candy. The first version, registered in 1891, displayed the logo with various emblems, acknowledgments and typological indications (no. 2094); it was followed in 1906, after the company went public, by a version that is very similar to the wrappers used today, with the name of the flavour highlighted inside a frame, and the wrapper ends to each side decorated with spiral ribbons bearing the names of all the flavours (no. 7860). Adhering to the practices of other businesses of the time, Baratti & Milano created its own trademark, wrappers, letterhead and advertising material to present the services offered by the company over time; warranted as an official Purveyor to the Royal Family, it made and sold candy, pastries, confectionery products, chocolate, wine and luxury liqueurs.

The company headquarters was equally representational, having moved in 1875 from Via Dora Grossa to the inside of the new Galleria dell'Industria Subalpina, and inaugurated a shop with tea rooms and a bar in the heart of Turin. When the spaces were renovated in 1911 with an addition designed by Giulio Casanova, an architect-decorator who trained at the school of Rubbiani in Bologna, in collaboration with the sculptor Edoardo Rubino, the shop became one of the most important documents of an "Italian" language that sought to recreate a union between the arts by combining the styles of the past with motifs from the floral arts. During the twenties, the company grew to an industrial scale with the construction of a large manufacturing plant in Corso Mediterraneo 132. As the business flourished, new advertising methods became necessary. The first conventional colour postcards were soon replaced by customized reusable metal boxes, which offered an alternative to bulk sales, and were supplied by manufacturers specialized in lithographic production located mainly in the area around Genoa, such as the Casanova company in Genova Sampierdarena. Furthermore, *affichistes* from the Art Nouveau and Déco periods were hired to design the images for the tin boxes produced by the Metalgraf company in Milan, for example, and for the printed material. There are remarkable posters and postcards designed for the Classica candy in the twenties by Pluto, the pseudonym for an artist who remains unidentified, which portray a ballerina-acrobat with a dress and hat made out of candy wrappers. Simplification and caricature, the distinctive features of illustration in the Piemonte area, were typical of the company's advertising at the end of the fifties, when Armando Testa in the early stages of his career designed two advertising posters, only one of which was ever distributed. He chose abstraction, simplification and irony—as may be seen in the wrapper for the Classica candy depicted as an oversized hat—as graphic and narrative devices to innovate the language of the advertising and combine it with an accredited idea of the "spirit" of the city, its capacity to merge advanced business practices and experimental ideas with traditional culture and lifestyle.

Baratti & Milano thus developed a comprehensive project over time, spanning from the urban scale to architecture, from the applied arts to communication; though it may not have been based on a deliberate strategy, it nevertheless succeeded in consolidating the fame of the company and that of Turin's most renowned establishments of yesteryear. The company changed hands many times over the years until 2003, when the brand was acquired by the Novi-Elah-Dufour group; at that time, the shop underwent a thorough restoration to preserve its original state. (fb)

M.S. Ainardi, P. Brunati, *Le fabbriche da cioccolata. Nascita e sviluppo di un'industria lungo i canali di Torino*, Allemandi, Turin 2008; E. Dellapiana, I. Massabò Ricci (edited by), *Baratti & Milano in Torino*, L'Artistica editrice, Turin 2010; C. and G. Padovani, *Cioccolatorino. Storie, personaggi, indirizzi, curiosità*, Blu Edizioni, Turin 2010; Archivio centrale dello Stato, Italian Patent and Trademark Office, n. 2094, filed 13.02.1891, reg. 6.03.1891; n. 7860, filed 25.12.1906, reg. 14.07.1907.

→The Classica candy (Baratti & Milano Historic Archives, Bra).

→Armando Testa, advertising poster, 1958 (Baratti & Milano Historic Archives, Bra).

CARAMELLE CLASSICHE

Pastiglie Leone Candy
Leone, Alba (Cuneo), then Torino
second half eighteenth century

Luigi Leone, who had produced colourful sugar candies since 1857 in his confectioner's shop at Alba (Cuneo), moved to Turin in the 1870s to Corso Vittorio Emanuele II 78. He expanded his business, and patented the trademark, first in 1900 when he registered the logo with the "L" at the centre, to be marked on every piece of candy (no. 4776), then again in 1911 when he rewrote the label defining the candy as "digestive and thirst-quenching" (no. 12025), a label still in use to this day. The company changed hands, but in 1934 it was purchased under the name of "Ditta L. Leone" by the brother and sister Celso and Giselda Balla (1896–1988), who was married that year to Innocenzo Monero, then a bank employee. They were the owners of a company that distributed confectionery products such as Dora, Talmone, Venchi and of course Leone. Giselda Balla, who was a dynamic and rather unconventional entrepreneur for the time, increased the company's production and sales capability by moving the premises in 1937 to the Art Nouveau-style building known as the former Fichet factory, in Corso Regina Margherita 242, and developed a distribution network that extended into the Liguria, Lombardia, Lazio and Veneto regions. At first the *pastiglie*, which were distinguished by their unusual pastel colours and small easy-to-make cylindrical shape, were sold in bulk out of glass jars. After 1880, they were packaged in pocket-sized boxes of golden yellow cardboard decorated with black lettering and Art Nouveau-style friezes that some years later, were wrapped in white paper with the name of the flavour printed in red letters. As an alternative, they were also sold in refillable metal tins. These too were initially produced in a single golden-metal version with black letters, later modified to a version with red letters. The communication of the product, introduced by the founder and documented by the company's participation in the International Exposition in Turin in 1911 and by the Art-Nouveau style poster illustrated by Giovanni Manca (1889–1984), was intensified over the following decade with a continued reliance on advertising, new forms of packaging and sales contests. During this period the company collaborated with Maga, one of the major advertising firms of the time, founded by Giuseppe Magagnoli in 1920, and with the Futurist artist Pippo Oriani (1909–1972). After World War II and the reconstruction of the production facilities, which had been seriously damaged by the bombings, the company remained in the hands of its current owners, the Monero family, and was directed by Giselda through the eighties. The Pastiglie Leone are the archetype of the sugar candy, and are a perfect example of a lasting product, with a well-defined identity and communication system that have remained substantially the same for over a century. Their enduring retro style has helped consolidate customer loyalty, as have the successful format, size and colour of the packaging, which have contributed to the brand recognition and distribution capacity.

C. Ruggiero, *L'oro d'Italia. Storie di aziende centenarie e famigliari*, vol. 3, Maggioli, Santarcangelo di Romagna (RN) 2013, pp. 277–85; P. Rugafiori, *Pastiglie Leone: artigianato dolciario per eccellenza*, in www.impreseneltempo-torino.it/index.php/imprese-nel-tempo/biografie-impresa/pastiglie-leone/dai-leone-ai-balla-e-monero; Archivio centrale dello Stato, Italian Patent and Trademark Office, no. 4776, filed 18.07.1900, reg. 10.10.1900; no. 12025, filed 8.12.1911, reg. 24.07.1912.

→Candies and package (Pastiglie Leone Archives, Collegno).

Caffarel Gianduiotto Chocolates

Caffarel, Turin; now Lindt & Sprungli

1865

The official birthdate of the name "gianduiotto" is 1869, when during Carnival in Turin, the popular *commedia dell'arte* stock character Gianduja apparently authorized Caffarel, in an official decree no less, to use this name for the famous chocolate fashioned in the shape of an upside-down boat.

The industrial production and marketing began in 1865 at Caffarel, the company founded in 1826 by the Waldensian Pier Paul Caffarel (1783–1845) and his son Isidor (1817–1867), to make chocolate using a new hydraulic-powered machine that ground the cocoa, sugar and spices. In 1852, Michele Prochet invented the mixture for the *gianduiotto*, though it is likely he must share authorship of the shape with Caffarel. Faced with the problem of the cost and scarcity of cocoa, in the light of the Napoleonic blockade, he replaced part of the cocoa with ground toasted hazelnuts (of the "round mild Langhe" variety) creating a new confectionery product called *givo*, which was adopted by many local artisans.

In 1878, the merger between Caffarel and Prochet, Gay e C., led to the foundation of the company known as Caffarel, Prochet e C., inaugurating a partnership which, through alternate fortunes, ended in 1930 with its acquisition by the partners Walter Bächstädt-Malan and Paolo Audiberti. To process the mixture for the *gianduiotti*, special machines and equipment were designed using advanced technology developed in the late thirties, which also included automatic machinery that wrapped the *gianduoitti* in the typical aluminium foil.

Today the shape is ensured by a machine that extrudes the chocolate mixture onto the conveyer belt, then clips it with two small mechanical "blades" that shut tight after the chocolate is poured. Fully aware of the importance of advertising at a time when industrial development was driving trade and the growth of non-essential consumer goods, the company hired two renowned illustrators such as Leonetto Cappiello (1875–1942) who designed advertising placards and posters, and Giacomo Malugani (1876–1942). Like other companies that contributed to the history of Italian food products, such as Lazzaroni or Baratti & Milano, Caffarel, Prochet e C. chose to use lithographed metal tins that combined functionality and remarkable potential for communication.

The decision to use the name Caffarel for the first time as a recognizable brand name, in 1876, was undoubtedly part of a strategy of brand identity; the first official document to transcribe and patent the brand or company trademark is dated 1902.

In 1968 the company moved from its ancient headquarters in Borgo San Donato in Turin to Luserna San Giovanni in the Waldensian valleys, where the founder was born; in 1998, it finally became part of the Swiss group Lindt & Sprungli. (fb)

C. Bächstädt-Malan, *Caffarel, 170 anni: avanti sempre più avanti: la meravigliosa storia del "cioccolato d'autore,"* Caffarel, Turin 1996; F. Fontanella, M. Di Somma, M. Cesar, *Come cambiano i marchi*, Ikon, Milan 2003, pp. 80–83.

→Detail of production; steel moulds for production by hand in various sizes, c. 1910 (Caffarel Archives, Luserna San Giovanni).

Bertolli Olive Oil

Bertolli, Lucca; now Deoleo
second half nineteenth century

Olive oil is a typically Italian food product. Of Italy's many recent and historic companies, Bertolli's specificity lies in its attention to the design of its communication but also—and this was very unusual for the time—to the design of the bottle that contains the oil, having filed a patent for an idea of shape as early as the fifties.

In 1865 Francesco Bertolli (1835–1895) opened a shop that sold local food products, including oil, wine and cheese, in San Donato, just a few kilometres from Lucca. Capitalizing on his commercial success and the decent amount of capital he had accumulated, in 1875 he founded the Banco e Cambio Bertolli in Piazza San Michele in the centre of Lucca, to serve as a money exchange and lending institution for emigrants on their way to the American continent. Their demand for local Italian products prompted Bertolli to open trades routes towards the United States. Upon the death of their father, his children developed an industrial group that was ahead of its time and by the turn of the century, stood out within the context of Italy's antiquated entrepreneurial system. It consisted in a company that produced and sold food products destined for exportation, supported by a financial intermediation system that had developed from the evolution of the original money exchange and lending office (which later became Banca Bertolli and was purchased in 1970 by the Banca Commerciale Italiana). The circle was closed with

the constitution, in 1912, of the Bertolli e Ponzi company, makers of the tin cans and wooden crates that were essential for exporting oil, which was absorbed in 1937 when the Società Anonima Bertolli gathered under its wing all the different phases of product preparation. Throughout the twenties and thirties the company invested heavily in various sectors so that by the outbreak of World War II, Bertolli was one of Italy's largest companies in the wine and oil sectors, with a brand name that enjoyed widespread international distribution.

The company's attention to the aspects of communication, which began in the 1900s when it registered a trademark with the image of the crowned eagle with open wings (no. 4790), became part of a more aggressive strategy in the fifties to develop a specific recognizable identity. It achieved this goal with the sophisticated solutions conceived by graphic designer Erberto Carboni (1899–1984), who was commissioned in 1952 to define the corporate image, from restyling the logo to give it greater impact to designing the installations for trade fairs, and with the decision to present the oil in a transparent glass bottle designed and patented for the occasion, as the advertising of the period was careful to point out, a move that initially caught the competitors off guard. Bertolli olive oil was naturally publicized for its health benefits; a 1954 advertisement read: "Man is a machine too and his body

requires constant and careful lubrication. Bertolli olive oil, extracted from the fruits of the ancient olive groves in Lucchesia, boasts incomparable flavour and nutritional properties. Light and easy to digest even for delicate stomachs, Bertolli olive oil will protect your health." Careful studies were conducted on the packaging and the proper preservation of the product. In 1967, Alberto Bertolli patented a plastic closure combined with a pouring spout to seal the central opening, made with a single mould, to be applied onto metal cans (no. US 3465925 A). After changing hands several times, from the family to Montecatini and, in 1972, to the Gruppo Iri-Sme, in 2008 the brand was purchased by the Deoleo Group and later by the CVC Capital Partners private equity firm. (fb)

VV. AA., *Erberto Carboni*, Electa, Milan 1985; L. Segreto, in *Dizionario Biografico degli Italiani*, vol. 34, Enciclopedia italiana Treccani, Rome 1988 (available online at www.treccani.it/enciclopedia/bertolli_(Dizionario-Biografico)/); Archivio centrale dello Stato, Italian Patent and Trademark Office, no. 4790, filed 5.08.1900, reg. 27.11.1900; United States Patent, *Combined plastic closure and pouring spout*, no. US 3465925 A, priority 01.02.1967; reg. 25.05.1967, publ. 9.09.1969.

→Erberto Carboni, advertisements, 1957, 1964, 1968 (Bertolli Archives).

è facile

prendere un granchio

è facile prendere un granchio
acquistando un olio qualunque....
La menta bastiglia a chiusura ermetica
garantisce l'assoluta genuinità
dell'olio d'oliva **Bertolli**

dal caratteristico delicato aroma
che conserva tutti i pregi del frutto.
Anche nella classica lattina l'olio
d'oliva **Bertolli** è l'alimento insostituibile
e il condimento insuperabile.

olio fino d'oliva

BERTOLLI
Lucca

il famoso olio di Lucca

L'aroma e la freschezza delle insalate e degli ortaggi rivivono nell'olio d'oliva Bertolli, insostituibile condimento della buona cucina italiana Il famoso olio d'oliva Bertolli, leggero, appetitoso, nutriente, dalla incomfondibile grazia toscana, è assolutamente genuino, garantito nelle sue qualità dalla secolare tradizione della Casa Bertolli.

OLIO D'OLIVA **BERTOLLI**

BERTOLLI
Lucca

condite sempre con olio d'oliva Bertolli   condite sempre con olio d'oliva Bertolli

QUESTA È LA TIPICA BOTTIGLIA DEL

purissimo olio d'oliva

BERTOLLI

LA MARCA PIÙ ESPORTATA NEL MONDO

Sasso Olive Oil

Sasso, Oneglia-Imperia; now Deoleo

1860

The P. Sasso e Figli company was founded in Oneglia, the port and oil capital of the Liguria region, in 1860 by Agostino Novaro (1837–1910), who chose to use his wife Paolina Sasso's surname for the company name. Novaro, who was determined to target an upscale consumer for his product, soon adopted a series of promotional tools that without a doubt anticipated more modern techniques.

First, he began in 1895, and continued through 1919, to publish the magazine "La Riviera ligure" which he sent to his clients with every can of olive oil. This was one of Italy's first *house organs*, edited by his children, first by Angiolo Silvio (1866–1938), a poet and author, and then by Mario (1868–1944) who was also a poet and intellectual, and transformed it after 1899 from a sort of company newsletter into a magazine with a culturally advanced editorial policy, which was reflected in both its literary contents and its graphic design and illustrations. An extremely important case study in the history of Italian publishing, and particularly representative of the Art Nouveau style, in 1899 it had reached a circulation of one hundred twenty thousand copies. Artists and graphic designers who worked for the magazine were also involved in the company communication which, in addition to the advertising pages, produced posters, calendars and illustrated postcards. They include the painters Plinio Nomellini (1866–1943), Giorgio Kienerk (1869–1948), Gabrio (Gabriele) Chiattone (1853–1934) and Franz Laskoff (1869–1921), the author of the logo with the woman reaching out towards an olive tree enclosed within a circle surrounded by a ribbon (registered in 1904,

no. 6676). At the same time, Sasso was well aware of the importance of packaging, and chose to use tinplate cans, produced by the metal industry of the Liguria region which had grown in proportion to the requirements of the olive oil industries. The company decided to characterize the cans, so that not only would they ensure perfect preservation of the product and make it easy to transport, fulfilling the need for example to supply olive oil to Italian emigrants, but they would also stimulate sales by standing out among the competition, with the bright olive green colour that still identifies the product today. The lettering, layout and graphic design—with the straight lines that divide the surface orthogonally—and the trademarks were all developed in the early decades of the twentieth century (nos. 11307; 12726; 37992).

Novaro's second idea was to emphasize the therapeutic and medicinal qualities of Sasso olive oil; at the end of the nineteenth century, his advertisements read: "The only Brand in Italy which has succeeded in obtaining a product so absolutely pure (chemically guaranteed) and exceptionally delicate, that it deserves to be endorsed by the most illustrious doctors Comm. S. Laura and Prof. Senatore P. Mantegazza as easily digestible even by the weakest of stomachs."

During the fifties, the meeting between Guido Novaro, the founder's grandson, and the adman and graphic designer Armando Testa gave a further boost to the brand's popularity. The communication was distinguished by its concision, irony and cheekiness, and included outstanding work, such as the series of posters in which people talk to the dishes they will eat, and the many

commercials for *Carosello* (1959–76), characterized after 1966 by the catchy little slogan "La pancia non c'è più" ("no more tummy!"), in the video performed by Mimmo Craig and produced by Delta Film, Testa's own production company. Sasso, which was first purchased by Buitoni then Nestlé, today, it is one of the brands, like Bertolli and Carapelli, controlled by the CVC Capital Partners private equity firm, which in 2014 purchased the Spanish food group Deoleo. (fb)

Z. Ciuffoletti (edited by), *Olivo: tesoro del Mediterraneo*, Alinari, Florence 2004, pp. 145–46; M. Gatta, "Un olio d'oliva artistico e letterario. Mario Novaro e 'La Riviera Ligure' della Ditta P. Sasso e Figli di Oneglia," *Mensa. Culture e piaceri della tavola*, January–February 2009 (available online at http://archivio.mensamagazine.it/articolo.asp?id=1165); C. and G. Padovani, *Italia Buon Paese*, Blu Edizioni, Turin 2011, p. 173; E. Cardinale, *Mario Novaro*, in *Dizionario Biografico degli Italiani*, vol. 78, Enciclopedia Italiana Treccani, Rome 2013 (available online at www.treccani.it/enciclopedia/mario-novaro_%28Dizionario-Biografico%29/); Archivio centrale dello Stato, Italian Patent and Trademark Office, no. 6676, filed 18.12.1904, reg. 9.04.1905; no. 11307, filed 30.04.1911, reg. 19.02.1912; no. 12726, filed 15.08.1912, reg. 29.10.1912; no. 37992, filed 16.12.1927, reg. 9.11.1929; www.fondazionenovaro.it.

→Product trademark, no. 12726, 15 August 1912.

→Armando Testa, advertising posters, 1955, 1970 (Sasso Archives).

l'ha mangiata tutta!

alimenti SASSO

→Armando Testa, advertisement,
1964 (Sasso Archives).

→Studio Testa, advertisement
(from *La Domenica del Corriere*,
3 May 1959, p. 31).

dica signor pesce,
per gustarla bene
e digerirla facilmente?...

Olio Sasso, signore,
l'olio d'oliva
supergenuino! •

OLIO SASSO

124   **the industrialization**   / **bottled**
       of traditional food products
       1850–1920

Carli Olive Oil

Carli, Oneglia – Imperia
1911

Of the many Italian companies that produce olive oil, the marketing and distribution strategy adopted by Carli, which sells its products by correspondence only and delivers them directly to the home, is both characteristic and identity-defining. A "sustainable" choice before its time, which reduces the cost and energy required for distribution. Fratelli Carli began to produce oil in Oneglia in 1911, when Carlo Carli's family (1854–1923), which owned a well-established print shop since 1908, decided to exploit the abundant production of oil from the family olive grove located in Costa Rossa. Putting together the print shop, the farm and the olive-press, Giovanni Carli, one of the six sons who had been put in charge of the olive oil business, relying on his brief experience as an oil broker—a figure who, in the olive oil supply chain in the Liguria region, sold a product that was harvested in other areas—, decided to skip the middleman and take his father's olive oil directly to the consumer. For the logistics, the company initially relied on the railway service, coming to an agreement that required the railways to deliver the demijohns or tins directly to the customers; after 1961, the company began to use its own fleet of marked company vans. Customers were contacted personally or, over time, handled by a network of door-to-door salesmen, and were kept constantly up-to-date with letters, brochures, catalogues, newsletters, special offers. In 1923 the company printed and sent out the first *Calendario Carli*, while in 1936, for the twenty-fifth anniversary of its foundation, the company published its *Ricettario*, a recipe book edited by Amedeo Pettini (1865–1948), head chef of the Royal House of Savoia, sent as a gift to customers with their first order for olive oil. So the printed page became the company's marketing "trademark." And in fact Fratelli Carli still has a company print shop dedicated to this purpose. A purveyor since the twenties to the Vatican and then to the Royal House of Savoia, in 1925 the company established its own analysis and quality control laboratory, and could count on an exclusive railway connection; by the thirties, after expanding and modernizing its production facilities, it had become one of Italy's most important olive oil producers. To support the sales strategy, based on an intensive stream of communication, a certain type of service offered by the company, its attention to the quality of the product and competitive prices, Fratelli Carli relied from the very beginning on the collaboration of artists and graphic designers. In 1922 it hired illustrator and *affichiste* Plinio Codognato (1878–1940), who also worked for Fiat and Pirelli, and produced the first Fratelli Carli logo; during the thirties the company commissioned illustrator and cartoonist Giuseppe Cappadonia (1888–1978), who designed the new Olio Carli lettering in 1934, which is still the company's signature trademark today, as well as the illustrations for the *Ricettario*. After resuming production in 1948, in the early fifties the packaging process became fully automated. In 1992 Fratelli Carli inaugurated the *Museo dell'olivo* at Imperia, which it expanded in 2002. (fb)

Storia d'impresa: Carlo Carli, "Fratelli Carli Imperia," from *Storie di ordinaria grandezza. Commercio, turismo e servizi: il terziario italiano raccontato dai suoi protagonisti,* Alinari-il Sole 24 ore, Florence 2009 (available online at www.reteimpreseitalia.it/Fondazione/Documenti/Voce-alle-imprese/Fratelli-Carli-Imperia/); C. Carli, R. Uboldi, *Straordinario quotidiano: 100 anni di storia, 100 anni di vita,* Stamperia Artistica nazionale, Trofarello (TO) 2011; C. Ruggiero, *L'Oro d'Italia. Storie di aziende centenarie e famigliari,* vol. 3, Maggioli, Santarcangelo di Romagna (RN) 2013, pp. 165–75.

→Giuseppe Cappadonia, *Ricettario Carli* recipe book, back cover (Fratelli Carli Photographic Archives).

→Demijohn storage, Fratelli Carli factory, Imperia, 1960 (Fratelli Carli Photographic Archives).

Mineral Water

Various bottlers

late nineteenth century

The natural mineral water industry, which bottles mineral spring water, developed in Italy at the close of the nineteenth century as it did in other European countries and in the United States, particularly in spa towns, known for the curative qualities of their waters. These locations, which were scattered throughout the country and had become elegant and elitist spa centres and vacation resorts, from San Gemini to San Pellegrino, from Recoaro Terme to Corticella, soon began to intensively exploit the possibility of bottling the water, to sell it for sanitary and therapeutic purposes.

One of the first to undertake this activity was the Sangemini company (now owned by the Norda-Gaudianello Group), which in 1889 began to bottle the water in its factory at San Gemini (Terni). Its slightly tart-tasting water was originally distributed in pharmacies because it was considered to be beneficial in feeding babies and delicate organisms, as indicated on the label which read "Water for children, old people and convalescents."

At the turn of the century, other spa towns began similar businesses, which they sustained not by creating a particular form of bottle, but by choosing to differentiate their communication strategies, from the labels to the advertising campaigns. The *Società anonima delle Terme San Pellegrino* (Bergamo), which owned the San Pellegrino spring, for example, inaugurated the Baths, the drinking rooms, the Grand Hotel and the Casino in the early years of the twentieth century, transforming the town of San Pellegrino Terme into a spa resort patronized by the European aristocracy. The water-bottling company (which has been owned by Nestlé since 1989) produced 35,343 bottles of mineral water in 1900, 5562 of which were intended for exportation. The label on the bottle, registered in 1906 (no. 7632), highlighted the Italian origin

of the brand and its connection to the territory, with a drawing of the Art Nouveau-style Casinò di San Pellegrino Terme. An equally significant example of label, after World War II, is Frisia, which in 1969 gave the traditional glass bottle a distinctive look with the new label conceived by graphic designer Max Huber (1919–1992).

Initially limited to the areas around the spas, the market for mineral water grew in the sixties, but developed far more significantly during the final decades of the century, when Italy became the world leader in both the production and consumption of mineral water, no longer considered for its therapeutic qualities but as a household beverage. An emblematic case in point is the notoriety achieved by Ferrarelle (since 2005 owned by LGR Holding). Founded in 1893 in Riardo (Caserta), the company, which bottled the water from ancient volcanic springs, renowned for its natural effervescence, was presented in 1900 at the *Esposizione nazionale d'igiene* in Naples where it was promoted as a beneficial source of water to drink at every meal. The first advertising campaigns were launched in 1903, in specialized medical and pharmaceutical publications, but also in more popular magazines such as "L'illustrazione Italiana." It definitively won over the markets in the eighties, with the advertising campaign "Liscia, gassata o... Ferrarelle?" created by Michele Rizzi, Lele Panzeri and Annamaria Testa (Michele Rizzi&Associati agency).

At the end of the decade, with the introduction of the bottle made out of PET (polyethylene terephthalate) which made it possible to keep production inside the company, using an unbreakable, more lightweight and economical material that could make a difference in the cost of production and transportation, company strategies began to reconsider the design of the bottles as well. They began

to differentiate the shapes, the formats, the caps, basically following one of two directions. The first replicated the original configurations of the glass bottles in PET. This was the case for San Pellegrino mineral water, which reproduced the shape and colour of the original green glass bottle in order to maintain the image for which it was recognized around the world; or San Bernardo mineral water, which in 1995 commissioned Giugiaro Design to work on an identical project for both a glass and a PET bottle, reproducing the tactile effect of eighty-eight drops of water on the surface of the two bottles. The second direction proceeded to experiment with configurations that were more congenial to plastic as a material. They exploited the lightness, malleability and mechanical properties of plastic to dismantle and simplify the form in order to respond to the requirements of production, seeking a balance between technical performance, economy of material and usability, and refining the configuration of the parts to achieve the greater resistance to pressure required by carbonated waters. Patents were filed, for example, by Fabio Chimetto for the Acqua Vera bottles in 1997 (with Loris Favero) and for San Pellegrino in 2002 (no. EP1348636 A1).

This design work led, at the turn of the millennium, to a general reconsideration of the glass bottle, which might also be conceived as an attempt to respond to the environmental issues raised by the production of immense quantities of plastic waste. Other examples include the fluid version designed in 2000 by Pininfarina for Lauretana, and the one with the transparent plastic cap, produced by F.lli Guzzini and designed in 2011 by Sottsass Associati for Lurisia (which is owned today by Invernizzi and Oscar Farinetti's Eataly), a brand linked to the *Stabilimento termale omonimo Lurisia* (Cuneo) founded in 1940.

→Plinio Codognato, Corticella
mineral water for the table,
advertising poster, 1920s.

→Stabilimento Tipolitografico
Mozzati, Acqua San Pellegrino,
advertising poster, 1931.

→Acqua minerale Lurisia,
advertising poster, 1930s
(Archivio Lurisia, Roccaforte
Mondovì).

E.-H. Guitard, *Le prestigieux passé des eaux minérales. Histoire du thermalisme et de l'hydrologie des origines à 1950*, Société d'histoire de la pharmacie, Paris 1951; M. Soresina, "Le acque minerali e le terme europee nel XIX secolo tra medicina, industria e modernità," E. Nocifora (edited by), *Turismatica. Turismo, cultura, nuova imprenditorialità e globalizzazione dei mercati*, Franco Angeli, Milan, 2000; D. Brignone, "Storia di un'acqua effervescente naturale: Ferrarelle dalle origini ai giorni nostri," *Ferrarelle: una storia effervescente*, Silvana Editoriale, Cinesello Balsamo (MI) 2001; P. Raspadori, "Bollicine. Per una storia dell'industria delle acque minerali in Italia dalle origini agli anni Ottanta del Novecento," *Annali di storia dell'impresa*, 13, 2002; G. Temporelli, *L'acqua che beviamo. Un viaggio nel mondo delle acque, naturali e trattate, destinate all'alimentazione e alla terapia*, Franco Muzzio Editore, Rome, 2003; A. Ciuffetti, "Industria delle acque minerali ed ambiente. L'acqua nella storia," *I frutti di Demetra, Bollettino di storia e ambiente*, 14, 2007, pp. 37–46 (available online at www.issm.cnr.it/demetrapdf/boll_14_2007/Pagine%20da%20demetra_imp%2014_ciuffetti.pdf); C. Folli, *San Gemini e le sue acque*, Armando Editore, Rome 2012; United States Patent, *Bottle for beverages with ergonomic grip*, n. EP1348636 A1, priority 27.03.2002, reg. 25.11.2002; publ. 1.10.2003; Archivio centrale dello Stato, Italian Patent and Trademark Office, no. 7632, filed 30.08.1906, reg. 30.10.1906.

→CBBPR, Sangemini, advertisement (from *La Lettura*, 1, 1939, np).

→Michele Rizzi, Lele Panzeri and Annamaria Testa/Agenzia Michele Rizzi&Associati, Ferrarelle, advertising campaign, 1980s (Ferrarelle Archives, Milan).

LISCIA?

GASSATA?

O FERRARELLE?

Effervescente naturale.

Chianti Wine in a Flask

Various producers, Tuscany

3rd century; then second half of the nineteenth century

In most cases, the excellent wines produced in Italy are bottled in the classic, standard and rather anonymous Bordeaux-style bottle; but there are some examples in which the content is totally identified with the container, such as Chianti wine and its flask. The history of the flask goes far back in time, and it has left traces in the art and literature of the Middle Ages. Its conception and production, which was concentrated primarily in Tuscany, respond to a number of practical necessities: on the one hand to provide a universal unit of measure, and on the other to contain the local wine, Chianti. Like many other containers, the flask has always served as a unit of measure. The bottom part, which is practically sphere-shaped and narrows progressively into a cylindrical neck, is sheathed in woven straw to protect it during transportation and, by weaving on a base that did not exist in ancient times, to keep it standing in a strictly vertical position. The straw originally covered the entire neck of the bottle, but in the mid-seventeenth century it was shortened when an emblem was applied to the glass to specify the volume of the container to help prevent the recurring frauds on the wine tax.

The need to produce glass containers, including the flasks, historically led to the development of glass furnaces and manufacturing companies in the area of Val d'Elsa and Empoli. In the early decades of the thirteenth century, the furnaces sprouted up where raw materials were available (sand and quartz minerals) and there were extensive woodlands for the fuel and vegetable ash they required. These were decisive factors for the development of glass production in this region, which in fact has almost always been utilitarian in nature: goblets, flasks, bottles, lamps, vials and glassware for medical purposes. At the turn of the twentieth century, the furnaces grew into large industries that produced flasks, demijohns, oil cruets and funnels, in the shade of green that was typical of Empoli glass, and was due to its high ferrous oxide content. The "bufferia" glass factories, where the glass was originally mouth-blown, later associated the new semiautomatic glass-blowing machines with the hand-weaving processes for the straw basket. The weaving was done primarily by female workers, in a production chain integrated with agricultural labour in terms of time and materials. The weaving techniques changed over time of course, from the earliest versions that wove the marsh grass horizontally in strips, to the later straw versions introduced in the nineteenth century, made with vertical strips tied together at the base with strands of straw.

Production is currently undergoing a problematic phase of transition, with quantities falling sharply for economic reasons, considering the expense of making the straw sheathing and because the shape of the flask makes it hard to store, package and transport. The interest of an object such as the Chianti flask lies in the evolution that led an ancient traditionally handcrafted artefact to a process of semi-mechanized industrial production, deeply rooted in the agricultural economy of the region, which fostered the growth of a vast entrepreneurial glassmaking cluster. Focusing more specifically on the design, it appears to be the result of a process of modification that perfected the technical and functional solutions over time, building a precise identity, based on the formal configuration, on the choice of materials and on the relationship with "the contents," Chianti wine. An innovative idea of packaging, *antelitteram*, that instantly identifies the product inside.

G. Cantelli, "La storia del vetro in Toscana," F. Burkhardt, C. Mantica (edited by), *Mestieri d'autore*, Camera di commercio, industria, artigianato e agricoltura di Siena – Electa, Siena–Milan 1993, pp. 25–35; S. Ciappi, "Il vetro d'uso comune in Toscana dal 1750 al 1950," *Il vetro dall'antichità all'età contemporanea, I Quaderni del giornale economico*, 5, 1996, pp. 83–86; S. Ciappi, *Il vetro impagliato a Empoli e a Montelupo Fiorentino (1900-1970)*, in D. Ferrari, G. Meconcelli Notarianni (edited by), *Il vetro fra antico e moderno. Le più recenti scoperte archeologiche. Un secolo di produzione e designer del vetro italiano (1897-1997)*, Milan 1999, pp. 91–94; A. Bassi, *Design anonimo in Italia. Oggetti comuni e progetto incognito*, Electa, Milan 2007, pp. 74–77.

→Chianti Ruffino, advertisement (from *Le Vie d'Italia*, 12, 1948, back cover).

→Glass factory Ditta Carlo Del Vivo, Empoli, pages from the price list, late nineteenth century.

on p. 132
→Cif – Commissionaria industria fiaschi, Empoli, advertisement (from *Il vetro*, II, 1, January 1939, p. XII).

130   **the industrialization**   **/ bottled**
         of traditional food products
         1850–1920

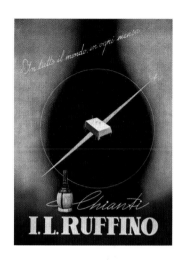

In tutto il mondo in ogni mensa

Chianti

I. L. RUFFINO

FABBRICA DI VETRI - DITTA CARLO DEL VIVO - EMPOLI		
DENOMINAZIONE e Numeri d'ordine	**CAPACITÀ** Litri	**PREZZO**
N. 1 Fiaschi e Fiaschetti uso Montecatini.	3½ a 3.	16
	2 a 2½	12
	1 a 1½	8
	½ a ⅜	7
	¼	6
N. 2 Fiaschi e Fiaschetti rivestiti uso Chianti.	2 a 2½	10
	1 a 1½	8
	1 a 1¼	7
N. 3 Fiaschi e Fiaschetti a doppio spessore con orlo alla bocca.	2 a 2½	16
	1 a 1½	13
	½ a ⅜	10

FABBRICA DI VETRI - DITTA CARLO DEL VIVO - EMPOLI		
DENOMINAZIONE e Numeri d'ordine	**CAPACITÀ** Litri	**PREZZO**
N. 4 Fiaschi Toscanelli a doppio spessore con orlo alla bocca e Bollo.	2 a 2½	17
	1 a 1¾	15
N. 5 Aspira Olio		28
N. 6 Ampolla per Olio		25

SOCIETÀ **C. I. F.** ANONIMA

COMMISSIONARIA INDUSTRIA FIASCHI

E M P O L I
(FIRENZE)

★

Vetrerie aderenti:

*L. & O. Ancilli, Poggibonsi - Vetreria Busoni, Livorno
Società Vetraria Certaldese, Certaldo-Empoli - Ditta
Alfredo Del Vivo, Empoli-Pontassieve - Elmi & Se-
rafini, Pistoia - Società Anonima Vetreria « Etrusca »,
Empoli - Fratelli Rigatti, Castelfiorentino - S. Mi-
niato - E. Taddei & C., Empoli-Figline Valdarno*

Rappresentante generale delle suddette vetrerie per la vendita di:

*Fiaschi nudi e vestiti di qualsiasi tipo - barili
damigiane - bottiglioni di tutte le capacità e di
tutti i tipi - fiaschi-bottiglia da esportazione
aspiraolio - ampolle da ghiaccio - pulcianelle
tipo Orvieto - piramidi da olio in vetro verde*

Fazi Battaglia Verdicchio Wine

Fazi Battaglia, Cupramontana (Ancona);
then Castelplanio (Ancona)
1953

In 1949 the Fazi Battaglia wineries at Cupramontana (Ancona) in the Marche region were purchased by Francesco Angelini, a pharmaceutical industrialist, from Fernando Fazi and Vittorio Battaglia who had founded it some years earlier. At the time it produced about sixty to eighty thousand bottles of Verdicchio per year, from a local grape that was still rather obscure, the quality of which the new owner desired to improve.

In 1953, he decided to give a signature look to his Verdicchio dei Castelli di Jesi Titulus, by launching a competition for the design of the packaging that was won by Antonio Maiocchi, an architect from Milan. The amphora-shaped bottle was distinguished by its curved shape, inspired by ancient Etruscan wine amphorae, by the typical emerald green colour and the equally recognizable label. Designed by engraver Bruno da Osimo (Bruno Marsili, 1888–1962), its lettering harked back to Antiquity, to ancient Greek letters actually, but it also included a separate scroll that illustrated the territory of production, rolled up and tied to the neck of the bottle with a string of raffia. Unchanged for over 50 years, the product was revised in 2007 by the communication agency Robilant & Associati; confirming the bottle—only the shape was slightly adjusted to make it more streamlined—the agency redesigned the central label, neck and collar, capsule and parchment scroll. Influenced by similar models from Provence, and protected by the 1953 patent (no. 45572), the bottle is not only a synonym of the Fazi Battaglia brand, but has become the symbol of Verdicchio dei Castelli di Jesi itself, and an icon of Italian wine.

Fazi Battaglia, which moved in 1956 to more modern facilities in Castelplanio (Ancona), is now run by the fourth generation in the family. (fb)

A.M. Sette, L. Sacchi (edited by), *Disegno e design. Brevetti e creatività italiani*, Fondazione Valore Italia, Rome 2009, pp. 226–27; L. Olivari (edited by), "Di generazione in generazione ma per via materna," *Il Corriere vinicolo*, 45, 14 November 2011, pp. 36–38; Archivio centrale dello Stato, Italian Patent and Trademark Office, no. 45572, filed 18.06.1953.

→Patent, no. 45572, 18 June 1953.

→Advertisement (from *Le Vie d'Italia*, 12, 1958, p. 1631).

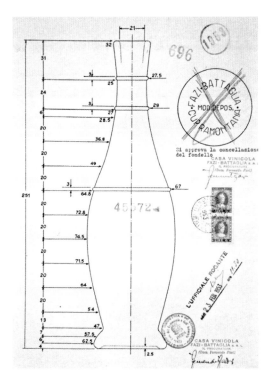

Vermouth Aperitif

Various manufacturers, Piemonte

early nineteenth century

Vermouth is a wine flavoured with absinthe (*arthemisia absinthium*)—*wermuth* in German, which is liqueur-like in consistency and slightly tart in flavour. Familiar to the Ancient Romans and available in various parts of Italy, it found particularly advantageous conditions for production in the Piemonte region, an area known for its dry wines and aromatic Alpine herbs. This tradition is one of the reasons for the existence, in the provinces of Turin, Asti and Cuneo, of a large number of manufacturers who built important industries in the nineteenth century to make and market vermouth.

More specifically, Giuseppe Bernardino Carpano founded the *Fabbrica di liquori e vermouth Giuseppe Carpano* in 1820, under the porticoes of Piazza Castello, to produce the liqueur industrially: his grandfather Antonio Benedetto Carpano (1751–1821) had been making it since 1786, mixing white Canelli moscato wine with alcohol, sugar and aromatic herb extracts, which he sold in the Merendazzo liqueur store in Piazza Castello. In 1870 Carpano introduced Punt e Mes, a bitter version of the vermouth "corrected" with half a dose of *china*, hence the expression in dialect "Punt e Mes," meaning a "point and a half" (the trademark was registered in 1916 as a bitter Vermouth, no. 16007). The company, which was sold by the Carpano family in 1939 to Silvio Turati, expanded its market by investing in advertising campaigns, designed in the twenties by the *affichistes* Marcello Dudovich (1878–1962) and Achille Luciano Mauzan (1883–1952) and after World War II, by Armando Testa. His was the remarkable three-dimensional image of Punt e Mes designed in 1960, a visual transcription of the name with outstanding iconic intensity and power of suggestion. Since 2001 Carpano has been owned by Fratelli Branca Distillerie.

In the second half of the nineteenth century, at least two other *maître licoristes* in Turin experimented with new recipes for vermouth: Alessandro Martini (1824–1905)—with Martini Bianco, Rosso, Rosato, Extra Dry—and Gaspare Campari (1828–1882). They were followed by many others in more peripheral areas, including Cinzano, Cora, Gancia, Grassotti, Cocchi, Calissano, Ballor or Fratelli Ferrero di Riccardo, just to the name the most renowned. The variety of manufacturers and the need to distinguish the different types of vermouths provided the impulse for the rapid development of corporate identity and communication tools, which brought many of the greatest *affichistes*, followed by graphic and visual designers, to work in this field. Then again, vermouth is the drink that originated the all-Italian ritual of the *aperitivo*, conceived as a way of filling time and setting the mood before a meal, as presented and visually interpreted by the manufacturers themselves since the nineteenth century, particularly in the Piemonte region.

Vermouth is also the basic ingredient for cocktails such as the Dry Martini, a world-class cocktail that mixes it with gin, the inevitable green olive, and a squeeze of lemon rind; to be sipped exclusively out of a classic martini glass.

G. Dalmasso, "Vermut," *Enciclopedia Italiana*, Enciclopedia Italiana Treccani, Rome 1937 (available online at www.treccani.it/enciclopedia/vermut_(Enciclopedia_Italiana)/); "Antonio Benedetto Càrpano," *Dizionario Biografico degli Italiani*, vol. 20, Enciclopedia Italiana Treccani, Roma 1977 (available online at www.treccani.it/enciclopedia/antonio-benedetto-carpano_(Dizionario-Biografico)/); B. and J. Sallé, *Dizionario Larousse degli alcolici e dei cocktails*, Gremese Editore, Rome 2001, pp. 145–46; Archivio centrale dello Stato, Italian Patent and Trademark Office, no. 16007, filed 16.05.1916, reg. 4.06.1916.

→Armando Testa, Punt e Mes, advertising poster, 1960.

ARMANDO TESTA

PUNTₑMES
APERITIVO
un punto di amaro e mezzo di dolce

→Cinzano, advertisement (from
La cucina italiana, September
1958, p. 777).

→Iper, Martini, advertisement,
1960.

→Max Huber, Vermouth
Grassotti, advertisement (from
Le Vie d'Italia, 12, 1948,
p. 1070).

136   **the industrialization**   **/ bottled**
        of traditional food products
        1850–1920

1872

grassotti

vermouth

torino

Aperol Aperitif

Barbieri, Padua; now Campari,
Sesto San Giovanni (Milan)
1919

The Aperol liqueur was created in Padua in 1919 by Luigi and Silvio Barbieri, the sons of Giuseppe, founder in 1880 of the company based in Bassano del Grappa (Vicenza), which also produced Ovos, a zabaglione-flavoured liqueur that was one of Vov's direct competitors [**Vov Egg Liqueur** p. 146]. It was introduced at the International Trade Fair held in Padua for the first time that year. Slightly alcoholic, bright orange in colour with a lightly bittersweet flavour, it was made with an infusion in alcohol of orange, rhubarb, cinchona, gentian and other aromatic herbs, with the addition of sugar and water. It was praised, as were many food products of the time, for the low alcoholic content that also made it suitable for female consumers, and for its beneficial health properties, as a "regulator of digestion," protection against influenza and as a tonic for convalescents.

Registered as a trademark in 1923 (no. 24591), from the twenties onwards Fratelli Barbieri featured its colour—a signature element to play against the bright ruby red of Campari Soda—in all the texts and images of its advertising campaigns. In the decade that followed, the company's graphic design work was commissioned to authors such as Erberto Carboni (1899–1983), who produced one of the first Modernist-looking ads for the company, or the Padua-born Futurist painter Dormàl (Carlo Maria Dormal, 1909–1938), selecting design magazines, among others, as a preferred means of diffusion. From the very beginning Aperol was very judicious in the selection of its advertising methods and strategies, which came to include television advertising in the seventies, particularly the commercials broadcast

for *Carosello*, and led the company to choose an interesting contemporary illustrator such as Lorenzo Mattotti for its new campaigns in the nineties. Starting in the fifties, Aperol became a key ingredient in making the *spritz*, an aperitif that probably originated in Austria and has become extremely popular in the Veneto area; it was originally a mix of sparkling white wine and water, which later evolved to include a shot of Aperol or Select, or Campari in a more alcoholic version, topped with a bit of seltz or soda water. It is no surprise that in 2011, this aperitif was marketed as the Aperol Spritz, in a bottled single-serving industrial version that has been very successful.

The experimentation with new products and the rejuvenation of the company's communication strategies in recent years, which included the restyling of the labels by Maurizio di Robilant in 2008, confirm the vitality of this Padua-based company, which became part of the Campari Group in 2004. (fb)

M. Scudiero and C. Rebeschini, *Futurismo veneto*, L'Editore, Padua 1990, pp. 204–08; B. and J. Sallé, *Dizionario Larousse degli alcolici e dei cocktails*, Gremese Editore, Rome 2001, p. 35; Archivio centrale dello Stato, Italian Patent and Trademark Office, no. 24591, filed 22.10.1923, reg. 4.11.1923.

→Erberto Carboni, advertising poster, 1931 (in *Il Dramma*, VII, 112, 1932).

→Advertisement (photo by Menotti Danesin), 1930s (from *Triennale di Milano 1933*, special issue, suppl. to *Lidel*, 1933, p. 11).

→Lorenzo Mattotti, Aperol, poster, 1988 (© Davide Campari-Milano).

APEROL

APERITIVO

L'APEROL è un dissetante aperitivo aromatico di gusto squisito poco alcoolico. Viene preparato con China, Genziana, Rabarbaro ed erbe aromatiche, e costituisce perciò la sintesi di antichi curativi vegetali. L'APEROL regola la digestione e mantiene il corpo snello ed elegante.

S. L. F.ˡˡⁱ BARBIERI - PADOVA

138   **the industrialization**   **/ bottled**
of traditional food products
1850–1920

Cynar Aperitif

G.B. Pezziol, Padua; now Campari,
Sesto San Giovanni (Milan)
1950

Of Italy's many liqueurs, Cynar (which derives its name from *cynara scolimus*, the Latin name for the artichoke), is considered to be particularly original because of its unusual artichoke-based recipe, and because it has become such a part of the collective imaginary thanks to the communicative power of its messages, and of course, its versatility. Made from a recipe based on the processing of artichoke leaves with a blend of herbs and spices, it was created by *G.B. Pezziol di Padova società per azioni*, the company that already produced the egg-based liqueur Vov, and was directed at the time by Angelo Dalle Molle. The trademark was registered in 1950 (no. 99835), and the following year a patent was filed for the label, a dark red rectangle dominated by the picture of an artichoke wrapped in the letters Cynar, with the words "The aperitif by Pezziol with active artichoke extracts" (no. 108192).

Launched as an aperitif, its very first advertisements established a promotional approach that placed the accent on its health benefits, which were "the product of long-term studies and ancient recipes" containing active extracts of artichoke and vitamin B, "universally" recognized for their specific effects on the liver and the nervous system. That is why it was presented as the finest "antidote to the wear and tear of modern life." After 1966 that slogan, "Against the wear and tear of modern life drink Cynar," became one of the primary catalysts for its popularity, thanks to the series of skits on *Carosello* that starred actor Ernesto Calindri, who recited the slogan sitting at a table in the middle of a busy thoroughfare. The affiliation between the actor and the brand lasted through 1984. Also marketed from the very beginning in the Cynar Soda version (a brand registered in 1953, no. 116784), over

the years it was reclassified in the category of liqueurs that also qualify it as a digestive. Since 1995 the Cynar brand has been a part of the Campari Group. (fb)

Archivio centrale dello Stato, Italian Patent and Trademark Office, no. 99835, filed 31.03.1950, reg. 28.12.1950; no. 108192, filed 16.03.1951, reg. 5.07.1952; no. 116784, filed 17.05.1953, reg. 8.04.1954; Australian Trademark, no. AUS 135433, reg. 23.01.1958 (available online at www.ipaustralia. com.au/applicant/pezziol-bv/ trademarks/135433/).

→Patent, no. AUS 135433, 23 January 1958.

→Advertisement, 1970s.

→Franco De Clementi, advertisement, early 1960s.

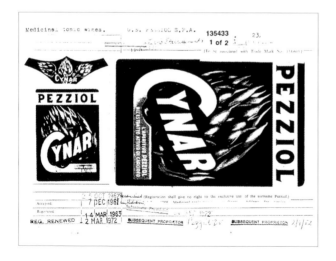

CONTRO IL LOGORIO DELLA VITA MODERNA...

CYNAR. L'AMARO VERO, MA LEGGERO.

CHI SI DIFENDE SI SALVA

PEZZIOL

CYNAR

La necessità di salvezza impo
all'uomo fin dalle origini
il problema della difesa, con
mezzi sempre più validi.
L'organismo invece ebbe
dalla natura un aiuto sempre
efficace per la sua difesa:
il carciofo, cui decotti salut
erano noti fin dalle più
antiche civiltà. Anche oggi
dal carciofo la difesa migliore
CYNAR
l'aperitivo a base
di carciofo e vitamina B.

CONTRO IL LOGORIO
DELLA VITA MODERNA

CHI SI DIFENDE SI SALVA

PEZZIOL

CYNAR

aperitivo

Difendete il vostro fegato
e i vostri nervi dal logorio
della vita moderna.
Bevete CYNAR,
l'aperitivo a base
di carciofo e vitamina B₁.

CONTRO IL LOGORIO
DELLA VITA MODERNA

Florio Marsala

Florio, Palermo; Cinzano, Santa Vittoria
d'Alba (Cuneo); now Illva, Saronno (Varese)
1832

Vincenzo Florio (1799–1868) belonged to a family that, in the early years of the nineteenth century, founded a number of different businesses. After settling in Palermo, he initially inherited a series of companies from his father and his uncle which he expanded over time, financing them with his own bank. These companies, which were later run by various members of the family (Ignazio Sr., 1838–1891; Ignazio Jr., 1868–1957; Vincenzo, 1883–1959), spanned many sectors, including navigation—with an intercontinental company that merged with Rubattino in 1881 to become *Navigazione generale italiana*—, steel mills and textile industries, as well as a sulphur industry, ceramics, and tuna fish, which was canned in oil and distributed throughout Italy as early as the mid-nineteenth century.

In 1832 Vincenzo Florio went into the winemaking business, building a winery made of tufo stone in Marsala to produce the local wine. The complex was sited near the modern distilleries built by two English entrepreneurs, of the many who had come to the island after 1806 when it became strategic for the control of the Mediterranean to contain the influence of Napoleon, John Woodhouse (1730–1813) and Benjamin Ingham (1810–1872), who with his nephew Joseph Whitaker, opened new horizons in his father's trade with the United States.

Credit for the production of this type of wine must be given to Woodhouse, who in 1794 added alcohol (rum or brandy) to the local wine, obtaining a stable new product that could thus be transported to England, where it was shipped almost exclusively at the beginning.

Marsala is a liqueur-like, aromatic, highly alcoholic wine, both dry and sweet at the same time, with an intense golden yellow colour tending to orange. In the 1820s, the Marsala produced in Sicily was still marketed as "similar to the wine of Madeira" or "Xeres," the Portuguese and Spanish localities that enjoyed a far more consolidated reputation at the time for their production of similar wines. Florio too stated his intent in 1934 to begin a "production of wine similar to Madeira." But he soon became the first producer to label Marsala with its Italian name, the Marsala Florio S.O.M. (Superior Old Marsala) in particular, and to gain access to international markets, thanks to his fleet of merchant ships and his trade network.

Unlike other areas of the country, in the first half of the nineteenth century a progressive separation took place between the cultivation of grapes, by farmers, and the wine-making process, which along with distribution was handled by industrial-scale enterprises.

Having reinforced his production facilities with new steam-powered equipment and mechanical bottling lines, by the end of the nineteenth century Florio had more employees than his major English competitors. In 1904, in response to a time of crisis, Florio gathered a group of capitalists and tradesmen from Marsala and founded a public company, *Florio e C. – Savi* (*Società anonima vinicola italiana*), setting up a financial operation that in 1907 would lead to a partial acquisition of the company by *Distillerie italiane* in Milan, and in 1924 to the purchase of the majority share by the owners of Cinzano, who also owned Woodhouse and Ingham-Whitaker. In 1929 the three companies Florio-Whitaker-Woodhouse were unified, creating an industrial concentration of companies that controlled the market.

As patrons of the Liberty-style in Palermo, an expression of Art Nouveau that had no equal in Europe, with a very active social life during the Belle Époque in Sicily, the Florio family commissioned architect Ernesto Basile to renovate the Grand Hotel Villa Igea (1899–1900) and to build Villino Florio (1899). The same influences permeate the advertising posters for Marsala Florio, designed by the most famous *affichistes* of the time, such as Plinio Codognato (1878–1940), Achille Mauzan (1883–1952), Leonetto Cappiello (1875–1942), Marcello Dudovich (1878–1962), Giorgio Muggiani (1887–1938) and Marcello Nizzoli (1887–1969). Vincenzo Florio had another idea for a potent publicity measure that brought international attention to the brand. As an enthusiast of automobile racing, he first promoted Coppa Florio, a series of automobile races that were run near Brescia, followed in 1906 by Targa Florio, an open-road competition for racing cars through the region of Sicily, a high-society affair and racing event that was held through 1977. In January 1998, the Saronno-based company Illva (*Industria lombarda liquori vini e affini*) took control over Florio's entire block of shares. (fb)

R. Giuffrida, R. Lentini, *L'età dei Florio*, Sellerio, Palermo 1985; R. Lentini, "Un inglese nel cuore del Mediterraneo: origini e caratteristiche del Marsala," *Douro. Estudos & Documentos*, 21, 2006, pp. 175–82; O. Cancila, *I Florio: storia di una dinastia imprenditoriale*, Rcs, Milan 2008; S. Candela, *I Florio*, Sellerio, Palermo 2008.

→Leonetto Cappiello, sketch for a poster, c. 11930 (Florio Archives, Marsala).

Maraschino Luxardo Cherry Liqueur

Luxardo, Zara; then Torreglia, Padua

mid-nineteenth century

In the case of "liquids" in general, and more specifically in the case of drinks, alcohol and liqueurs, it is not always easy to find a bottle that is totally identified with its contents. That is, a bottle or other type of container that becomes synonymous with the product it contains. This is the case—just to cite a few examples in Italy—with the chianti wine flask or the Campari Soda and Aranciata San Pellegrino bottles, or with Maraschino Luxardo and its typical straw-covered bottle.

Founded in 1821 in Zara, on the Dalmatian coast, by Girolamo Luxardo (1784–1865), a trader in rope and coral born in Santa Margherita Ligure who had come to Zara to expand his market, the Luxardo company opened with the production of a typical local drink, a distillate made from cherries known as "rosolio maraschino," which was known in the area since the Middle Ages. Luxardo perceived the potential for this liqueur to be produced industrially, and exploiting his commercial relationships—he had been named vice-Consul for the Kingdom of Savoia in Zara—in 1829 he was granted an exclusive fifteen-year concession from the Hapsburgic authorities to produce the liqueur. Over the years, to complement the original production of Maraschino, Luxardo introduced other distillates and varieties of rosolio with varying degrees of alcoholic content. By the mid-nineteenth century, his products were popular on the local and foreign markets, from the Kingdom of Savoia to that of the Two Sicilies, from Central Europe to the Danube River, in Russia,

on the Mediterranean, in the Americas, in India and Australia.

Since its very foundation, the company was actively engaged in advertising and other communication strategies; in 1885 it filed a patent for a label (no. 1223) which was later modified to include the red "Luxardo" logo at the top (registered in 1924, no. 29248), and has remained substantially unchanged to this day.

Another unique signature element, which has also remained basically unchanged, is the bottle. To make certain that the Maraschino would reach its destination in one piece, the long-neck glass bottle with the slender body was protected with a layer of woven straw, made with a handcrafting technique that had developed around Zara, and been associated with the production of maraschino since the early nineteenth century.

The vicissitudes of Italian history in its relations with the city of Zara, which became part of Yugoslavia after World War II, led to the nationalization of the company, which had been seriously damaged during the 1943 bombings. Giorgio Luxardo (1897–1963), the family's fourth generation, decided to start all over again in Torreglia (Padua), where he purchase an unfinished factory from the Pezziol company. He selected the area of the Colli Euganei, where he deemed he could successfully cultivate the cherries, his raw material, near the processing plants. After grafting the Marasca cherry onto sour cherry trees from Pescara, in just a matter

of years Luxardo obtained a fruit that ripened rapidly and was suitable for mechanical harvesting and industrial processing.

In the meantime, the old factory in Zara was renamed "I tvornica likera maraska," and the Yugoslavian government began to produce Maraschino and sell it in bottles that were identical to those of Luxardo. It was not until the sixties, after a long court case, that the paternity of the Italian company was acknowledged. Today the production of Maraschino, still controlled entirely by the company, is run by the sixth generation of the family. (fb)

N. Luxardo De Franchi, I Luxardo del Maraschino, Libreria Editrice Goriziana, Gorizia 2004; G. Roverato, Luxardo (Girolamo) S.p.A., in id., L'industrializzazione diffusa. Storia dell'economia padovana 1923-2003, Appendix I casi aziendali, Esedra editrice, Padua 2005; M. Barbot, Giorgio Luxardo, in Dizionario Biografico degli Italiani, vol. 66, Enciclopedia Italiana Treccani, Rome 2007 (available online at www.treccani.it/enciclopedia/giorgio-luxardo_(Dizionario-Biografico)/); Archivio centrale dello Stato, Italian Patent and Trademark Office, no. 1223, filed 4.09.1885, reg. 21.10.1885; no. 29248, filed 15.02.1924, reg.15.02.1925.

→The bottle today and advertisements from 1890 and 1900, (Girolamo Luxardo spa Archives, Torreglia).

144   **the industrialization**   / **bottled**
of traditional food products
1850–1920

Vov Egg Liqueur

G.B. Pezziol, Padua; now Molinari, Rome

1910

The recipe for an egg-based liqueur was probably invented in 1845, when Padua-born pastry chef Gian Battista Pezziol needed to find a use for the egg yolks left over from his production of *torrone*, and so he mixed them with Marsala, alcohol and sugar. He founded the company G.B.Pezziol, located in Via dei Servi, and in 1881 participated in the Italian Exposition in Milan. The company had given its liqueur many different names (such as Zabajone or Zabaione "delle benedettine"), but in 1910 it filed a patent for the trademark Vov, which appeared between quotation marks (no. 10390), and the product became established under this name, borrowed from the word *vovi*, which meant "eggs" in the Venetian dialect.

It was then, in the first decade of the twentieth century, that Vov made the transition from a drink made to order, though the recipe was quite exclusive, to an industrial product that would be produced by other companies as well under similar names. This transformation coincided with the introduction of the unmistakable bottle and an intense advertising campaign launched by the company, which was owned in the twenties by the Pezziol family and directed by Amabile and Antonio Palamidese, vice-president of the Padua trade fair, succeeded, in 1935, by the brothers Angelo and Amedeo Dalle Molle.

The cylinder-shaped bottle, which could be grasped by the small characteristic handle near the neck, was white to preserve its sun-sensitive contents, and initially made out of ceramic; it was later produced in glass, though it maintained the opaque white colour as a signature element. The label, which has remained basically unchanged over the years, but was not registered until 1931 (no. 44366), features the word Vov in yellow against

a blue sky at sunset, with the Basilica of Sant'Antonio in Padua in the background.

Advertising announcements and posters, which focus primarily on the invigorating, tonic and comforting power of Vov, were commissioned to some of Italy's finest *affichistes*. In 1910, Aldo Mazza (1880–1964) emphasized the nutritional value of the egg yolk by drawing all the diners to look like chickens, roosters and chicks sipping their drinks in elegant evening dress; Leonetto Cappiello (1875–1942) relied on one of his classic character ideas in 1922, identifying the brand with a dark Pierrot against a yellow background, while in the thirties Marcello Nizzoli (1887–1969) set the bottle on a shelf that was actually a perspective extension of the logo.

After World War II, Vov grew extremely popular, thanks in part to the many other versions of egg-yolk based liqueurs, such as the Bombardino, a cocktail that was a big hit at ski resorts.

In 2012 the Vov trademark and recipe were purchased by Molinari and production was moved to Moncalieri (Turin). (fb)

G. Simone, *Il guardasigilli del regime: l'itinerario politico e culturale di Alfredo Rocco*, Franco Angeli, Milan 2012, p. 92; *Chi è? Dizionario degli Italiani d'oggi*, vol. 6, Rome 1957, p. 207; Archivio centrale dello Stato, Italian Patent and Trademark Office, no. 10390, filed 24.04.1910, reg. 25.08.1910; no. 44366, filed 18.08.1931, reg. 15.12.1932.

→Marcello Nizzoli, preliminary sketches, 1930s.

→Marcello Nizzoli, advertising poster, 1939.

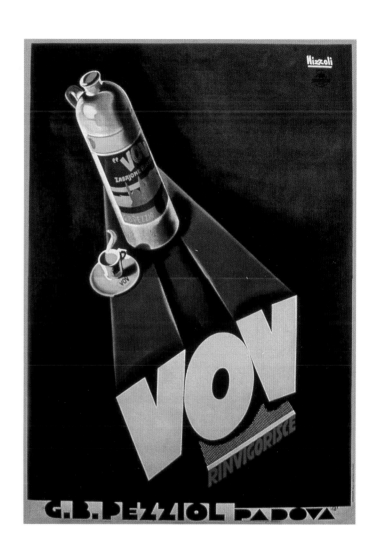

Vecchia Romagna Brandy

Buton, Bologna; now Montenegro,
San Lazzaro di Savena (Bologna)
1939

The historic fame of Italian brandy is linked to a number of products such as Stock, made by the Stock company founded in Trieste in 1884, and Vecchia Romagna, produced by Buton in Bologna. This distillate of Trebbiano grapes in the unusual thick glass "triangular" bottle featuring a label with the image of Bacchus, was conceived in 1939 within the company headed by the sons of Filippo Sassoli de Bianchi, Achille in particular, who took over the company upon the death of their father, who had inherited it himself from his wife Maria Rovinazzi. The Distilleria Gio. Buton & C. originally belonged to the Rovinazzi family: it was founded in 1820 by the pastry chef Giacomo Rovinazzi and Jean Bouton, a veteran of the Napoleonic wars exiled after the Restoration in France, where he had owned a distillery in Gentilly, in the Cognac area. Filippo Sassoli de Bianchi turned the business around, improving the production facilities and enhancing the company's international vocation and marketing strategies. The company won a gold medal at the Universal Exposition in Paris in 1900, in which it participated with a lavish Art Nouveau-style kiosk, and intensified its advertising campaigns. The promotion of the products, among them Buton Cognac and the elixir Coca Buton, obtained by distilling a blend of herbs that included coca leaves, and rather successful in terms of sales, was entrusted to important poster artists who expressed themselves in the Art Nouveau style of the era. The company collaborated with the Officina di arti grafiche Chappuis and the Maga agency, both based in Bologna, and commissioned posters from Giovanni Mataloni (1869–1944), Nasica (Augusto Majani, 1867–1959) and Marcello Dudovich (1878–1962).

In the early forties, painter Doro Falchieri provided the illustrations for the Buton Vecchia Romagna cognac, which was reclassified as a brandy after 1948, in compliance with the convention between Italy and France which established that the name *cognac* and *Armagnac* could only apply to products made in France. The characterization therefore concentrated on the shape of the bottle, a triangle flattened at the centre of each of the three sides, inspired by a similarly-shaped bottle of Scotch whiskey, though the company's specific attention to bottles is demonstrated by a patent filed in 1906 for a long-neck bottle (no. US D38139 S).

After World War II, as the company grew from the artisanal to the industrial scale—in the sixties Buton was one of the few liquor companies to be quoted on the stock exchange—, Vecchia Romagna became one of its best-selling products. In 1960, the name was changed to Vecchia Romagna Etichetta nera (the new name was registered, no. 161882), which was rather effectively developed to create a rhyming couplet between the words "etichetta nera," black label, and the slogan "Il brandy che crea un'atmosfera," persuasively used after 1958 in the television advertising campaigns on *Carosello*, directed by Giuseppe Bacci (1921), head of the advertising department through the sixties. The warm local accent by actor Gino Cervi and the creation of a relaxed family setting, in a middle-class environment presented as unequivocally modern, associated the brandy in the eyes of the viewer with its capacity to make any social situation exclusive. In 1989, the bottle was slightly modified and patented for the company by Lorenzo Sassoli de Bianchi (no. US D321478 S), though it was later sold to the international corporation Diageo. In 1999 the Vecchia Romagna brand became part of the Bologna-based Montenegro Group, controlled by the Sergnoli family. (fb)

P.E. Rubbi, *Gio. Buton & C.: un'azienda tra storia e cronaca*, Calderini, Bologna 1982; L. Papo, *Il brandy italiano*, Alinari, Florence 1987; M. Marozzi, "'L'atmofera' non è più quella ma almeno l'azienda va avanti," *La Repubblica*, 30 January 1993; G. Lonardi, "Vecchia Romagna etichetta italiana," *La Repubblica*, 21 September 1999; G. Pedrocco, "Bologna industriale," *Storia di Bologna*, R. Zangheri (edited by), Bononia University Press, Bologna 2013, book 4., vol. 2., *Bologna in età contemporanea 1915-2000*, edited by A. Varni, pp. 1112–13; United States Patent, *Design for a bottle*, n. US D38139 S, reg. 17.04.1906, publ. 31.07.1906; *Bottle*, n. US D321478 S, priority 13.04.1989, reg. 3.10.1989, publ. 12.11.1991; Archivio centrale dello Stato, Italian Office of Patents and Trademarks, no. 161882, filed 4.07.1960, reg. 12.07.1963.

→Advertisement (from *Fili*, 95, November 1941, p. 2).

→Advertisement, 1960s.

Nonino Grappa

Nonino, Percoto (Udine)
1973

The products of the Nonino distillery in Friuli paved the way for what became a radical "innovation of meaning" in the consideration of grappa as a spirit. For a distillate that originated as a home-made or artisanal product of rural Italy, and was considered "poor" in terms of quality and value, this meant opening up significant possibilities for enhancing status and appeal. To begin with, in December 1973, Nonino decided to switch to a single-variety grape production, convincing the grape growers to separate the pomace, and select the Friuli region's most famous variety, *picolit*. This transformation—which aimed to put grappa on the same footing with other great distillates—occurred at a moment in time when the wine sector was moving towards an appreciation for finer wines and the distinction between artisanal and industrial production, a process sustained by vehicles of cultural dissemination such as those linked to the figure of wine critic Luigi Veronelli, with whom Nonino began a constructive dialogue. The meticulous distillation process, developed over the years in a family tradition that began in 1897 in Percoto (Udine), guaranteed quality

and excellence throughout the procedure, under controlled organoleptic and hygienic conditions, using partially mechanized production systems. Ensuing from the change in the "contents" of the product were the choices to be made with regards to methods and instruments for the presentation: from the packaging to the label, to the commercial and communication strategies. In lieu of the traditional "anonymous" bottles, a small ampoule (250 ml) was designed, with an essential form that reflected the limited quantity of the initial production, and at the same time accented the value of the contents. The trademark, the original "tag" label, the cardboard box and the metal cork were designed by architect Franco Vattolo; the photographic representation was commissioned to Aldo Ballo, one of the great Italian photographers who worked with design furniture manufacturing companies and magazines. Whereas Benito Nonino's family legacy—he represented the family's fourth generation—centred on competence and operative expertise, his wife Giannola Bulfani's family legacy lay in its appreciation of the design culture and culture in general, as demonstrated by the institution in the

seventies of the International Nonino Literary Prize. Her father owned a mechanical manufacturing company, but after he was joined by his son-in-law Dario Del Maestri, the company began to produce design furniture under the brand name Mobil Italia, working with important architects, designers, graphic designers and photographers, such as Aldo Ballo and his son-in-law, Oliviero Toscani. Over the years, Nonino introduced further innovations to the content, process and form of its products, inaugurating an approach that was followed in diverse ways by other companies and contributing to the international success of a typically Italian spirit.

G. Turani, "Quella cara, carissima grappa d'autore," *La Repubblica*, 24 February 1985; C. Compagno, *Il caso Nonino*. *Lo spirito dell'impresa*, Isedi, Turin 2000; F. Bruni, "A dynamo and her daughters turn leftovers to gold," *The New York Times*, 6 December 2003; conversation by the author with Giannola Nonino, CEO of Nonino, 8 October 2014.

→The Nonino Distillery.

→Single-varietal Picolit grappa, 1973.

the modern food product
1920–60

Recipe Collections, Cookbooks, Food and Wine Guides

Historically, recipe collections and cookbooks have played an important part in building the food culture, and in the diffusion of food patterns and practices. Originally written in manuscript form, and later published, they were long available only to a restricted elite.

The twentieth century introduced other editorial forms that contributed to the democratic objectives of knowledge and uniformity of tastes and habits, as well as the introduction and consolidation of new products. These publications (which covered living, health, home economics and nourishment), were addressed to the general public, and also included the booklets printed by food companies with the purpose of introducing their own innovative products, which offered a whole range of new possibilities that needed to be illustrated.

→Elio Luxardo, photographer, 1940 (© Fondazione 3M photographic archives).

There can be no discussion on this subject without mentioning *La scienza in cucina e l'arte di mangier bene* by Pellegrino Artusi, published for the first time in 1891, but reprinted many times over the course of the twentieth century: a "national" recipe collection, initially published at the author's own expense, which developed and grew as a sort of collective work with the contributions of his readers, with whom he established a dialogue.[1] Addressing himself to the lower and upper middle class, Artusi reconstructed a common heritage in a sort of map that reinterpreted the country food of feast days, codifying the "primo" as an opening dish and placing particular emphasis on pasta, which became the very foundation of Italian cuisine. Piero Camporesi writes: "*Scienza in cucina* did more for national unification than the *Promessi Sposi*"; he also sustains that "Artusi's 'gustemi' succeeded in creating a code of national identification where Manzoni's 'stylemi' and 'fonemi' failed"[2] (N.d.T: "gustemi" is a play on the Italian word "gusto," taste, that mimics the form of the word "fonemi," phonemes.) A new editorial trend in the general press, for a mid-to-upper middle class audience, links the recipe books (including those published by food industries such as Cirio, Carli, Bertolini, etc.) to the themes of the modernist designs for living and the economy of the home (they even featured the same authors, like Ada Boni or Lidia Morelli[3]). A similar direction was taken by "La cucina italiana," the first magazine dedicated entirely to food which came out in 1929,[4] or the sophisti-

[1] P. Artusi, *La scienza in cucina e l'arte di mangiar bene*, Landi, Florence 1891; since then, over one hundred editions have been printed. Another recipe book that inaugurated the line of regional cookbooks was V. Agnetti, *Nuova cucina delle specialità regionali*, Società Editoriale Milanese, Milan 1909.
[2] P. Camporesi, "Introduzione," P. Artusi, *La scienza in cucina e l'arte di mangiare bene*, Einaudi, Turin 2001, p. XXII.
[3] See, among others, A. Boni, *Il talismano della felicità*, Preziosa, Rome 1929; L. Morelli, *Le vostre giornate. Agenda 1936*, Alfieri & Lacroix (for Richard Ginori), Milan

1936; *Nuovi orizzonti della vostra mensa*, preface by L. Morelli, Società generale delle conserve alimentari Cirio, Portici (NA) 1936. In general, D. Musci, *Credere, obbedire, cucinare: i ricettari italiani fra le due guerre*, Ananke, Turin 2009.
[4] Edited by Umberto Notari, the publisher of the daily newspaper *L'Ambrosiano* and founder of the Istituto Editoriale Italiano; writer, friend and best man at Filippo Tommaso Marinetti's wedding; married to Delia Pavoni, the widow of engineer Giuseppe Magnaghi, who founded and owned the Terme di Salsomaggiore.

→*La Cucina Italiana, rivista di gastronomia per le famiglie e i buongustai*, XII-XIII, 1934, cover.

→Società Generale delle Conserve Alimentari "Cirio," Naples-S. Giovanni a Teduccio, *Nuovi orizzonti per la vostra mensa*, with preface by Lidia Morelli, 1936, cover.

cated cookbook printed in 1931 and entitled *La cucina elegante ovvero il Quattrova illustrato*, illustrated by architects Gio Ponti and Tomaso Buzzi, for Domus publishers.

Another trend (which would prevail after World War II) expressed an interest in the first culinary *vademecums*, such as the guides published by the Touring Club Italiano in 1931. This line of publications would soon show great vitality in the guides to restaurants and to food and wine, such as the Michelin (1956) and later the Espresso (1979) or Gambero Rosso (1991) guides, which proliferated side by side with recipe books and cooking magazines; in the wake of changing lifestyles in all spheres including eating patterns, they were basically an indication of the decline in cooking and home-making skills, and the transition from cooking at home to the pleasure of eating out (and not just on Sunday).

New Domestic Organization

In the industrial era, lifestyles and habits concerning food were influenced by the evolution of domestic and collective living spaces.

The Modernist design culture, for the first time, dedicated its full attention to the organization of the kitchen.[5] In a forced synthesis, the starting point was the model of the Frankfurt kitchen by Margarete Schütte-Lihotzky presented in 1927 which was rational and efficient in its approach to circulation, movement and spatial organization, in the separation between kitchen and dining room, and the first timid introduction of home appliances.

These choices interpreted the role of the housewife in a partly traditional manner (household staffs were dwindling or disappearing entirely), within a functional-productivist perspective linked to a consumer-driven logic. This kitchen model was picked up in Europe and in Italy, first by design magazines such as "Domus," "Casabella" or "Edilizia moderna," and then by the exemplary Casa Elettrica for the IV Triennale di Milano in 1930, designed by Gruppo 7 (L. Figini, G. Pollini, G. Frette, A. Libera), with the kitchen by Piero Bottoni.[6] In 1945, the book *La cucina* by Marco Zanuso for Domus publishers provided a theoretical basis and examples of design based on this concept, which would become consolidated and endure over time.

[5] On these themes, see among others, G. Origlia (edited by), *Album, annuario di progetto e cultura materiale diretto da Mario Bellini, 1 Progetto mangiare*, Electa, Milan 1981; M. Boot and M. Casciato (edited by), *La casalinga riflessiva. La cucina razionale come mito domestico negli anni '20 e '30*, exhibition catalogue, Multigrafica Editrice, Rome 1983; T. Favarelli Giacobone, P. Guidi, A. Pansera, *Dalla casa elettrica alla casa elettronica. Storia e significati degli elettrodomestici*, Arcadia Edizioni, Milan 1989; M. Romanelli, M. Laudani, L. Vercelloni, *Gli spazi del cucinare,* appunti per una storia italiana 1928-1957, Electa, Milan 1990; R. Poletti, *La cucina elettrica. I piccoli elettrodomestici da cucina dalle origini agli anni settanta*, Electa – Alessi, Milan 1994.

[6] M. Romanelli, M. Laudani, L. Vercelloni, *Gli spazi del cucinare...*, cit., p. 15. About the Triennale see A. Pansera, *Storia e cronaca della Triennale*, Longanesi, Milan 1978; L. Ciagà, G. Tonon (edited by), *Le case nella Triennale. Dal parco al QT8*, Electa, Milan 2005.

[7] F. Picchi, *Standard alimentari: i pionieri dell'industrializzazione*, in G. Bosoni, F. Picchi (edited by), "Food design. Il

As early as the forties, but more prominently in the decade to follow, the "American-style" kitchen represented an industrial version of functionalist principles, embodied in the home appliances, in which the spatial organization, based on technologically accessorized running countertops and cabinets, changed the dynamics of roles and the time spent in the kitchen and created a new domestic economy. Since then the spatial changes, as always ensuing from a design process, would become more a matter of size than organization (if we exclude the expansion towards the dining area in the open kitchen, and towards the living room in an integration of kitchen and lounge areas), though it was the evolution of home appliances that had the strongest impact. Prompted by the innovations in technology and production, the social, economic and cultural transformations, as well as consumer spending and lifestyles, eating spaces began to serve a variety of functions above and beyond traditional conviviality, where the methods and possibilities of preservation (first the refrigerator, then the freezer) dialogue with those of "production" (the gas range, the oven, followed by pressure cookers, microwave ovens, steamers, etc.) to influence one another, inspired by the idea of *labour-saving food* that required less time and effort.[7]

While during the period between the two world wars, the gas-fired kitchen range had already made cooking more functional and practical (though it did not influence its basic philosophy or management model), after the fifties, the refrigerator would radically alter the calendar of available foods, buying, cooking meals, handling leftovers, reflecting a trend that evolved with the introduction of freezing systems and frozen products.[8] Frozen foods would challenge the integrity and the shape of food (at least temporarily, until they were defrosted), boosting the process of artificializing and manipulating nature which had already erased the physical and organoleptic identity of the new foods created during the modernist period.

Within this technological and functionalist rationale, the kitchen and domestic organization ended up constituting a sort of extension of the industrial food production networks into the home; and women, from the rational homemakers they were (when the Modernist culture

→E.V. Quattrova, *La cucina elegante ovvero Il Quattrova illustrato*, Editoriale Domus, Milan 1931, cover and drawing by Gio Ponti, *Remigia o la cuoca letterata* (p. 105).

progetto del cibo industriale," *Domus*, 823, 2000, p. 74.
[8] The result of scientific and technological research into freezing conducted by biologist and naturalist Clarence Birdseye, who sold his first products in the United States as early as 1929. Before frozen foods could become a household item, they required the construction of a "cold chain," i.e. a system for preparing and freezing foods in specially-equipped factories, with vehicles that could transport the foods at a temperature below –20 °C, freezers available in stores and in the home. But most of all they would have to defeat cultural resistance. It should be noted that Findus Italia, the largest frozen foods industry, opened in 1962. See, among others, A. Lupacchini, *Food design. La trasversalità del pensiero progettuale nella cultura alimentare*, List, Trento 2014, 71–84; Istituto italiano alimenti surgelati, *Quarant'anni di storia sociale e alimentare attraverso l'evoluzione dei surgelati*, Rome (2004); T. Favarelli Giacobone, P. Guidi, A. Pansera, *Dalla casa elettrica alla casa elettronica…*, cit.; M. Nacci (edited by), *Oggetti d'uso quotidiano: rivoluzioni tecnologiche nella vita d'oggi*, Marsilio, Venice 1998.

D O M U
N O V

MOBILI - ARR
OGGETTI D'A
MODERN

★

L'asse da stiro ribaltabile   L. **390**

Cucina in abete a vernice forte in azzurro,
composta di tavolo con due cassetti e piano
in linoleum due sedie, credenza con piano a
sporgere ed ante con fondo mobile L. **2110**

★

REPARTO ARREDAMENTI
M O D E R N I   D E

LA RINASCENTE

P. DUOMO - III PIANO

M I L A N O

10

L'ALLUMINIO PURO E LE SUE L... ...ERE
ANTICORODA... ...ÌAN

...ono il materiale
...to alla fabbrica-
...i lampadari, delle
...a per porte e fine-
...elle finiture dei mo-
... radica e di essenze
...ate, e degli oggetti
...decorazione di gusto
...derno: perchè il loro
...ore è inalterabile e di
...no più morbido di quello
...el cromo e del nichel.
...La lucentezza dell'alluminio non è ottenuta per de-
posizione di una sottile
foglia metallica e non è
quindi soggetta a macchiar-
si od a lasciar trasparire
il metallo di base come
negli ottoni cromati, niche-
lati od argentati.

l' **ALLUMINIO**
l' **ANTICORODAL** e
l' **ALUMÀN**

sono **saldabili, fucina-
bili** ed atti alla punzona-
tura ed al conio. L'Allu-
minio è l'unico metallo
da decorazione che non
debba essere importato
dall'Estero poichè è pro-
dotto con minerale e mano
d'opera italiana in stabilimenti italiani.

**Lamiere e profilati
in leghe di alluminio**

L. L. L.
" SOC. LAVORAZIONE
LEGHE LEGGERE

Direzione:
Via Principe Umberto, 18 - Milano

Stab. in Porto Marghera (Venezia)

A L L ... M I N I O

designed their kitchens) frequently became an "instrument" at the service of the logic of capitalist consumption (rather docile and fulfilled, or antagonistic, inside the kitchen and out).

This is, more generally, a situation in which, explain Capatti and Montanari, "the relationship between edible objects, manual labour and machines, far from simplifying things made them more complex… Hygiene, functionality, safety, speed, savings and the very notion of progress now appear as generic ideals, which are not necessarily compatible with the values of fine food."[9]

on the previous pages
→**Domus Nova kitchen furniture,**
advertisement (from *Domus*, **41,**
May 1931, pp. 10–11).

From Modernist Food to the Consumeristic Product

The period between the two world wars, from a cultural point of view, was distinguished by its awareness and pride in the role that could be played in the construction of a modern society not only by the tools of design (from city planning to architecture, to design), but also by the tools of expression (art, music, film, photography or theatre), because they could dialogue with the epoch-making transformations in the fields of science, technology, economics and society.[10]

The food artefacts designed at that time are, for all intents and purposes, products of the modernist rationale, with little or no trace of the typologies and morphologies of tradition. These products were conceived in relation to the different technological production systems, based on research studies and solutions frequently protected by patents,[11] to the new living and eating habits in domestic, collective and public spaces, and to the new patterns of behaviour and social, economic and cultural conditions.

Two different typologies may be distinguished, which correspond largely to the *pre* and *post* conflict eras, respectively: one, the products determined by the necessities of design and production, the result of a somehow "absolute" idea of the modernist food product (with an explicit reference to their artificial nature and geometric morphology[12]); two, the products befitting to the new consumer dynamics, forerunners and effect of the transition from need to desirability, appeal and seduction.[13]

Many Modernist artefacts are conceived within a logic of "abstraction" with respect to natural ingredients, in a process of reinterpretation that

[9] A. Capatti and M. Montanari, *Cucina all'italiana, storia di una cultura*, Laterza, Rome – Bari 2005, p. 312.
[10] About Italian design during and after World war II, V. Gregotti, *Il disegno del prodotto industriale. Italia 1860-1980*, Electa, Milan 1982; *Anni Trenta. Arte e cultura in Italia*, exhibition catalogue, Mazzotta, Milan 1983 (II edition expanded); R. De Fusco, *Storia del design*, Laterza, Rome – Bari 1985, pp. 257–315; M.C. Tonelli Michail, *Il design in Italia 1925-43*, Laterza, Rome – Bari 1987;

G. Bosoni, A. Nulli, "Italia: storie parallele fra progetto e consumo," E. Castelnuovo (edited by *Storia del disegno industriale*, 3 vols., Electa, Milan 1989–91, pp. 122–47; A. Pansera, *Storia del disegno industriale italiano*, Laterza, Rome – Bari 1993.
[11] About patents in Italy, including those for food products, see VV.AA., *Brevetti del design italiano, 1946-1965*, Electa, Milano 2000; A.M. Sette (exhibition catalogue curated by), *Disegno e Design. Brevetti e creatività italiani*, Fondazione Valore Italia, Rome 2009.

considered the form independent of the content, like the bouillon cube in relation to meat. They were constructed to respond to specific requirements, sometimes embodying the principles of medical research in the area of health, psychophysical wellbeing and dietary supplements, in an age of subsistence diets with a shortage of the substances and physical-chemical elements required for proper nutrition.

While during the first phase in industrial history, the design of the food artefact was motivated by the need to define a product made from "natural" ingredients, within a domestic and/or artisanal production system, which was then "translated" into an industrial version within the limits of production constraints, in this phase it was driven primarily by the requirement of "functionality" and/or "total" reconfiguration. Culminating in the *hubris* of being created "out of nothing," like the bouillon cube which was both ingredient and product, and when water was added, became broth ("double broth," Star called it). This was the case with powdered milk, yeast, freeze-dried products, chocolate and instant coffee, products which broke the continuity between the artisanal and the industrial product, and existed in an exclusively industrial version, asserting the supremacy of the new model: "Thanks to these magic packets – write Capatti and Montanari – industry asserted its power, in terms of speed and ease of execution."[14]

It is no coincidence that, in borrowing the aesthetic codes and visual languages of the time, the "abstraction" of design and the development process together led to the elaboration of geometric forms, such as the square, the rectangle, the triangle, the cylinder, the cube or the cone section. "The development of industrial food directly involves food technology, which has made it possible to create safe and long-lasting foods, but has also led to "unnatural" visual and tactile configurations of the products," Alfonso Morone has rightly sustained.[15]

At this point, the product represented a "promise of uniformity," of permanent high quality, ensured by constant testing and improvement, guaranteed by the standardization of the industrial process. On the other hand it was a "programmed object," built by processes of addition and transformation, the value of which lay in its requisites (sensorial, vitamin-fortified, economic) and its appearance. As Marco

[12] "The standardization process of the industrial system has often been characterized by the frequent imposition of geometric forms as an aesthetic and functional principle of edible products" (G. Bosoni, "Il progetto del cibo industriale," G. Bosoni, F. Picchi (edited by), *Food design...*, cit., p. 42).
[13] In the words of Giovanni Siri: "The consumer follows a logic of desire and not need, of impulse and not necessity, of aesthetics and not ethics, of play and not rationality" (G. Siri, *La psiche del consumo*, Franco Angeli, Milan 2001, quoted also in G. Fabris, *Il nuovo consumatore: verso il postmoderno*, Franco Angeli, Milan 2003, p. 49).
[14] A. Capatti, M. Montanari, *Cucina all'italiana...*, cit., pp. 317–18.
[15] A. Morone, "Dall'artigianale all'industriale," *Diid-disegno industriale*, monograph issue *Food design*, 19, 2006, p. 34.

opposite and on the following pages
→**M. Zanuso, *La cucina*,
Quaderni di Domus, 4, Editoriale
Domus, Milan 1945, double
pages.**

Riva writes: "The aspect, the form and the colour of food are anything but secondary aspects in eating food: their perception triggers a complex psychological and physiological mechanism... The visual information communicated by food is subconsciously compared to the archetypes housed in our memory, and in just a few milliseconds, determines whether or not we are ready to "hone" the rest of our sensorial systems."[16]

This approach led to the design of recognizable iconic forms (such as the Plasmon and Pavesino biscuits, the Formaggino Mio cheese cubes, etc.) and to a unitary design of form/product/company trademark. Company strategies, marketing, advertising and design become the instruments of a coordinated series of actions, in which the choice of priorities among the factors to be emphasized and the importance of the professional expertise determined the general characteristics of company identity (quality, economics, communication, etc.).

The tools of visual design, communication and advertising were essential to the formulation of the modernist, and later consumer product. Food industries either created their own in-house departments to handle these aspects, or commissioned independent firms or agencies.

After World War II, in addition to the modernist products, new artefacts were being conceived to respond to the change in living conditions brought about by the growing importance of the strict rationale behind a capitalist consumer-driven economic organization. This translated into the need for a constant and rapid turnover of goods, fuelled by a steady stream of new products supported by "scientific" tools of marketing, communication, publicity and sale.

During the fifties and sixties, the dietary model changed as a consequence, eagerly opening up to packaged and canned products sustained by the cultural homologation set in motion by the mass media. Instrumental in this process were the commercials broadcast on television—RAI television began broadcasting nationwide in 1954—especially on the programme Carosello, which premiered in 1957.

The most significant new products were desserts and soft drinks, which are covered extensively in the Inventory (along with some of the modernist icons, such as the bouillon cube, yeast packets and additives), and are emblematic for an understanding of the change in eating habits that took place in the fifties.[17] The excellence of Italian

[16] In the sequence: perception, appearance, attraction, sensorial desire, stimulus and the search for gratification (M. Riva, "Parametri e tecnologie del progetto alimentare," G. Bosoni, F. Picchi (edited by), *Food design...*, cit., pp. 70–71). There are interesting considerations which are also applicable to food in A. Corbin, *Storia sociale degli odori*, Bruno

Mondadori, Milan 2005.
[17] G. Gallo, R. Covino, R. Monicchia, *Crescita, crisi, riorganizzazione. L'industria alimentare dal dopoguerra ad oggi*, in A. Capatti, A. De Bernardi, A. Varni (edited by), *Storia d'Italia, Annali 13. L'alimentazione*, Einaudi, Turin 1998, p. 276.

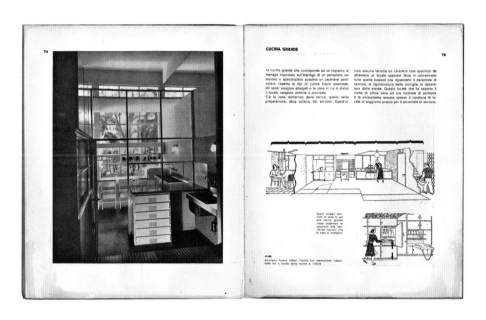

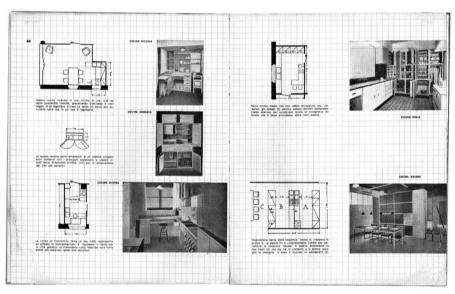

La distribuzione e i tipi della cucina. Abbiamo già accennato sulla parte generale ai nuovi orientamenti dello studio che il problema distributivo della cucina ha assunto in questi ultimi anni.

Si è partiti dal concetto fondamentale di esaminare il lavoro delle massaie da un punto di vista scientifico esaminando i percorsi, gli spostamenti, i movimenti che essa deve compiere durante il suo lavoro nella cucina.

Tale concetto è sinteticamente ed efficacemente espresso nello schema sottoriprodotto che fu pubblicato in occasione della Esposizione dell'abitazione di Parigi 1935.

Lo schema (1) mostra chiaramente su quali concetti e con quale metodo il problema sia stato affrontato e risolto fino ad arrivare, attraverso numerose esperienze, alle ultime soluzioni.

In base a questi concetti e attraverso a tutte le più

sti ad un estremo della seguenza, sono tolti gli alimenti e i recipienti che, attraverso i tavoli di preparazione e l'acquaio, giungono, per la cottura, ai fornelli, posti all'altra estremità della seguenza. Il processo di pulitura delle stoviglie, segue in senso inverso la stessa via e termina allo scaffale dove le stoviglie adoperate vengono riposte.

In funzione delle dimensioni e del tipo di servizio, la cucina può essere distinta in cinque tipi:

a) cucina grande; b) cucina media; c) cucina piccola o minimum; d) cucina nicchia; e) cucina armadio;

a) La cucina grande corrisponde ad un andamento di casa di una certa importanza; si prevede personale di servizio anche numeroso, e un locale annesso con funzione di credenza e di pranzo per la servitù detto office. Mentre per la cucina propria-

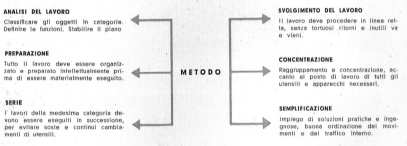

ANALISI DEL LAVORO

Classificare gli oggetti in categorie. Definire le funzioni. Stabilire il piano.

PREPARAZIONE

Tutto il lavoro deve essere organizzato e preparato intellettualmente prima di essere materialmente eseguito.

SERIE

I lavori della medesima categoria devono essere eseguiti in successione, per evitare soste e continui cambiamenti di utensili.

METODO

SVOLGIMENTO DEL LAVORO

Il lavoro deve procedere in linea retta, senza tortuosi ritorni e inutili va e vieni.

CONCENTRAZIONE

Raggruppamento e concentrazione, accanto al posto di lavoro di tutti gli utensili e apparecchi necessari.

SEMPLIFICAZIONE

Impiego di soluzioni pratiche e ingegnose, buona ordinazione dei movimenti e del traffico interno.

(1) Schema d'impostazione

interessanti esperienze e realizzazioni degli ultimi anni si è potuto, arrivare ad uno schema (2) che riproduciamo che può essere considerato come definitivo per la soluzione del problema.

Sistemazione dei mobili a parete secondo una disposizione che riproduce nella sua seguenza il ciclo di preparazione e cottura dei cibi in un senso e il ciclo di lavatura scolatura nel senso inverso.

Dal refrigerante e dallo scaffale delle stoviglie, po-

mente detta valgono quei concetti di massima sopra esposti, in questo caso assume un valore particolarmente interessante l'office. Esso impedisce almeno in parte che gli odori e i rumori della cucina si diffondano nell'alloggio. Accoglie gli armadi per stoviglie, cristallerie e biancheria da tavola liberando la zona del pranzo, oggi molto spesso conglobata nell'ambiente di soggiorno, dalla necessità di mobili destinati a tale uso e dalla soggezione del-

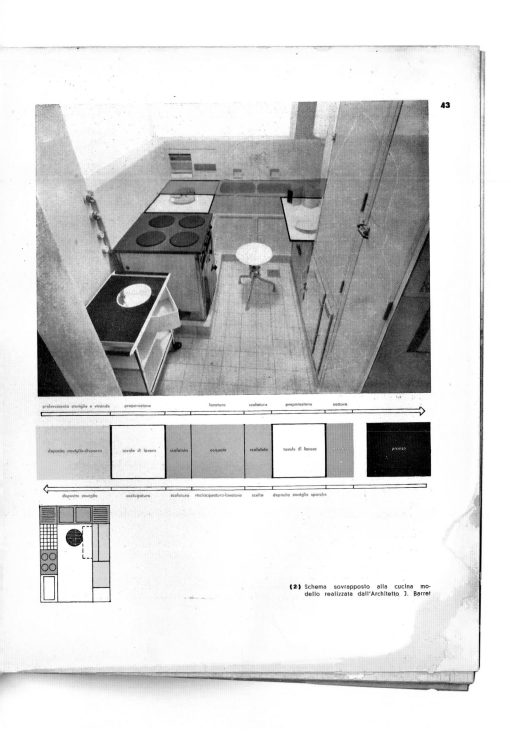

(2) Schema sovrapposto alla cucina modello realizzata dall'Architetto J. Barret

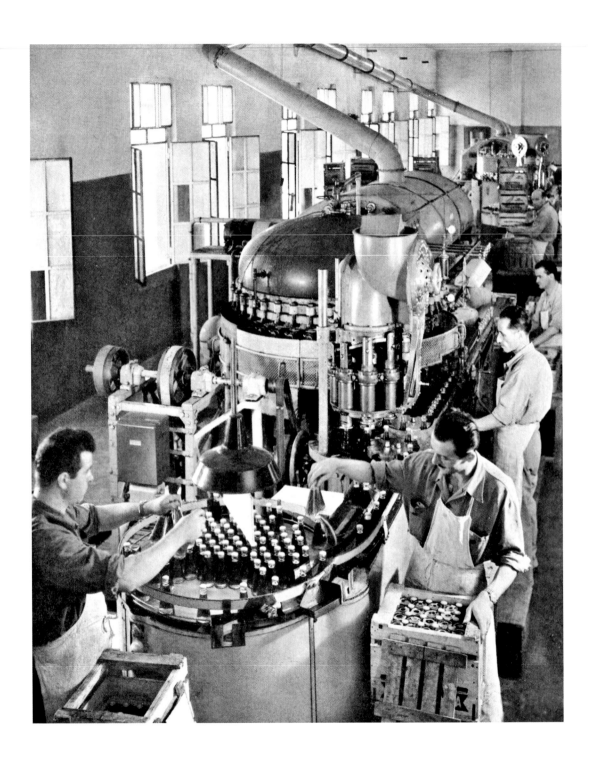

ice-cream also broke into the field of highly desirable quick snacks, in the "homemade" products of ice-cream shops or industrially-produced ice cream, from ice-cream bars on a stick to frozen dessert cones. The same was true for the evolution of soft drinks made from fruit or citrus juices, such as orangeade, *cedrata* and *chinotto*.

The aperitif, yet another Italian speciality, was developed industrially as a *premixed* ready-to-drink beverage, a sign of the interest in new social patterns and behaviours, consequent to the evolution of new lifestyles, and confirmed by the rising popularity of the single-serving typology in food products and *snacks* (from potato chips to saltine crackers).

Pre-packaged single-serving snack cakes, ice cream, non-alcoholic beverages and so on have become the "voluptuary" foods of the modern age. Coffee, chocolate, beer and spirits[18] have been considered in this category throughout history, and now many new food typologies (at least for part of the wealthy West) are coming to share this fundamental characterization in that they are non-essential—though indispensable—and typical of the contemporary consumer lifestyle.

The Food Industry: from Autarchy to the Economic Boom

The long and complex period in history that went from the end of World War II through the post-war period—relatively to the construction of an industrial system, with the implications involved in the role of the design culture—may be divided into two interconnected phases that began before the end of the conflict, and may be defined respectively as "foundation" and "development."

For manufacturing companies, the period that followed World War I (with the due differences in methods and timeframes, for each geographical area and technological-manufacturing context) brought with it the rise of a mature economic, productive and organizational system, a necessary premise to the nationwide distribution and the development of the remarkable range of food typologies that emerged in the years of the economic boom.[19]

There are analogies between the food industry and the evolution of industry in general as far as the context and constraints of autarchy

→Control and packaging department for Campari Soda, 1950s (from *La "Campari" oggi*, Sezione Arti Grafiche Ariel, 1953, p. 27).

→Production of plastic wrap for packaging (from *40 anni di imballaggio*, suppl. to *Imballaggio*, 418, December 1990).

[18] The theme and the field of "historical" voluptuary goods, which is understood to mean *stimulants* in English (bordering on the area of *drugs*), deserves to be explored, along with contemporary voluptuary goods/stimulants/drugs and their relevant social and psychological implications. See VV.AA., *Necessario indispensabile. Oggetti ed eventi che hanno cambiato la nostra vita 1952-1991*, Arnoldo Mondadori Arte, Milan 1992; W. Schivelbusch, *Storia dei generi voluttuari, Spezie, caffè, cioccolato, tabacco, alcol e altre droghe*, Bruno Mondadori, Milan 1999.
[19] On the history of industry, see, among others, R. Romeo, *Breve storia della grande industria in Italia 1861-1961*, Il saggiatore, Milan 1988; A. Colli, *Storia della piccola impresa in Italia nel Novecento*, Bollati Boringhieri, Torino 2002; N. Crepax, *Storia dell'industria in Italia. Uomini, imprese, prodotti*, Il Mulino, Bologna 2002. On the food industry, see chap. II, note 1. And, E. Cavallero, *Il Duce, il cibo e l'autarchia*, Araba Fenice, Boves (CN) 2009.

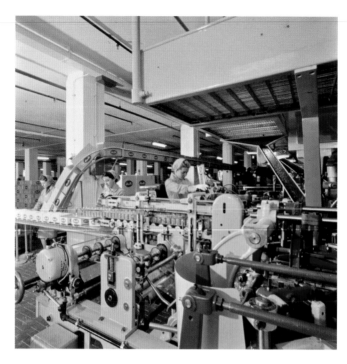

→Boxing machines and
packaging department at
Barilla, 1955 (Barilla Historic
Archives, Parma).

→Armando Testa, Carpano,
advertisement (from *Motor
Italia*, 40, 1957, p. 25).

→Giorgio Tonti, Sangemini,
advertisement, 1961 (from
VV. AA. (edited by), *Due
dimensioni*, Editype, Milan
1964, n.pag.).

are concerned; this similarity also extended to the experimentation, research and innovation on artificial raw materials and to the "new" products linked to social and economic transformations and the evolution of technology and production systems. Though the autarchic phase of the Italian economy and the preparation for war spurred the growth of the production system and in some cases the modernization process, especially in the steel and electro-mechanical industries, the food sector was anything but on the path to true modernization. As Giampaolo Gallo, Renato Covino and Roberto Monicchia write: "It appears mostly as a sponge sector for employment… for the mostly small or tiny companies working primarily on local markets, the conjuncture that developed out of the constraints of the autarchic regime and the war effort allowed them to operate in a context that ensured high prices, and to avoid having to use expensive raw materials imported at high costs from international markets."[20] And: "The food industry prospered thanks to the difficult access to foreign markets and a pay scale that encouraged high profits, that is to say a context in which the regime's protectionist policies were extremely permissive and allowed entire artisanal or semi-artisanal sectors to survive and grow on the national market."[21]

CARPANO
VERMUTH **RE** DAL 1786

As it were, the sector branched out in two different directions: on the one hand, the development and consolidation of large industries, many of them specialized in the production of low-cost food staples (pasta, peeled tomatoes, etc.); on the other the subsistence of the characteristic Italian fragmentation, based on family-run businesses with low capitalization and a small number of employees and specializations;[22] they did however ensure a particular capacity for variation and flexibility in production. And like in many other manufacturing fields, clusters began to form within specific territories, based on the common knowledge of traditional crafting skills, and strong family and social relations.[23]

This capacity to cultivate local expertise, while working within a comprehensive global system, is one of the major characteristics of Italian manufacturing, common to many different sectors such as furniture and fashion, motors and the mechanical industry, in addition of course to food.

In concurrence with these economic, entrepreneurial, manufacturing and technological conditions, the years between the two World Wars brought with them, though in a partial and non-linear fashion, new

[20] G. Gallo, R. Covino, R. Monicchia, *Crescita, crisi, riorganizzazione…*, cit., p. 271.
[21] Ibidem, p. 272.
[22] Ibidem, p. 274.
[23] This was the beginning of the development of the clusters that underlies the economy of small-to-medium entreprises in Italy. See G.G. Becattini, *Dal distretto industriale allo sviluppo locale, svolgimento e difesa di una idea*, Bollati Boringhieri, Turin 2000; A. Colli, *I volti di Proteo, storia della piccola impresa in Italia nel Novecento*, Bollati Boringhieri, Turin 2002.

→Arrigoni / Mario Cappellato
propaganda office,
advertisement, 1938.

→Federico Seneca, Perugina
Chocolates, advertising poster,
1930s (from *Tavole di Federico
Seneca*, preface by L. Borgese,
Edizioni Vendre, Paris c. 1950,
n.pag.).

prerequisites in the fields of culture and design, which responded to the new conditions arising from patterns of behaviour and lifestyles within a consumer market still under construction.

Despite these limitations, the pre-war situation may be considered the foundation for the unbridled growth of the fifties when, as confirmed by statistical data, "the semi-artisanal forms" gave way to "more markedly industrial forms and a process of cautious but not insignificant modernisation." Even though, write Gallo, Covino and Monicchio, "there was a persistent prevalence, in terms of both companies and employees, of traditional productions, symptomatic of a still-foundering national market and a slow transition to a true industrial dimension."[24]

A wilful but geographically contradictory process, affected by the sector of production and the methods of labour organization: "The sectors with the greatest number of employees are still flour mills, olive oil, bread baking. The more specifically industrial sectors, such as pasta, pastry, chocolates, fruit and vegetable preserves, dairy products, butchery and meat processing, are inferior."[25]
It is worth drawing attention to the consolidation of the gap that had become evident in recent years, between the development of production systems and the state of agriculture (crops and livestock). In the mid-fifties during the economic boom, in comparison with the increase in the production and sales of industrial goods—which were beginning to compete at the European level in a process that came to a head in the late sixties on the level of production, industrial organization, of the relationship between sectors and concentration—, agriculture was unable to satisfy the needs of the national market.[26] The question of the relationship between the agricultural and manufacturing systems in Italy remained a constant that protracted a contrast between underdevelopment and attempted and/or successful modernisation, even in its most intensive forms, and in the end, paradoxically and not always intentionally, would prove to be functional to the preservation of traditional-original-local characteristics and the products they expressed. The continued existence, even under the surface, of this sensibility was the necessary premise for the consolidation of a food culture that would give rise to the "mixed" model of economics-manufacturing-design-distribution and consumption (distinguished from the mass market) that would prevail in Italy in the last decades of the twentieth century.

[24] G. Gallo, R. Covino, R. Monicchia, *Crescita, crisi, riorganizzazione…*, cit., p. 275.
[25] Ibidem.
[26] Ibidem, p. 273. This was a question destined to reappear with the many contradictions and conflicts it implies; it just recently surfaced in proposals that offered a new cultural, economic and operative rapport and balance.

→Advertising panels for
Perugina and Ambrosoli
at the Fiera di Milano, 1938
(Fondazione Fiera Milano
Historic Archives, Milan).

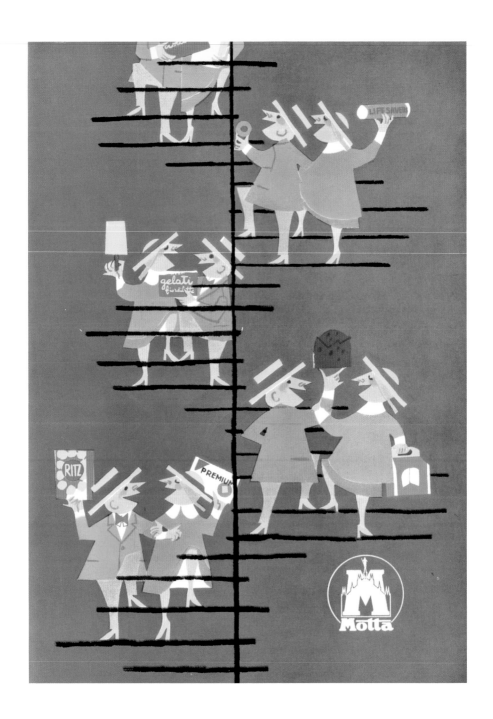

After World War II, the scientific innovations, technical and formal solutions, and materials introduced into the systems for preserving and packaging food products, contributed significantly to the development of new trends in food production and consumption.

A particularly significant example are the advances in the research conducted in the thirties in Sweden by Ruben Rausing on the possibility of packaging milk in paper and plastic coupled together, which led him in 1954 to invent the Tetra Pak, a carton lined on the inside with a thin watertight polyethylene film. Initially used for milk, it was later adopted for many other foods. This solution was the prelude to a radical transformation not only of materials and production technology, but of behavioural patterns as well. Without returnable bottles, containers became portable, and could be used on the go: this was the dawn of disposable packaging, and more in general of quick and economical solutions for serving and enjoying food.

Transparent plastic, which was coupled with other materials to make Tetra Paks, became widely available in packaging and as a system to wrap and preserve food. In both cases, it left the product visible, forever modifying the way we perceive, enjoy and choose. Also conceived for wrapping and preserving were the aluminium foil wraps, produced for example in 1965 by Domopak (a name that combines the words *domus* and *pack*).[27] Another breakthrough, in the same decade, came with the aluminium cans for liquids, an evolution of the tinplate or tin can: they served as an effective barrier against light, cooled quickly, were lightweight and easy to manufacture. The plastic bottles made of PVC or PET, introduced in Italy in the eighties, provided rigid and watertight containers for liquids, paving the way for yet another revolution in food packaging and consumer practices.

Equally significant, in this case, especially in the area of domestic habits, was the introduction of reusable polyethylene containers with special seal systems, like the ones conceived by Earl Silas Tupper in 1947 and available on the American market since 1951. During those same years, in Italy, Kartell, one of the largest contemporary design product manufacturers, was just beginning to experiment specifically with polyethylene and polypropylene, and how they could be applied to kitchenware. These methods for preservation and containment offered new possibilities for producing and selling food products, especially after the advent of freezing systems and more particularly in self-service mass retailing. At the same time, they introduced new practices and habits based on the possibility of maintaining the organoleptic properties of food (over a certain period of time), by wrapping them in plastic or sealing them in containers, not just glass jars or aluminium cans, but the cheaper and more modern plastic bowls.

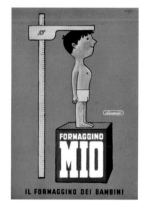

→Motta, advertisement (from *Pubblicità in Italia, 1954-1956*, suppl. to *L'Ufficio Moderno – la pubblicità*, 11, 1957).

→Raymond Savignac, Formaggino Mio Locatelli, poster (from *Pubblicità in Italia, 1954-1956*, suppl. to *L'Ufficio Moderno – la pubblicità*, 11, 1957).

[27] The story of the Domopak company is quite interesting. It was founded in 1965 in Frosinone by Italian-American Mark Antonucci to produce wrapping film made from PVC and later from aluminium.

→Olio Sasso, set of advertising posters (from *Pubblicità in Italia, 1954-1956*, suppl. to *L'Ufficio Moderno – la pubblicità*, 11, 1957).

→First Supermarket store (later Esselunga), Viale Regina Giovanna, Milan, 27 November 1957 (Esselunga Archives, Milan).

→Giulio Confalonieri, Magazzini Standa Milano, advertising poster (from *Pubblicità in Italia, 1969-1970*, suppl. to *L'Ufficio Moderno – la pubblicità*, 11, 1969, p. 44).

→Food section inside the Standa department store, Milan, October 1956.

From the Supermarket to Vending Machines

As for distribution, the two directions that emerged before World War II with the coexistence of large and medium-to-small enterprises, often part of traditional clusters, are reflected in the divergence between the two different ways of marketing food, with fresh or handcrafted foods available in boutiques and small shops, and industrial products sold in a variety of different versions in supermarkets, shopping malls and cafeterias.[28]

The modernist and/or consumeristic industrial food is de-contextualized with respect to its origins and distribution, so that (non-)places such as mass retailers are its perfect channels.

This is not the place to investigate the history of mass retailing, which in the area of food products, developed in the United States before coming to Europe. In Italy the phenomenon appeared in the late fifties with the special food departments located inside department stores such as Standa in 1956, and then grew to include dedicated stores such as the Supermarket supermarkets, later renamed Esselunga, which first opened in Milan in 1957. Mass retailing offered new opportunities for architects, visual and product designers. For example, Max Huber worked for Esselunga, Albe Steiner and later Bob Noorda for the Coop system of cooperatives (which inaugurated its first supermarket in Reggio Emilia in 1963). A radical change was produced in the way consumers began to relate to products, looking at them in new ways, understanding and choosing products without the intermediation of a salesperson, relying solely on the constituent elements and components of the products themselves (visible content, form, package, brand, communication, colours, size and so on).

In regards to the idea of self-service, it is worth focusing for a moment on vending machines, which in exchange for a coin or some other form of payment return a product or a service. They are important from the perspective of how we relate to industrial food products, but also as a design problem, as they embrace the design of machines, technological systems and methods of interaction from both a mechanical and cultural point of view.

They are part of the panorama of contemporary artefacts that populate the public and private spaces of our cities, and which we tend to use distractedly, often without noticing their functional or aesthetic characteristics.

Machines establish an impersonal commercial relationship, that eschews a connection between two people – the buyer and the seller – a rapport that was generally as anonymous as the aspect of vending machines, until advertisements began to appear on them and their appearance gradually improved. The same product thus displays a minimal degree of formal characterization and a maximum degree of advertising and communication: this is an example of total identification between object and brand image. Quite popular in the fifties, the first vending machines sold chewing-gum balls or soft drinks in bottles, soon to be followed by coffee and many more products. They document how the relationship with food developed very different physical and psychological dynamics, cold, mechanical, artificial, anticipating the dynamics of self-service cafeterias and fast-food restaurants.[29]

[28] E. Colla, *La grande distribuzione in Europa*, Etas, Milan 1995; Emanuela Scarpellini describes it as an "integral element of the concept of modernity" (E. Scarpellini, *La spesa è uguale per tutti. L'avventura dei supermercati in Italia*, Marsilio, Venice 2007, p. 107); see also idem, *Comprare all'americana. Le origini della rivoluzione commerciale in Italia 1945-1971*, Bologna, Il Mulino 2001).
[29] See A. Bassi, "Nonoggetti, superoggetti: tre generazioni di vending machine," *Casabella*, 716, November 2003, p. 85 and ff.; A. Bassi, *Il design dell'artefatto tecnologico*, in T. Gregory, *XXI secolo. Gli spazi e le arti*, Istituto Enciclopedia Italiana Treccani, Rome 2010, pp. 453–61.

Ice Cream Cone

Antonio Valvona (United Kingdom);
Italo Marchiony (USA)
1902–03

The story of the wafer cone made to hold ice cream—a food product that originated in Italy—is rather controversial, as is its authorship, claimed by many. One of the first references to an edible cone is contained in the book *Mrs. A. B. Marshall's Cookery Book* published in 1888; but there are patents to support the machines to produce small cones for ice cream invented by two Italian immigrants: Antonio Valvona in Manchester in 1902 (no. US 701776) and Italo Marchiony in the United States in 1903 (no. US 746971 dated December 15th, 1903). The latter in particular seems to stake the claim for the intellectual paternity of take-away ice cream, which was sold on the streets of New York as early as 1896, originally in a small glass jar, then in a folded piece of paper, and finally in an edible sugar cone. He thereby solved the hygienic problem that arose from using a glass jar (which could be returned by the consumer to be used again, but still required washing), by patenting a machine that with a single metal mould could produce ten sugar wafers shaped like a cone, similar to the ones we see today. He would later open a company that manufactured the cones in Hoboken, New Jersey. Another version (though it is based on the story told by the man himself in the "Ice Cream Trade Journal" in 1928) attributes the invention to the Lebanese pastry chef Ernest A. Hamwi who sold ice cream at the St. Louis World's Fair, in 1904, in a "zalabia"—a crunchy wafer soaked in syrup, baked in a hot waffle press, and rolled up in the shape of a cone. The industrial acceleration came when machines were built that could produce the cone automatically, such as the one patented in 1912 by Frederick Bruckman from Portland, Oregon. In Italy the forefather of the ice cream cone may be considered the "parigina,"

a dessert consisting in a portion of ice cream pressed between two round, square or rectangular wafers, which was popular in the late nineteenth century, particularly in Milan. Italy may also be credited with the solution for freezing the ice cream cone. In 1959, Spica (*Società partenopea imbottigliamento confezione alimenti*), an ice cream factory located in Naples (bought by Algida – Unilever), invented a process that isolated the ice cream from the wafer with a layer of oil, sugar and chocolate. In the same year, the name Cornetto was registered, which would thereafter designate one of the most popular ice cream dessert cones in the world. The cone is both a functional and ergonomic as a form— which eliminates the need for a spoon to eat the ice cream with—for a food product-container that is pleasing to the touch and delicious to taste, distinguished by a surface texture that also serves a structural purpose.

P. Dickson, *the Great American Ice Cream Book*, Atheneum, New York 1972; J. Gustaitis, "Who Invented the Ice Cream Cone?," *American History Illustrated*, 23, 4, summer 1988, pp. 42–45; C. Liddell, R. Weir, *Frozen Desserts*, St. Martin's Press, New York 1995; L. Wardlaw, *We All Scream for Ice Cream*, Harper-Collins Publishers, New York 2000; P. Antonelli, *Humble masterpieces. 100 every day marvels of design*, Thames & Hudson, London 2005, pp. 24–25; A. Bassi, *Design anonimo in Italia. Oggetti comuni e progetto incognito*, Electa, Milan 2007, pp. 104–05; United States Patent, *Apparatus for baking biscuit-cups for ice-cream*, no. 701776, priority 12.07.1901; reg. 12.07.1901, publ. 3.06.1902; United States Patent, *Mold*, no. 746971, priority 22.09.1903; reg. 22.09.1903, publ. 15.12.1903.

→Patent, no. US 746971, 15 December 1903.

I. MARCHIONY.

MOLD.

APPLICATION FILED SEPT. 22, 1903.

NO MODEL.

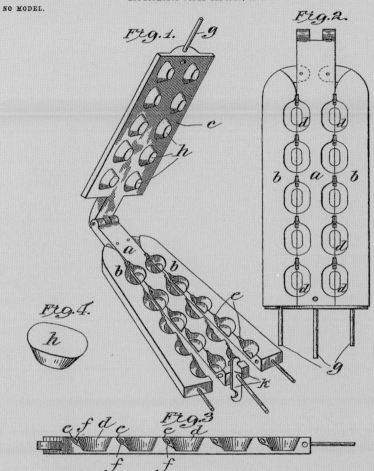

Fig.1.

Fig.2.

Fig.4.

Fig.3.

Witnesses

Edgworthbrune

Lucius Varney

Inventor

Italo Marchiony

By his Attorneys

Redding Keover Greeley

Pinguino Ice Cream Bar

Gelati Pepino, Turin
1938

Domenico Pepino, a master sorbet-maker from Naples, founded the company Gelati Pepino in Turin in 1884 to make frozen desserts, which were quite difficult to produce at the time because refrigerators had not yet been invented. He became an official purveyor to the royal court and famous among the local aristocracy. After participating in the *Esposizione internazionale dell'industria e del lavoro* in Turin in 1911, a lavish celebration of Italy's industrial progress, he moved the company to Piazza Carignano and sold it in 1916 to Giuseppe Feletti, an entrepreneur in the confectionery industry, and his son-in-law Giuseppe Cavagnino. The extended partnership led to an expansion of the company, which opened a new kitchen and introduced a different production technique. Using dry ice—a process in which carbon dioxide in its solid form releases cold when it sublimes to its gaseous state—to cool and preserve the ice cream, they made it possible to transport, and hence to ship it anywhere. They introduced a further innovation in 1938 with their project for the Pinguino, a chocolate-coated ice cream bar on a stick, and patented the name: the lower white part contrasts with the chocolate, bringing to mind the black and white plumage

of the penguin after which it is named (no. 58033).
This was the design of a new form and a new way of eating take-away ice cream: available in a variety of flavours, and enclosed in a characteristic semi-transparent parchment paper wrapper, it could be produced and replicated using processes that guaranteed its homemade quality. Not an ice cream cone, which was introduced in the early twentieth century, to be filled with scoops of ice cream, but a brand-new typology: by moulding the ice cream around a stick, it was easier to hold and to eat on the move. Without forgetting that the production process delivered a ready-to-eat ice cream, which could be sold as a single serving, not only in ice-cream parlours but potentially in other types of stores as well. Ice cream on a stick constitutes the design of a typology that may be said to be "definitive," and which since World War II and even now, continues to be a benchmark for all ice-cream manufacturers. Its first and most famous imitator and competitor was the Mottarello by Motta, which won even greater recognition and diffusion as a result of its fully industrialized production. It certainly was no easy endeavour in 1938 to perfect the light coating: "The only food oil that responds

to our needs is coconut oil because while it remains solid at 18 degrees it melts at 22, so that the coating on the ice cream is perfect," wrote Feletti to the Minister of Agriculture and Forests in 1939. During the phase of autarky enforced by the regime, materials that did not originate in Italy, such as coconut oil, were unavailable. Feletti did not need much, around 80 quintals a year to produce 800 kg of ice cream per day. His request was granted, and thanks to the dry ice that kept the product frozen, he was able to export his ice cream and become famous beyond the borders of Italy. Pepino Gelati still belongs to the Cavagnino family.

B. Gambarotta, "Storia del Pinguino," in *La Stampa*, 26 April 2002; R. Rossotti, *Storia e storie di Torino*, Newton Compton, Milan 2008, p. 59; Archivio centrale dello Stato, Italian Patent and Trademark Office, no. 58033, filed 21.06.1938; reg. 27.11.1938.

→Production kitchen, 1930s (Gelati Pepino 1884 Historic Archives, Avigliana).

→Advertisement, 1930s (Gelati Pepino 1884 Historic Archives, Avigliana).

Mottarello Ice Cream Bar

Motta, Milan; now Nestlé Italiana,
Assago (Milan)

1950

The Mottarello, a moulded ice cream bar on a stick available in vanilla or chocolate, was conceived by Angelo Motta (1890–1957) who patented its shape and name in 1950 (nos. 35997; 103862)—the name itself was registered ten years earlier (no. 62503)—and began to produce it with advanced machinery. While the Pinguino ice-cream bar on a stick (1938) produced by Pepino in Turin unequivocally came first—though it would always remain substantially an artisanal product in terms of production process and distribution, packaging and advertising—, the Mottarello marks the debut of industrial ice-cream in Italy. It should be noted that in the fifties, cafés and restaurants were becoming equipped with refrigerators which allowed them to preserve and sell these products without being ice-cream makers themselves. The expansion of this model was also fostered, among other things, by Motta's distribution system, which in 1950 counted as many as 2000 retailers in Italy alone; they were supplied by centres of distribution called "cells," large refrigerated warehouses owned by the company (almost 50 in 1951), which served as an intermediate step between the company and the retailers. From then on production increased by 80–90% annually, and in 1954 reached a peak of 750,000 pieces a day. The Mottarello

thus became a mass consumer product, like the *panettone* before it. Compared to its predecessor Pinguino, and to distinguish itself from it exploiting the possibilities and processes of production offered by industrial machinery, Mottarello was first released with a more wavy form, with three characteristic grooves on the surface that are easy to recognize in the patented design. It later adapted to the model of the chocolate-coated vanilla ice-cream bar, which became a standard that inspired every ice-cream manufacturer. No further innovation was brought to ice-cream bars until the project for the Magnum Algida, which raised the standard for the entire sector. Considered a symbol of the new economic prosperity, it was described in the early advertising campaigns as a product that is "delicious, nutritious, refreshing and thirst-quenching"; it was also sold in multi-packs and could be taken home ("minimum preservation around two hours"). Its importance was underlined by writer Michele Serra: "The mottarello (in the lower case, like aspirin, like nutella, like moka: these are proper names that have had the honour of becoming household words, and this is a promotion on the field) is one of the few trans-generational products that has challenged the passing of time and styles (...) and couldn't care less about trends and about the fickle tastes of the

masses." Following the acquisition of Motta by the Iri-Sme group in 1968, the company division that produced ice-cream was sold in 1993 to the Nestlé corporation.

VV.AA., *Brevetti del design italiano 1946-1965*, Electa, Milan 2000, p. 136; A. Colli, "La Motta: da bottega artigiana a impresa di Stato," *Annali di storia dell'impresa*, XI, 2000, pp. 571–629; M. Serra, "Castelli di sabbia e calcio balilla: i mille usi del mottarello," *L'Espresso*, 6 July 2010 (available online at http://espresso.repubblica.it/food/dettaglio/castelli-di-sabbia-e-calcio-balilla:-i-mille-usi-del-mottarello/2130313); A. Colli, "Angelo Motta," entry in *Dizionario Biografico degli Italiani*, vol. 77, 2012 (available online at 3_3 Mottarello_en.doc3_3 Mottarello_en.dochttp://www.treccani.it/enciclopedia/angelo-motta_(Dizionario-Biografico)/?stampa=1www.treccani.it/enciclopedia/angelo-motta_(Dizionario-Biografico)/; Archivio centrale dello Stato, Italian Patent and Trademark Office, no. 62503, filed 9.08.1940, reg. 19.10.1940; no. 103862, filed 2.07.1950, reg. 19.10.1951; no. 35997, 30.11.1950.

→Advertising poster, 1948 (Gelati Motta-Nestlé Archives, Milan).

→Patent, no. 35997, 30 November 1950.

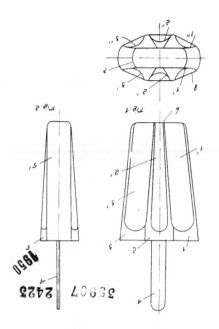

Sammontana Ice Cream

Sammontana, Empoli (Florence)
1955

In 1946 Romeo Bagnoli bought a dairy bar in Empoli and began to make ice cream on a small scale. With the help of his two sons Renzo and Sergio, the production facilities were mechanized and the fame of his ice cream parlour grew, tying its name to the nearby farm Sammontana—located in the eponymous town in the municipality of Montelupo Fiorentino—which supplied its fresh milk. In 1955, as the success of their ice cream grew, the Bagnoli family decided to expand: they began to supply their ice cream to other bars and dairies—delivering it in a lithographed 6-litre canister. At the same time, they decided to move up to the industrial scale, and inaugurated a new production plant. In the sixties, when refrigerators and sometimes freezers had become commonplace in most households, Sammontana introduced the 1-litre

canister of ice cream, a domestic version of the 6-liter container. Ice cream could now be enjoyed in the privacy of one's own home, and not just in bars and cafés.
The lithographed metal canister, enclosed in a transparent bag with the flavour of the ice cream printed on it, was replaced around 1975 by a plastic carton without the bag, and with the flavour of the ice cream specified directly on the carton.
The Sammontana brand adopted the slogan "Gelati all'italiana" from the very outset, with the specific intent to distinguish its ice cream from more industrially-produced products or international models.
The graphic design of the original trademark was by Sineo Gemignani, a painter from Empoli who conceived the image of a pirate winking as he licked an ice cream cone. But it was the famous American graphic designer

Milton Glaser who developed the current trademark in 1981, featuring the ice cream cone with the red tongue licking its lips. Still run by the Bagnoli family, since 2008 Sammontana has also acquired the Sanson, Mongelo and Tre Marie brands.

C. Lapucci, *Renzo Bagnoli. Fondatore della Sammontana*, Polistampa, Reggio Emilia 2008; VV.AA., *Sammontana, per passione dal 1946*, Maschietto Editore, Florence 2012.

→Preparation and Packaging departments, Sammontana factory in Empoli, 1960s (Sammontana Archives, Empoli).

→Milton Glaser, trademark, 1981.

→The original version of the canister, 1959 (Sammontana Archives, Empoli).

Cornetto Ice Cream Dessert Cone

Società partenopea imbottigliamento
confezione alimenti, Naples;
now Algida-Unilever, Rome – Naples

1959

In 1959 the *Società partenopea imbottigliamento confezione alimenti* (Spica) in Naples began the industrial production of the Cornetto ice-cream cone, after solving the problem of the cone becoming soggy when filled with ice cream. By coating the inside with a layer of oil, sugar and chocolate, the ice cream inside the cone was isolated, preventing the cone from soaking it up. The Cornetto is therefore a crispy wafer cone filled with vanilla ice cream, and topped with a layer of chocolate and ground hazelnuts. Registered under the name Cornetto by Spica in 1959 (no. 147387), after 1976 it was produced by Algida (which had incorporated Spica and been acquired two years before by the English-Dutch group Unilever), a company founded in Rome in 1945 by Italo Barbiani and Alfred Wiesner, a Yugoslavian engineer, and later moved to Naples. Both had worked at the Gelateria Fassi, an ice cream parlour founded in Rome in the late

nineteenth century that was always receptive to the latest transformations in production technology. Algida's leading product was initially the Cremino, a vanilla ice cream bar coated in chocolate, yet another interpretation of the ice-cream-on-a-stick typology which began with Pinguino and Mottarello. The Cornetto was advertised from the very beginning on television (with a series of commercials produced between 1958 and 1966 by the artist Pino Pascali (1935–1968) with Lodolo Film), but its real fame came with the advertising campaigns of the eighties and compelling slogans such as "Cornetto, cuore di panna." Its unmistakable Italian origins, and the advantages in terms of economics, production, organization and development that came with being part of a large group, led Algida and its subsequent projects, such as the Magnum with its innovative form and alimentary qualities, to become

international leaders in the field of industrial ice cream products. *Think local and act global*, as the economists say.

D. Bargellini, *Costruire un'azienda design-oriented. I 12 principi del design management*, Franco Angeli, Milan 2014, pp. 98–99; M. Avagliano, *Alfred, il partigiano che inventò il gelato Algida*, in http://moked.it/blog/2012/03/27/storie-alfred-il-partigiano-che-invento-il-gelato-algida/; Archivio centrale dello Stato, Italian Patent and Trademark Office, no. 147387, filed 30.01.1959, reg. 17.02.1960.

→Virgilio Milana, advertisement, 1958 (from VV.AA. (edited by), *2 Mostra Nazionale Artisti Pubblicitari*, exhibition catalogue, Milan 1959, n.pag.).

→Giuseppe Colombo, advertisement, 1962 (from VV. AA. (edited by), *Due dimensioni*, Editype, Milano 1964, n.pag.).

→Advertising poster
(from *Pubblicità in Italia
86-87*, suppl. to *L'Ufficio
Moderno – la pubblicità*, 11,
1986).

Plasmon Biscuits

Plasmon, Milan; now Heinz Italia, Latina
1902

The *Sindacato italiano del Plasmon* was a company founded in 1902 in Milan by Italian doctor Cesare Scotti, who began that year to import and sell Plasmon—a milk-protein based dietary supplement that was the product of a joint English-German scientific research study—with the purpose of exploring its possible applications in the field of nutrition. The factory trademark was registered in Italy in 1904 with the following description: "Pure water-soluble albumin derived from milk and called Plasmon and food products based on it. The picture represents a nude sculptor shown from behind holding a hammer in his right hand and a scalpel in the left as he engraves the word Plasmon on the capital of a Doric column, reproduced in Greek on the base. The trademark is completed by the inscription *s.a. an.a Italo-Svizzera del Plasmon* arranged in an arch at the top and the word *Milano* at the bottom" (n. 6341). This illustration would remain forever associated with the company in the collective imaginary, while the name, derived from the Italian word "plasmare"—to shape—suggests the product's potential for moulding the body and refers to the supplement's aim to foster strong and healthy growth. From the very beginning, the health factor became a distinctive characteristic of the products, which were always innovative and on the cutting edge of research in the fields

of health and nutrition. In 1916 the company changed its name to *Società del Plasmon* and in 1932 inaugurated its plant in Milan in Via Archimede 10. It began exporting its products to Egypt and Brazil, pasta, cocoa, cream of rice, wheat semolina and cookies, which it had been selling since the 1910s. In particular, in the newsletter "Bollettino della Società del Plasmon" dated April 1934, the cookies were described as "Biscuits with Plasmon. Exquisite – Supernutritious – Easy to digest. For the sick, frail, convalescent and children," emphasizing its therapeutic properties. But above all, they were well-designed from a functional point of view: shaped with rounded edges, easy to grip, solid and not at all brittle so that they would not crumble into little pieces, they could be recognized by the name engraved into them in capital letters. After World War II, in response to growing market needs, the first automatic production line was inaugurated in 1948 and in 1953 a new plant was built in Via Cadolini, to produce the now popular cookies. At the same time, a new logo was added to the classic illustration that reproduced the shape of the cookie and the inscription on it, to make the trademark more recognizable and identity-defining. Many advertising campaigns were developed in the 1950s, which continued to emphasize the nutritious properties

and tolerability of the products, because: "Plasmon foods, by virtue of the animal proteins they contain, are the only foods to be particularly rich in A.P.F. (Animal Protein Factor), the new vitamin principles that have been shown to be essential to growth and reproduction." Over the following decade, the advertising adopted a more essential and iconic language, as in the artefacts designed by Bob Noorda (1927–2010) or the Young&Rubicam agency. The company—famous for having introduced baby foods in Italy in 1961, during the economic and demographic boom—was purchased in 1963 by the Heinz group and in 2013 by Berkshire Hathaway and 3G Capital. (fb)

G. Ginex, G. Lopez, G.P. Massetto (edited by), *I marchi di fabbrica a Milano*, Camera di Commercio di Milano, Milan 1992; R. Monachesi, *Marchio*, Lupetti & Co., Milan 1993; F. Fontanella, M. Di Somma, M. Cesar, *Come cambiano i marchi*, Ikon, Milan 2003, pp. 190–93; C. and G. Padovani, *Italia Buonpaese*, Blu Edizioni, Turin 2011, p. 178; Archivio centrale dello Stato, Italian Patent and Trademark Office, no. 6341, filed 7.06.1904, reg. 4.09.1904.

→Bob Noorda, advertisement (from *Pubblicità in Italia, 1968-1969*, suppl. to *L'Ufficio Moderno – la pubblicità*, 11, 1968, p. 20).

→Wrapping paper for Plasmon pasta, 1950s.

ipernutritive

PLASMON

...ERALIMENTO - TUTTE LE ...TEINE ANIMALI, I PRINCIPI ...FORATI ED I SALI MINERALI ...LATTE IN COMBINAZIONE ORGANICA NATURALE

Le PASTINE AL PLASMON per Il PLASMON contenuto sono le più ricche oltre che di proteine vegetali ed animali anche di fosforo e calcio. I sali indispensabili per la ricostituzione del sistema nervoso ed osseo.

La PASTINA più completa di amino acidi essenziali.

MATASSIN **PLASM** *ipernutri*

3 STELLINE — 1 OCCHI DI PERNICE — 5 ASTRINI — 7 PERLINE — 2 ANELLINI — 4 FILI D'ANGELO — 9 GRANELLINI D'ANGELO — 8 MICRON — 13 TAGLIERINE BEBÉ — 10 MACCHERONI BEBÉ — 12 GEMMINE

PASTINE *al* **PLASMON** *ipernutritive*

PLASMON

SUPERALIMENTO - TUTTE LE PROTEINE ANIMALI, I PRINCIPI FOSFORATI ED I SALI MINERALI DEL LATTE IN COMBINAZIONE ORGANICA NATURALE

MAMME!
La PASTINA AL PLASMON dà vigoria e salute. Non manchi mai nella dieta del vostro bambino. Crescerà bello, sano, ed intelligente.

MATASSINE *al* **PLASMON** *ipernutritive*

PLASMON

...ERALIMENTO - TUTTE LE ...TEINE ANIMALI, I PRINCIPI ...FORATI ED I SALI MINERALI ...LATTE IN COMBINAZIONE ORGANICA NATURALE

Le PASTINE AL PLASMON per Il PLASMON

Pavesini Biscuits

Pavesi, Novara; now Gruppo Barilla, Parma

1937; 1951

After moving to Novara in 1934, Mario Pavesi (1909–90) opened a bakery in 1937 and began to produce a traditional typology of local biscuits, known as "biscottini di Novara." Traditionally rectangular with rounded corners, and extremely light, these biscuits are rooted in an ancient seventeenth-century recipe perfected by the nuns in the convents around the city. They owe their fame to local bakers, including Luigi Camporelli who began to produce them in 1852. Compared to the traditional version, Pavesi's biscuit was smaller and not as moist so that it could be packaged and preserved more easily. Pavesi had always been aware of the extraordinary potential of advertising as a factor in accelerating company development; so to design the new wrappers, he hired Aldo Beldi (1922–2000), a young advertising artist, but also worked with the well-established Gino Boccasile (1901–1952).

In 1951 Pavesi patented the shape describing it as the "Biscottino di Novara with a form that is basically rectangular, with rounded corners and the longer sides slightly curved" (no. 37569) and baptized them with the name "Pavesini" (no. 107039). Their shape and name instantly became the company trademark, with the contribution of Bob Noorda, who initially added the words "Biscottini di Novara" in script at the top, almost instantly abandoned, in favour of the word "Pavesi." The company, which went onto the stock market in 1953 while maintaining its base in Novara, initiated the industrial production of other bakery products, such as the Crackers Soda in 1954 [**Gran Pavesi Saltine Crackers** p. 207] or Ringo in 1967, a vanilla-chocolate sandwich cookie with a cream filling. Even with the economic recovery of the fifties, Pavesi continued to hire illustrators and graphic designers that could bring an innovative contemporary language to the communication strategies of a major Italian industry and reinforce its brand dentity: they included Gian(Carlo) Rossetti, Armando Testa and Erberto Carboni, and for television commercials, Luciano Emmer, Maria Perego or Marco Biassoni. These freelance professionals were coordinated by Mario Troso, a young engineer who joined the Pavesi advertising and development department in 1953 and directed it for over thirty years, assisted by a team of specialists.

The prolonged collaboration with Carboni—who was already working with Barilla and Bertolli, among others— began in 1958. He was responsible for the sophisticated graphic design of the slogan "It's always time for Pavesini," whereas it was the mascot Topo Gigio, a mouse conceived by Perego in 1959 and featured in the popular children's television show *Carosello*, who rocketed it to fame. Other advertising campaigns of the seventies were developed by Studio Pentagono, led by Gianni Venturino, by Ccp with Gabriele Ferrari and Alberto Olivieri, Studio Garant or the Leader Agency in Florence. Pavesi's long-sighted entrepreneurial vision contributed decisively to expanding the market for food products in Italy, which he also advanced with the construction of roadside restaurants known as Autogrill Pavesi, designed by the major Italian architects, along the newly-built Italian highway network. In particular, the innovative typology of the bridge structure, introduced in the first buildings by Angelo Bianchetti, is an original contribution to the history of architecture: inspired by a commercial concept, it made good use of this opportunity to leave a significant mark on the territory that would affect lifestyles and consumer spending, in Italy and abroad. After 1972 Pavesi changed hands many times, after it was sold to Iri-Sme, leading ultimately to its acquisition by the Barilla Group in 1993.

VV.AA., *L'Italia dei Pavesini. Cinquant'anni di pubblicità e comunicazione Pavesi*, Archivio Storico Barilla, printed by Amilcare Pizzi, Parma 1997; VV.AA., *Brevetti del design italiano 1946-1965*, Electa, Milan 2000, p. 132; F. Fontanella, M. Di Somma, M. Cesar, *Come cambiano i marchi*, Ikon, Milan 2003, pp. 172–99; S. Colafranceschi, *Autogrill. Una storia italiana*, Il Mulino, Bologna 2007; Archivio centrale dello Stato, Italian Patent and Trademark Office, no. 37569, filed 19.04.1951; no. 107039, filed 27.08.1951, reg. 21.04.1952.

→Gino Boccasile, advertising poster, 1948 (Barilla Historic Archives, Parma).

the modern food product / **sweet**
1920–60

above
→**Erberto Carboni,**
advertisement (from *Pubblicità*
in Italia, 1964-1965, **suppl. to**
L'Ufficio Moderno – la pubblicità,
11, 1964, n.pag.).

above right
→**Erberto Carboni,**
advertisements, 1964 and 1968
(Barilla Historic Archives,
Parma).

opposite
→**Angelo Bianchetti, Autogrill**
Pavesi on the Milan-Turin
highway, Veveri (NO), 1962
(Barilla Historic Archives,
Parma).

Bucaneve Biscuits

Ditta Fratelli Zanin, Orsago (Treviso)
now Gruppo Bauli, Castel d'Azzano (Verona)
1950

The story of the cookie with the hole in the middle and the sugar glaze shaped like petals on top, which inspired a whole range of gestures for an eating ritual that entered the collective imaginary of entire generations, began in 1950 when the Ditta Fratelli Zanin bakery first put Biscotti Doria on the market. It registered the trademark immediately (no.102744), as it did later for the Bucaneve (no.141147).
The production of baked goods had actually been started over a century earlier by Alessandro Zanin, a baker in Sarmede (Treviso) just a few kilometres from today's factory. In 1903, his son Ugo expanded the company's range of breads to include cakes and cookies, and after World War II, changed the name of the company to Doria, to commemorate his friendship with Swiss baker René Doria, a biscuit manufacturer in the Alta Savoia region, whose surname brought to mind the celebrated aristocratic family from Genoa.
In the sixties, the Doria brand grew rapidly in Italy and beyond, but it was the famous jingle ("Con la ricetta della nonnina zucchero latte e fior di farina")

sung by Miranda Martino in 1965 that forever fixed the Bucaneve in the minds of television viewers, who were reminded by the grandmother in the commercial that Doria biscuits are made with sugar, milk and flour "the old-fashioned way," but in "the most modern of factories."
In addition to the Bucaneve's form and special recipe, one of the characteristic elements in the project was the choice of a paper tube for the packaging, which made it easy to recognize on the shelves. It was also relatively simple to close, unlike other packaging typologies, so that the product stayed fresh longer.
In 2006 the company became part of the Bauli Group.

A. Filippini, "Biscotto Bucaneve," G. Iacchetti, *Italianità*, Corraini, Mantua 2008, pp. 21–22; B. Ga., "Biscotti Doria: addio al fondatore Zanin," *Il Sole 24 Ore*, 11 January 2014; Archivio centrale dello Stato, Italian Patent and Trademark Office, no. 102744, filed 20.02.1950, reg. 21.06.1951; no. 141147, filed 13.11.1957, reg. 3.02.1959.

Gran Turchese Biscuits

Colussi, Venice-Vittorio Veneto (Treviso);
then Fontivegge (Perugia); now Gruppo Colussi, Milano
1955

The Gran Turchese shortbread biscuit was conceived in 1955 by Giacomo Colussi, who was inspired by a round gridded Roman-era mould that he noticed in a museum in Pompei.
At that time, Colussi's business spanned the entire country, in an entrepreneurial experience that began back in 1911 when Angelo Colussi, the owner of a bakery in Venice that produced the traditional local *baicoli* biscuits, inaugurated his artisanal biscuit production in Vittorio Veneto, in the province of Treviso. By the twenties, it had become a full-fledged factory with a new oven, two baking chambers, a kneading machine and other avant-garde machinery that raised the volume of production to over 100 kilograms of biscuits per hour, a considerable amount for the time. Over the following decade Colussi expanded its production of biscuits to include *panettoni*, wafers and small pastries, creating a direct sales network with 14 stores located throughout the Triveneto area and in Milan, when his son Giacomo joined the company.
After World War II, Giacomo founded Colussi Perugia in Fontivegge, in the province of Perugia, while his brothers Alberto and Sandro stayed behind to manage the factories in Vittorio Veneto and later in Voghera, united under the brand name Colussi Milano. A few years later, the Gran Turchese, produced on foreign machinery imported especially to make shortbread biscuits, boosted the fame of the brand throughout Italy. Not only

because it reflected the new eating habits of part of the population that could now, in the mid-fifties, afford store-bought biscuits for breakfast, but also because it was a well-designed biscuit with an unusual gridded surface that had holes in it, perfect for dipping in milk. In Colussi's mind, this was to have been just one of the products in a complete line of shortbread biscuits with names inspired by gemstones, but the first product in the line, the Gran Rubino, was not as successful as it should have been, and so the Gran Turchese stood alone. In 1961, a new plant was built in Petrignano di Assisi (Perugia) to optimize production and distribution; the first advertising campaigns were broadcast on television, and, in a parallel effort, special attention was focused on the packaging for promotional purposes, devising new tin containers for the biscuits.
Following the acquisition of several important brands in the food industry, the Colussi Group was founded in the nineties to gather all the brands under one wing, including Misura, Agnesi, Riso Flora and Sapori Siena 1832. In 2000 Angelo reunited the two branches of the family, buying Colussi Milano and the factory in Vittorio Veneto from his cousins.

F. Melli (edited by), *Colussi 100. Piccole dolcezze del vivere*, Ticom, Piacenza 2011.

→Packaging assembly line, 1968
(Colussi Historic Archives, Milan).

Oro Saiwa Biscuits

Saiwa, Genoa; now Mondelez International
1956

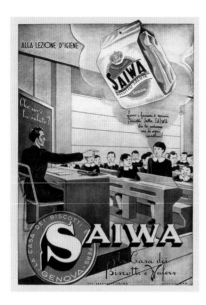

In 1900 Pietro Marchese opened a pastry shop in Genoa, the capital of the Liguria region, in which he produced dessert wafers, imitating the sugar wafers he had eaten during a trip to Great Britain.

As production grew, in 1922 he founded a company in Genoa and called it Saiwa, an acronym for *Società accomandita industria wafer e affini*, which three years later became a public company as it began to expand into an industrial dimension. Perfectly aware of the importance of communication, it distributed various types of cookies in large silkscreened tin cans—which were produced in-house after 1934—and obtained a warrant as Official Supplier to the Royal House of Savoia, using the emblem on its letterhead, press campaigns, packaging and boxes. Saiwa was one of the first Italian companies to package biscuits, which traditionally were sold in bulk, in several different types of boxes: recognizable tin cans, cardboard boxes and bags (an idea that was innovative at the time, and

has been replicated with great success in our own time. By the onset of World War II, it was one of the leading confectionery industries in Italy. During the reconstruction years, after the 1942 bombing that destroyed the plant, the buildings and machinery were renovated, new ovens and packing machines were installed. In the fifties, Saiwa became one of the largest industrial bakeries with products for every hour of the day that everyone could afford: from cookies to crackers, to Kellogg's cornflakes, a product from America that they distributed.

In 1956, it named its breakfast biscuits (which were already in production) Oro Saiwa, associating the product with a gold-coloured package which was patented (no. 132170), tying it to the *naming* and the graphic design (nos. 132002; 132173), and supporting it with resolute advertising campaigns, that turned it into a mature industrial product in terms of strategy, organization of production and advertising methods. The biscuit is no

longer identified by a generic name alone, as Oro Saiwa has become a synonym, replacing the words themselves, for a dry breakfast or snack biscuit. It was then fashioned into its "definitive" square shape that also made it easier to package.

In 1965 the company was purchased by the American group Nabisco (National Biscuit Company), and later changed hands again from Danone to Kraft, before being sold to its current owner, Mondelez International.

L. Piccardo, "Saiwa. Storia," https://www.yumpu.com/it/document/view/16278348/saiwa-storia-centro-on-line-storia-e-cultura-dellindustria; Archivio centrale dello Stato, Italian Patent and Trademark Office, no. 132002, filed 6.07.1956, reg. 29.03.1957; no. 132170, filed 24.06.1956, reg. 23.04.1957; no. 132173, filed 24.06.1956, reg. 23.04.1957.

→Advertisements (from *Tempo*, 1940).

Buondì Snack Cake

Motta, Milan; now Gruppo Bauli,
Castel d'Azzano (Verona)
1952

After developing the project for production of the traditional *panettone* at the industrial scale, building one of the largest Italian companies in the food industry, in 1952 Angelo Motta (1890–1957), conceived the idea for an innovative food product: the Buondì single-serving snack cake. Fated to become a new eating ritual, the mid-morning snack at school or at work, it partly replaced the traditional breakfast or afternoon snack that Mother made, with bread and jam or honey. The Buondì, loosely the Italian for "Good day!," and a registered name (no.112100) intended as a greeting to start the day off right, was originally conceived as a small snack cake, a sort of "mini-*panettone*" without raisins or candied fruit but covered with a sugar glaze, in a single-serving wrapper sealed to keep it fresh. This was the first example of an industrial "between-meals snack," sweet, clean, convenient, a quick snack that could be eaten without sitting at the table. Highlighting new eating patterns, the advertising campaigns often show it next to the breakfast bowl or a glass of fresh-squeezed orange juice, to emphasize freshness, fragrance and flavour. Significantly, the year it made

its debut, the commercials recommended the new Motta product as a remedy for "hidden hunger," the source of health problems and illnesses caused by inadequate nutrition, and pointed out that it was made from a yeast dough "produced by highly modern automated factories; made of flour, sugar, butter and the freshest eggs; protected by a special wrapper that guarantees total hygiene." A number of different versions with chocolate or fruit flavouring were introduced after 1970. The brand is currently owned by Bauli.

Necessario indispensabile: 1952-1991 oggetti ed eventi che hanno cambiato la nostra vita, Arnoldo Mondadori Arte, Milan 1991, p. 39; A. Colli, "La Motta: da bottega artigiana a impresa di Stato," *Annali di storia dell'impresa*, XI, 2000, pp. 571–629; A. Colli, "Angelo Motta," entry in *Dizionario Biografico degli Italiani*, vol. 77, 2012 (available online at www.treccani.it/enciclopedia/angelo-motta_(Dizionario-Biografico)/); Archivio centrale dello Stato, Italian Patent and Trademark Office, no. 112100, filed 16.10.1952, reg. 15.06.1953.

→Advertisement, 1966.

Cremino Fiat Chocolates
Majani, Bologna
1911

Majani was founded in 1796 as the *Laboratorio delle cose Dolci di Teresina Majani* and in 1830 opened a kitchen in Bologna with a storefront and tearoom. In 1856, after buying steam equipment for processing chocolate, it began to produce jams and chocolate. Throughout the nineteenth century, the company won an array of awards at the Universal Expositions; it became an Official Purveyor to the Royal House of Savoia, and was granted the right to use the royal emblem on its signs. In 1908 Majani commissioned architect Augusto Sezanne (1856–1935), one of the leading architects of the Italian Art Nouveau style, to design a building in the centre of Bologna, the interiors of which would be renovated in 1938 by Melchiorre Bega (1898–1976), which soon became a parlour for the gatherings of the aristocratic and cultural society in Bologna. Winning a competition against other chocolate-makers, in 1911 the company won a commission to create a chocolate that would serve as a publicity measure for the launch of the Fiat Tipo 4 automobile. And so it invented the Cremino Fiat, made with toasted hazelnuts and almonds, in the shape of a cube with four layers of alternating types of chocolate. Until 1913, the automobile company had the exclusive right to distribute these chocolates during its car presentations; Majani was later allowed to sell it in its stores, under the condition that it display the name and logo of Fiat in white letters with gold outlines, using a typeface that was similar to the automobile company's logo and inscribed within a blue circle with a gold edge. In 1950 Giuseppe Majani spa patented two trademarks that identified the *cremino* "shaped like a cube with dark and light layers" (nos. 98744, 98775). A rather interesting production system, also patented (no. 203149), was devised to make it possible to cut a large number of perfectly-shaped chocolates, all at the same time, from a single large "slab" of soft chocolate, applying mechanized standard-production concepts to traditional methods for producing chocolates. (fb)

A.M. Pradelli, *Bologna fra storia e osterie*, Pendragon, Bologna 2001, pp. 69–71; E. Mazzolini, A. Mendolesi, *L'Italia del cioccolato*, Touring Club, Milan 2006, pp. 100–01; Archivio centrale dello Stato, Italian Patent and Trademark Office, nos. 98774, and 98775, filed 2.02.1950, reg. 29.10.1950; Ministry of Agriculture and Commerce, Office of Intellectual Property, Certificate of Industrial Property Rights, no. 203149, 26.12.1921.

→Certificate of industrial property rights, no. 203149, 26 December 1921 (Majani 1796 Historic Archives, Valsamoggia).

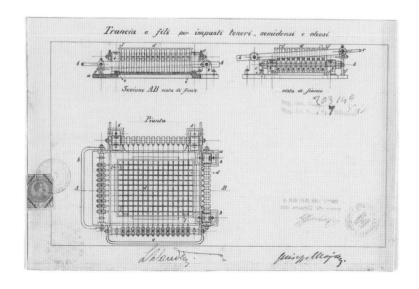

Bacio Perugina Chocolates

Perugina, Perugia; now Nestlé Italiana,
Assago (Milan)
1922

Francesco Andreani, Leone Ascoli, Francesco Buitoni and Annibale Spagnoli founded the company *Società Perugina per la Fabbricazione dei Confetti* in 1907, opening an artisans' workshop in the centre of Perugia dedicated to the production of sugared almonds and jams. When Giovanni Buitoni joined the company, it began to evolve towards a more consummately modern approach to production and marketing, and in 1914 moved to a new plant in Fontivegge (Perugia). After World War I, the growing experimentation with new products, which came to include candy, chocolate and products made with cocoa powder, led in 1922 to the creation of the Bacio, the longest-standing emblem of the brand.

Credit for the idea must be given to Luisa Sargentini (1877–1935), who assisted her husband Annibale Spagnoli in the technical direction of the company, though she herself was an entrepreneur in the fashion industry. She conceived a praline made with *gianduia* crowned with a whole hazelnut, and coated in dark Luisa chocolate (named after her), as a way to reuse the chopped hazelnuts left over from the production of other confectionery products. Because its irregular form was reminiscent of a knuckle, it was initially called "Cazzotto," the Italian word for a punch in the face, but was later renamed "Bacio" by Giovanni Buitoni.

Starting in the mid-twenties, in an effort to increase its market share, the company undertook a series of operations to rationalize the more labour-intensive production processes, such as the bonbon sector—which made filled chocolates—and the packing and wrapping. The latter was considered essential to the commercial strategies envisioned by the company: if it was to earn recognition in the sector of "fine products out of competition"—luxury

and gift items, it was compelled to guarantee the quality of the packaging and appropriate publicity. The first step was to increase the machinery and introduce an assembly line, as well as systems to monitor productivity—even though the actual automation of production, first and foremost for the Bacio, did not begin until 1956; the next step was to absorb the Borrani printing company in Florence, which had collaborated with the company for years, thereby securing a complete production cycle that included packaging and boxes. Furthermore, its relationship with the company *S.a.Maioliche Deruta & Consorzio italiano maioliche artistiche* (Cima) led to the creation of a series of ceramic accessories and containers to associate with the confectionery products.

The decision to significantly escalate the advertising logically led to the institution of the role of artistic director in 1923, entrusted to poster artist Federico Seneca (1891–1976) who had been working with the company since 1919, and who became head of the Buitoni Advertising department in 1925, soon after the Buitoni family took control over Perugina.

In particular, Seneca designed the advertising for the Bacio relying on a number of visual tools. In 1922 he first designed a wrapper made out of silver paper, followed a year later by the image that became a crucial element in the innovative illustrated packaging scheme (patents nos. 24944 and 26022). With an explicit reference to Francesco Hayez's famous painting *the Kiss*, he conceived the unmistakable silver and blue box, with the image of a couple kissing, and beside it the name, written with smooth rounded calligraphic letters that highlight the capital B. In the early thirties, the same designer conceived the idea of wrapping the Bacio chocolates in a scroll printed with

quotes and aphorisms about love, on sophisticated semi-transparent paper; similarly, for the many posters advertising Perugina products, like the image for the Bacio, he chose to focus on highly distinctive characters built around essential lines, for greater impact.

The packaging, which is immediately recognizable though it has been restyled several times, remained essentially unchanged over the years, even when the new signature tube pack was introduced, supported by a media advertising campaign that led with the slogan "Tubiamo...?," an Italian play on words that associated the tube to the cooing of doves, and was both a romantic invitation and an allusion to the new form.

In 1969 the company merged with Buitoni before being sold to Cir, and in 1988 was purchased by the international corporation Nestlé. (fb)

Tavole di Federico Seneca, preface by L. Borgese, Edizioni Vendre, Paris c. 1950; G. Buitoni, *Storia di un imprenditore*, Longanesi, Milan 1973, p. 44; G. Gallo (edited by), *Sulla bocca di tutti. Buitoni e Perugina una storia in breve*, Electa Editori Umbri, Perugia 1990; F. Milesi (edited by), *Federico Seneca. Mostra antologica*, exhibition catalogue, Grapho5 Litografia, Fano (PU) 1998; L. Masia, *Buitoni la famiglia, gli uomini, le imprese*, Silvana Editoriale, Cinisello Balsamo (MI) 2007, p. 119; F. Chiapparino, R. Covino, "La fabbrica di Perugia. Perugina 1907-2007," *Quaderni storici del Comune di Perugia*, Icsim – Comune di Perugia, Perugia 2008; Archivio centrale dello Stato, Italian Patent and Trademark Office, no. 24944, filed 10.12.1922, reg. 11.05.1924; no. 26022, filed 14.06.1923, reg. 2.07.1924.

→Cutaway of the product; trademark, no. 24944, 10 December 1922; wrappers, 1930s (Perugina-Nestlé historic museum Archives).

→Perugina Factory, 1930s
(Perugina-Nestlé historic
museum Archives).

→Federico Seneca, advertising
poster, 1920s (from *Tavole
di Federico Seneca*, preface
by L. Borgese, Edizioni Vendre,
Paris c. 1950, n.pag.).

Rossana Candy

Perugina, Perugia; now Nestlé Italiana,
Assago (Milano)
1926

The Rossana candy came out of the Perugina factory in 1926 and was patented the same year (no. 33505). Presented four years after the equally famous Bacio [**Bacio Perugina Chocolates** p. 196], it was just as successful, as demonstrated by a news item in a magazine of the time that boasted: "the predicted annual production was sold within a month."

At that time the company, run by the Buitoni family, offered a wide range of products—chocolates made in different shapes and different ways, chocolates with sophisticated fillings (cream, liqueur, Bitter, Cordial Campari, Gancia sparkling wine), cocoa in powder or bean form, special jams, candy—of medium to medium-high quality because they never used surrogates, in every possible price range. The periodic introduction of new products served Giovanni Buitoni's (1891–1979) ambition to come across as a commercially dynamic company, an unusual strategy in a market that did not yet cater to the masses.

Known as Rossa Perugina or simply Rossana, the name was inspired by Roxanne, the woman loved by Cyrano de Bergerac in the play by Edmond Rostand. It was distinguished on the outside by its bright red wrapping with gold lettering and geometric motifs, demonstrating the importance that the company attributed to the experimentation with packaging conducted by the art department under the guidance of *affichiste* Federico Seneca, who joined the company in 1919 and served as the head of the department from 1923 to 1932.

Its physical characteristics were just as meticulously designed: its consistency, hard outside and soft inside, with a filling made of hazelnuts, almonds, apricot, liqueur and milk, and its light cream colour won the hearts of consumers. Compared to the more common morphology of traditional handcrafted candies, which were generally produced in simple round or oval shapes, Rossana alluded to the production potential of mechanized industrial systems with its elongated shape, characteristic raised "edges" and the name embossed on the surface. The unexpected boom in sales led the company to optimize the facilities and manufacturing processes in the candy production lines as well.

Equally innovative were the new ways of savouring candy that it induced in the consumer, focused upon the relationship between the hard outer surface and the dense filling inside. Advertised in print, radio and television—relying after World War II on Italian advertising agencies such as Armando Testa, and some foreign agencies—it became one of the most famous candies in Italy.

In 1969 the company merged with Buitoni before being sold to Cir, and in 1988 was purchased by the Nestlé multinational company. (fb)

Rivista dell'economia umbra, XXXVIII, 10 October 1926, p. 174; F. Chiapparino, R. Covino, "La fabbrica di Perugia. Perugina 1907-2007," *Quaderni storici del Comune di Perugia*, Icsim-Comune di Perugia, Perugia 2008; Archivio centrale dello Stato, Italian Patent and Trademark Office, no. 33505, filed 3.05.1926, reg. 7.06.1926.

→Advertisement (from *La Rivista illustrata del popolo d'Italia*, 11, November 1926, p. 61).

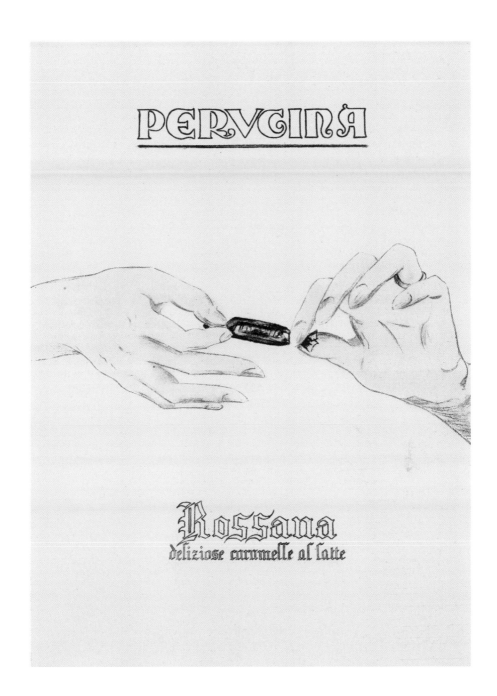

Golia Candy

Davide Caremoli, Milan;
now Perfetti Van Melle, Lainate (Milan)

1932

The Golia name and brand, which identify "gummy liquorice drops," were registered simultaneously in 1932 (nos. 45403 and 45404) by the Davide Caremoli company, founded in Milan in 1913.

The biblical reference to Goliath, probably chosen to contrast with the tiny size of the candy, the similarity to other drops with beneficial balsamic qualities, the hand-twisted candy wrappers, the design of the six-point green star with the name in the middle, the chewy consistency, the fresh taste, all concurred to its surge in popularity. And the compelling advertising campaigns, developed throughout the century by the Acme-Dalmonte agency, Carlo Dradi, the Clan agency and Young & Rubicam, made it a household name by developing images and slogans that lingered in the collective memory of Italians, like the famous paraphrase of a traditional children's rhyme: "Chi non mangia la Golia è un ladro o una spia."

Initially the liquorice-flavoured balsamic candy was sold in bulk, then in the early fifties, it was packaged in sealed bags, while it became habitual for shopkeepers to use it as change for their customers, given that the suggested retail price was 1 lira. The growth in sales raised the production to 60 quintals per day in 1954 and in 1965, the year the factory was moved to Lainate, to 12 tons per day. That same year the company introduced Golia Bianca, a small liquorice square with a hard mint coating, which was sustained, starting in 1981, by an innovative advertising campaign created by Lele Panzeri and Anna Maria Testa (Michele Rizzi & Associati agency). In 1987, the *Dolcificio Lombardo* company, owned by the brothers Ambrogio and Egidio Perfetti, who had also settled in Lainate in 1946 and founded their company Perfetti spa, bought out Caremoli, marketing the Golia candy along with their own best-selling product, the Brooklyn

"bridge chewing gum." In 2001 Perfetti bought a majority share of the Dutch company Van Melle, creating Perfetti Van Melle, and becoming one of the leaders in the "globalized" confectionery industry.

VV.AA., *L'ingegno e le opere. Esperienze di produzione nel milanese*, Jaca Book, Milan 2006, pp. 164–65; L. Panzeri, *C'ero una volta. Vita di un creativo*, Lupetti, Milan 2006, n.pag.; Archivio centrale dello Stato, Italian Patent and Trademark Office, no. 45403 and no. 45404, filed 1.04.1932, reg. 26.05.1933.

→Dalmonte, advertisement (from *La Domenica del Corriere*, 31 March 1946).

→Advertisement (from *Le Vie d'Italia*, 12, 1948, p. 1068).

→Advertisement, 1977 (Perfetti Van Melle Historic Archives, Lainate).

**bella voce
bella gola**

di Golia ce n'è una sola

Ambrosoli Honey-Filled Candy

Ambrosoli, Ronago (Como)
1932

Giovanni Battista Ambrosoli, a graduate in industrial chemistry from the Technikum in Winterthur (Zurich), with professional experience in the chemical field in Switzerland, returned to Ronago (Como) in 1906 to run his paternal grandmother's farm, and developed a passion for beekeeping. In 1923 he registered his company "G.B. Ambrosoli" with the Chamber of Commerce of Como, turning his personal interest into a business. In the twenties, he adopted an original and rational system of production and logistics which allowed him to increase production and make the most of the flora in bloom: he purchased a number of vehicles, and transported the hives from the plain areas to the mountainous zones, thereby inaugurating what is known as nomadic apiculture. The name of his honey, Miele Ambrosoli, was registered in 1928 (no. 39671) and by the thirties, the company's production included honey, honey-filled candies, floor and furniture waxes made with beeswax (nos. 44757 and 45498).

In the years between the two World Wars, his following grew steadily thanks to his participation, for example, in the trade fairs in Milan with his own company stand, to the advertising campaigns he launched that emphasized how important it was to have honey on hand, highlighting its "soothing healthy exquisite" properties, to the commercials he broadcast over the radio—a budding means of communication in those years. At the same time, he improved distribution in 1934 by opening a warehouse in Milan and offices in Rome. The business grew with the help of his son Costantino and the new machines that were acquired to produce candy. Benefitting from a countrywide sales network, the company expanded beyond the borders of Italy before World War II, consolidating its position after the war by sponsoring sports teams and events. Its fame grew in the sixties thanks to the collaboration with Studio Testa and the commercials for the television show Carosello, filmed between 1965

and 1976 by Tomislav Spikic/Zagreb Film, which featured the reassuring jingle "Dolce cara mammina," "Dear sweet mommy."
In 1977, when the company was structured into its current legal form (G.B. Ambrosoli spa), the top-selling product was honey, representing over 55% of total sales, followed by candy (38%).

G. Pizzorni, page on *G.B. Ambrosoli spa*, in http://www.lombardiabeniculturali.it/archivi/soggetti-produttori/ente/MIDB0019CD/; Archivio centrale dello Stato, Italian Patent and Trademark Office, no. 39671, filed 26.10.1928, reg. 25.08.1930; no. 44757, filed 30.11.1931, reg. 27.03.1933; no. 45498, filed 4.03.1931, reg. 4.06.1933.

→Dalmonte, advertisement, 1930s (G.B. Ambrosoli Historic Archives, Ronago).

→Advertising totem at the Fiera Campionaria di Milano, 1936 (Fondazione Fiera Milano Historic Archives, Milan).

Tic Tac Mints

Ferrero, Alba (Cuneo)

1969

The design of Tic Tac is an expression of the innovative choices made by Ferrero for his products and communication strategies, at a time when the company founded by Pietro Ferrero (1898–1949) in 1946 in Alba (Cuneo), was becoming firmly established following the success of Nutella, launched in 1964. The mints, conceived in 1969 to diversify production, which had concentrated almost exclusively on chocolate and hazelnuts until then, were initially called Refreshing Mint, but that was changed to the onomatopoeic name Tic Tac, which reflected the noise made by the candies in their plastic box. This attention to packaging, a strategy adopted by Ferrero in the early seventies for a series of different products, including the single-serving packs of Nutella, Estathé ice tea or the Kinder Sorpresa, distinguished this product as well. The Tic Tac box was designed by Amilcare Dogliotto, a childhood friend of Michele Ferrero (1925–2015) son of the founder Pietro, who had worked in the company since 1955 and held many other international patents for packaging and production methods for the confectionery industry.
The revolutionary mini-dispenser is described in the American patent filed in 1972 (no. US 3872996) as a container for granular materials "comprising a flat parallelepipedic body having an open end into which a generally rectangular cover or plug is inserted." What makes it so special is the slightly protruding flap that flips up with a flick of the thumb to open the box, creating a whole new gestural approach. Tic Tac is one of the products that brought Ferrero widespread international distribution, particularly in the United States.

V. Marchis, *150 (anni di) invenzioni italiane*, Codice Edizioni, Turin 2011, pp. 115–16; United States Patent, *Container for granular materials*, no. US 3872996, priority 11.04.1972; reg. 9.04.1973, publ. 25.03.1975.

→Patent, no. US 3872996, 11 April 1972.

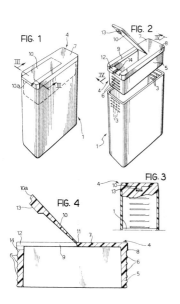

San Carlo Potato Chips

San Carlo, Milan;
now San Carlo Unichips, Milan
1936

San Carlo was one of the first companies in Italy to introduce *potato chips* or *crisps,* as they are known respectively in the United States and in Great Britain, where they were created in the mid-nineteenth century, and which in the first decade of the twentieth century were on their way to becoming a mass consumer product, thanks to the circumstance that they could be packaged in a cellophane bag. This was a product, manufactured within a mechanized mass production process, that could be eaten on the go, ideal for supplementing meals or as a side dish, the forerunner of snack foods, and a quick yet gratifying means of nourishment.

In 1936, Francesco Vitaloni opened a deli in Via Lecco in Milan which, in honour of the church nearby, he named San Carlo. His speciality was "patatine croccanti," potatoes that were peeled, sliced very thin, fried in hot oil and lightly sprinkled with salt. Due to increasing demand, in 1940 the deli moved to larger premises and changed its name to *San Carlo...le patatine* (the three suspension points in the middle are conceived to elegantly distinguish gourmet food from sainthood).

The package extolled and described the qualities of the crisps, and suggested how to eat them: "the most exquisite crisps with guaranteed quality... the most digestible potato crisps," "the healthiest food of all alkaline fare," "always fresh, always deliciously crunchy the Chips bring joy to the table... and delight to those who eat them," with Vitaloni's own signature underneath. The trademark was registered in 1952 (no. 115280) and, in the sixties, the picture of Mr Crocc, the smiling potato chip wearing a chef's hat, was introduced as yet another marketing tool, and was even produced as a promotional toy.

When Alberto Vitaloni took over in the fifties, production increased as the technology was upgraded and grew to include savoury snacks, breads and bakery goods. In the same period, Dante Vernice of the CPV agency designed the San Carlo logo with the yellow letters against a red background. It was restyled in 2002 by Ginette Caron, a graphic designer who also worked on the packaging for the potato chips. Her project was based on the perceptive experience of the product as it appears on supermarket shelves, leading to the decision to use opaque white for the bag and photos of the project by Oliviero Toscani, highly distinctive elements when compared to the loud colours of the competition. The profusion of messages that crowded the original bags was discarded in favour of the few elements that were essential to the communication: the matte paper that conveyed a sense of purity, flavour, lightness and health, and the starkness of the layout, focusing on the subject, the potato, featured at the very centre of the bag.

In the early nineties San Carlo purchased Pai, another historic brand in this sector. The San Carlo potato chips are emblematic of the diffusion of new products and eating habits in Italy, linked to new patterns of consumption that reflect a faster pace of life, with foods intended to be both appetizing and enticing, such as snacks in general and potato chips in particular.

Archivio centrale dello Stato,
Italian Patent and Trademark Office,
no. 115280, filed 22.05.1952,
reg. 19.01.1954.

→Ginette Caron, product packaging, 2002.

Gran Pavesi Saltine Crackers

Pavesi, Novara;
now Gruppo Barilla, Parma
1954

Dry, thin and crispy, crackers were first made in the United States in the early nineteenth century as an evolution of the hardtack supplied to soldiers or sailors in lieu of bread during their long voyages. The name crackers derived from the crackling sound they made while baking. They were first brought to Italy in 1954 when upon his return from a trip to the United States, Mario Pavesi (1909–90) tested the market and developed the production technology, which he then adopted in his new factory in Novara, inaugurating a new typology in the baked goods sector.
"In September 1954 we began to devise our advertising campaign for the crackers and shortly thereafter for the Chips and the round Thins as well. Our primary target group was women; our goal: to become part of the family diet at home or on the go; our slogan: 'The most modern expression of the oldest of foods'" wrote Mario Bellavista in 1997, the author of Pavesi's communication from 1948 to 1959, who was responsible for the advertising that launched the Crackers Soda Pavesi and several years earlier, the Pavesini [**Pavesini Biscuits** p. 186].

The decision to package them in single servings, one of the first in the country, with obvious advantages in terms of convenience and freshness, was made possible by the installation of a packaging line that filled the cracker boxes as they moved along the conveyer belt, and of packaging equipment designed to handle the single-servings (patents nos. 125087, 137075).
In 1964 the Crackers Soda Pavesi changed their name to Gran Pavesi and the advertisements, not coincidentally, featured the image of a large loaf of homemade bread, the slices of which turned into crackers, reflecting the dietary concerns of a society that wished to break free of traditional foods, and suggesting a connection between the lightness of the product and the fitness of the body. Pavesi's goals were thus substantiated: the introduction of pre-portioned savoury snacks on the Italian market brought with it a new eating habit, inspired by a product that offered an alternative to bread, but was more frugal and essential, and more convenient to eat during coffee breaks, study breaks or on the go.

In 1954, some months after Pavesi, Motta began its production of Ritz crackers, under license by the National Biscuit Company (Nabisco) in the United States, which had been marketing them since 1934.
Pavesi has been part of the Barilla group since 1993, the latest in a line of owners that also included Iri-Sme.

M. Bellavista, "Uomo di marketing prima del marketing," VV.AA., *L'Italia dei Pavesini. Cinquant'anni di pubblicità e comunicazione Pavesi*, Amilcare Pizzi, Parma 1997, pp. 58–64; Archivio centrale dello Stato, Italian Patent and Trademark Office, no. 125087, filed 23.03.1955, reg. 21.09.1955; no. 137075, filed 7.02.1957, reg. 2.06.1958.

→Advertisement, 1956 (Barilla Historic Archives, Parma).

Crackers Pavesi...

CHIPS AL MAIS - Un gusto nuovo, un piacere nuovo. Squisiti con l'aperitivo, deliziosi con i succhi di frutta.

CHIPS CRACKERS - Sapore dolce-salato. Particolarmente adatti con il the, con l'aperitivo e per preparare croccanti tartine.

CRACKERS SODA - Leggermente salati. Si accompagnano deliziosamente ad ogni pietanza e ne rendono più vivo il sapore. 6 pacchetti sigillati in ogni scatola.

sempre croccanti
come appena sfornati!

igiene garantita
dall'automatismo
della produzione.
Perfetta conservazione
grazie allo speciale
involucro isolante
a chiusura termoadesiva

crackers **PAVESI** 100 LIRE

→Studio Sigla, advertisement, 1955 (Barilla Historic Archives, Parma).

→N. Pizzorno, advertisement for Ritz crackers, Motta 1959 (from *Pubblicità in Italia, 1959-1960,* suppl. to *L'Ufficio Moderno – la pubblicità,* 11, 1958).

→Elio Luxardo, portrait with a box of Ritz crackers, 1956 (© Fondazione 3M Archivio fotografico).

Aranciata San Pellegrino Soft Drink

San Pellegrino, San Pellegrino Terme (Bergamo);
now Nestlé Italiana, Assago (Milan)

1932

Aranciata San Pellegrino in its distinctive bottle was conceived by Ezio Granelli, owner of the company since 1925, and introduced at the Fiera campionaria in Milan in 1932. Made with San Pellegrino mineral water [**Mineral Water** p. 126], orange juice and sugar, it was the first drink released on the market by the company.
The production process, in synthesis, involved juicing the oranges that came from Sicily in the factory in Milan, to be transformed into a soft drink and bottled at San Pellegrino Terme.
The icon of its success was the club-shaped glass bottle, patented in 1934 (no. 11771), which starting with a circular base first swells outward then stretches up into the short narrow neck. The textured surface was an explicit reference to the peel of the orange from which the juice was squeezed. Emblematic of the different expressive languages of their time, advertising artefacts were designed to publicize

the product through the years, from the hand-drawn posters in which it was shown in exclusive surroundings—"everywhere ... it is the latest thing"—which also underlined its health benefits and its natural composition based on mineral water, to the campaigns that allusively connected the ideas of fruit and thirst, like the ones developed by the Armando Testa agency in the late seventies.
Demonstrating the existence of a mature market for this type of single-serving soft drink, there was a drink in Algeria in the early thirties made out of concentrated orange juice that Léon Beton had named Orangina, inspired by a similar Spanish drink known as Naranjina. After 1951, it was sold by CFPO, *Compagnie Française des Productes Orangina*, in a bottle with a granular surface similar to that of Aranciata San Pellegrino, restyled by Jean-Claude Beton, the son of the company founder, to be a little more

rotund. The bottle continues to be a signature element of the product to this very day, as are the advertising campaigns, designed by *affichiste* Bernard Villemot. (fb)

"The Orangina Bottle," VV.AA., *Phaidon Design Classics*, Phaidon, London 2006, entry 398; A.M. Sette, *Disegno e design. Brevetti e creatività*, exhibition catalogue, Fondazione Valore Italia, Rome 2010, pp. 306–09; Archivio centrale dello Stato, Italian Patent and Trademark Office, no. 11771, filed 1934, reg. 28.02.1935.

→Advertisement, 1950s (Gruppo Sanpellegrino Historic Archives).

→Armando Testa, advertising poster, 1979.

→Advertising cardboard cutout and patent no. 11771, 28 February 1935 (Gruppo San Pellegrino).

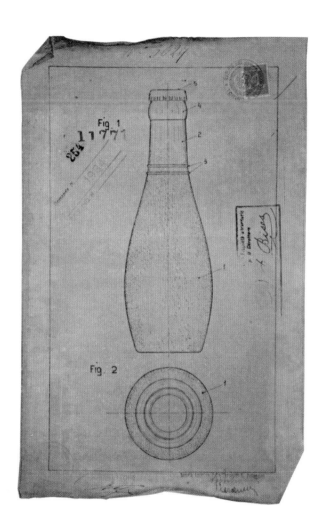

Chinotto Soft Drink
Various manufacturers
1930s

Chinotto is a soft drink derived from the extract of *Citrus myrtifolia*, commonly known as *chinotto*, a small fruit that originally came from China—hence the name—and was imported to Europe in the sixteenth century. Initially used to produce an essence for perfumes and as a vitamin supplement for seafaring crews, because it lasted long without perishing, in the nineteenth century it was adopted by the confectionery industry, and used prevalently as candied fruit, in alcohol or for juice. It is distinguished by its tart and slightly acerbic aftertaste.

In the thirties, *chinotto* evolved from an "artisanal" drink to an industrial product, in the category of refreshing non-alcoholic soft drinks such as orange drink or tamarind. They were marketed mixed with water and carbonated, as a drink for leisure or vacation time, which Italians were just beginning to enjoy. And because of the similarity in colour, *chinotto* was considered the Italian response to the growing popularity of Coca-Cola, first imported to Italy from America in 1927.

The first documents in which it appears as a trademark are dated 1938, registered by the *Industria liquori e sciroppi Enrico Porzio* in Udine as Aranciata al Chinotto (no. 59081), though the original industrial version was credited to San Pellegrino and was introduced together with their Aranciata in 1932 [**Aranciata San Pellegrino Soft Drink** p. 210]. And because the *chinotto* extract must be mixed with water, after World War II the drink was included in almost all the assortments of soft drinks produced by the manufacturers of mineral waters. There were in fact many different versions on the market, other than San Pellegrino, such as Recoaro, Sorgente Panna or Terme di Crodo [**Mineral Water** p. 126]. The most distinctive version—which was the expression of a specific design for the bottle and for the advertising artefacts—known throughout Italy was the version produced by the Leonina

Neri company in Rome, which changed its name to Chinotto Neri srl in 1950, and moved the factory to Capranica (Viterbo) to exploit the mineral water spring of San Rocco. Soon after patenting the trademark in 1948 (no. 93172), the company introduced a small bottle, presented in 1949 along with the design of the trademark (no. 94289), characterized by alternating grooved and textured surfaces—reminiscent of citrus rind—and the trademark embossed on it. It was 1950 when Chinotto Neri chose to exploit a graphic-mnemonic device and became Chin8 (no. 100192), using the number 8 instead of the letters "otto," which spell the Italian word for eight, and launching a name with remarkable communicative impact. The drink has been equally successful in the version produced by San Pellegrino, which was renamed Chinò in the eighties and supported by a graphic design that reversed the "n" to face backwards and coloured it red. Another product of interest is the more recent Lurisia chinotto, a Slow Food Presidium for *chinotto di Savona*, a product made with the citrus fruit grown on the Riviera Ligure di Ponente, in keeping with the idea of preserving the specific production of each geographical region: since World War II, production of this citrus fruit has become consolidated in the Liguria region, and in several areas of Sicily.

www.chinotto.com; Archivio centrale dello Stato, Italian Patent and Trademark Office, no. 59081, filed 26.09.1938, reg. 27.04.1939; no. 93172, filed 21.12.1948, reg. 18.12.1949; no. 94289, filed 18.05.1949, reg. 14.02.1950; no. 100192, filed 26.04.1950, reg. 26.01.1951.

→Ditta Leonina Neri e F.llo, patent no. 94289, 18 May 1949.

→Stabilimenti Demaniali Recoaro Milano, patent no. 95993, 14 March 1950.

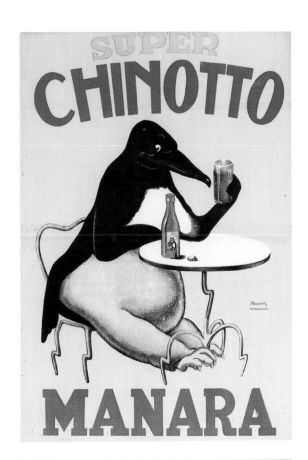

→Giovanni Manca, Super
Chinotto Manara, advertising
poster, 1950s (Club Amici
del Chinotto Archives).

→R. Paltrinieri, Aranciata
Chinotto, San Pellegrino,
advertising poster, 1950s.

Con i recenti ampliamenti, lo Sta
bilimento Demaniale di Recoaro
produce ogni ora 60.000 bottiglie di squisite, sane ed igieniche
bevande Recoaro. Lo Stabilimento Demaniale di Recoaro ha oggi la potenzialità gior-
naliera di un milione di bottiglie e, benché
dotato del più moderno automatismo di produzione, dà lavoro ad oltre 650 operai.

bevande
RECOARO

CHINOTTO RECOARO
ARANCIA RECOARO
LIMONE RECOARO

*deliziosi succhi naturali di agrume
nella famosa acqua minerale di Recoaro*

RECOARO TERME: OASI DI SALUTE E DI RIPOSO

→Bevande Recoaro,
advertisement, 1950s; Mariano
Congiu; S. Pellegrino,
advertisement, 1958 (Club
Amici del Chinotto Archives).

→Chinotto Lurisia, 2008
(Lurisia).

→Ferrarelle, advertisement,
1950s (Club Amici del Chinotto
Archives).

Cedrata Tassoni Soft Drink

Tassoni, Salò (Brescia)
1955

Tassoni Soda, known as Cedrata and on the market since 1956, is a soft drink with a sweet and slightly acerbic taste, conspicuous for its bright yellow colour and transparent glass bottle with a surface textured like the citron rind, in a single-serving size and devoid of a label. The logo was initially moulded directly into the glass, but later both the brand and ingredients, printed in yellow and green, were indicated on the bottle cap alone. Its origins date back to the artisanal distilleries documented in the eighteenth century along the Riviera Gardesana—the coast of Lake Garda in the province of Brescia—and was made by apothecaries who distilled hydro-alcoholic infusions to obtain an extract from the citron rind, the basic ingredient in the preparation of *Acqua di cedro*, a slightly alcoholic drink.

In Salò, in the province of Brescia, one of the apothecary shops that was also a distillery, and was certified as a pharmacy in 1793, in 1868 became the property of Bartolomeo Castelli and nobleman Nicola Tassoni—who would give the company its name.

In 1884 ownership passed on to Paolo Amadei, who chose to separate the pharmacy from the distillery, and organize the latter on a more strictly industrial basis. The product that launched the *Stabilimento farmaceutico Tassoni*—and won the bronze medal of the Universal Exposition in Paris in 1900 for the design of its stand—was Cedral, Tassoni's version of the traditional *Acqua di cedro*, which would also become the name of the company. In the twenties, when his son Carlo Amadei joined the company, a new phase of expansion was inaugurated that began with the production of Cedrata in 1921, distinguished from all others by the addition of citron syrup—a name patented the very same year (no. 22021). Fully aware of the dynamics of Italy's nascent industry, Amadei launched his first advertising campaigns; the posters for Cedral Tassoni are classics of a certain type of advertising characteristic of the twenties and thirties. With didactic intent the Cedrata is described as a "complete and exquisite thirst-quencher" full of vitamins to fortify sportsmen and

children alike. During the economic boom, which led to the growth of leisure time and the spread of refreshing soft drinks such as orange drink or *chinotto*, in 1955 the company introduced its Tassoni Soda (patent no. 122001), "the ready-to-drink Cedrata in just the right amount"—as the advertising read—in a transparent glass bottle with a shape and texture that were easily recognizable and highlighted the citron yellow colour of the drink. (fb)

G. Iacchetti, *Italianità*, Corraini, Mantua 2008, pp. 99–100; Archivio centrale dello Stato, Italian Patent and Trademark Office, no. 22021, filed 11.07.1921, reg. 29.10.1923; no. 122001, filed 9.01.1955, reg. 15.03.1955.

→Peeling the citrus fruit, 1960s
(Cedral Tassoni Archives, Salò).

→Advertisement, 1926
(Cedral Tassoni Archives, Salò).

→Advertising poster, 1956
(Cedral Tassoni Archives, Salò).

Campari Soda Aperitif

Campari, Sesto San Giovanni (Milan)

1932

Davide Campari (1867–1936) chose Sesto San Giovanni in 1923—"the city of factories" at the gates of Milan—to build the plant for his company (founded in 1862) which he commissioned to architect Luigi Perrone, the designer of the Circolo filologico in Milan, in the neo-Romanesque style, with brick walls adorned with ceramic decorations on the outside; on the inside he used reinforced concrete, which was rather innovative for the time. The choice of architect confirms the company's unflagging interest in the aspects of art and design, which over the years would orient the decision not only to hire the best *affichistes* and graphic designers to create the posters—from Marcello Dudovich to Leonetto Cappiello, from Marcello Nizzoli to Nicolaj Diulgheroff and Bruno Munari—but also to make a series of promotional items that proved essential to the diffusion of the brand around the world.

The company's most famous product was its Bitter; in 1932 production began on Campari Soda, which offered the Bitter in pre-mixed ready-to-drink servings. It was sold in the unmistakable cone-shaped bottle, originally manufactured by Vetrerie Bordoni in Milan, featuring a design that may be in part attributed to Fortunato Depero (1892–1960): while he was not directly involved in the actual design and technical development of the bottle, he undoubtedly inspired this original and innovative shape.

As co-author with Giacomo Balla in 1915 of the manifesto *Ricostruzione futurista dell'universo*, in which he theorized the contribution of artists to every field of human creativity, Depero was one of the most active Futurists in the field of visual communication and the applied arts. In Rovereto, he ran the Bottega d'arte with his wife Rosita, which produced fabrics, carpets, tapestries and furniture. He collaborated with many companies, especially in the field of graphic design, but his most significant work was produced for Campari, for which he created posters, individual issues of magazines, promotional objects and much more. In the thirties, he contributed significantly to the design of the Campari Soda bottle.

The shape of the bottle was in fact derived from similar morphologies—created by breaking down and recomposing the geometric-machinist forms typical of Depero's artistic experimentation and that of many other Futurists—to those found in the posters and in the promotional articles (the first of which date back to 1926–27) conceived by Depero: the cone or upside-down goblet shape was developed at a later date by the glass factory and the company. It was a small bottle, that tapered gradually in the top third of the body and was crowned by a slightly billowing aperture; made out of transparent frosted glass, the lower part contained information about the product and the company embossed on the glass, and therefore did not require a paper label. There are many elements of interest here: the unusual conic form, which in fact makes it easier to store in crates; the choice of material, a transparent frosted glass with a special surface texture that emphasized the deep red of the drink; and the words embossed on the glass. This was an object that packed remarkable communicative substance and power.

Like the drink itself, the container is clearly the result of a design process, which developed a specific configuration based on methods of industrial organization and production.

It is worth noting that a few years after Campari Soda was launched on the market, an automatic vending machine was designed to distribute the drink in public spaces. This forefather of today's vending machines, with its rectangular body set on a trapezoidal base, featured a publicity sculpture by Depero on the top: an anthropomorphic figure drinking with a straw out of a bottle shaped like an upside-down goblet.

The name and shape of the bottle were patented respectively in 1944 and in 1955 (nos. 75284, 76416, 548789.

B. Schonteich, "Campari Soda," M. Scudiero (edited by), *Depero per Campari*, Fabbri, Milan 1989, pp. 19–23; G. Belli (edited by), *La casa del mago. Le arti applicate nell'opera di Fortunato Depero*, exhibition catalogue, Charta, Milan 1993; AA.VV., *Brevetti del design italiano 1946-1965*, Electa, Milan 2000, pp. 138–39; *999 Phaidon Design Classics*, vol. I, Phaidon, London 2006, entry 212; Archivio centrale dello Stato, Italian Patent and Trademark Office no. 75284, filed 24.09.1944, reg. 19.08.1947; no. 76416, filed 24.09.1944; reg. 26.11.1947; no. 54878, 18.07.1955.

→Franz Marangolo, advertising poster, 1950 (© Davide Campari-Milano Spa).

→Vetrerie S.A. Angelo Bordoni e Figlio, drawing of a bottle for Campari Soda, 1932 (© Davide Campari-Milano spa).

→Patent no. 54878, 18 July 1955 (© Davide Campari-Milano spa).

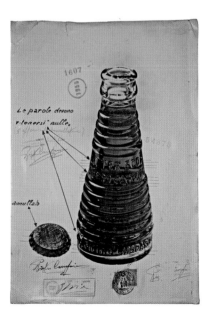

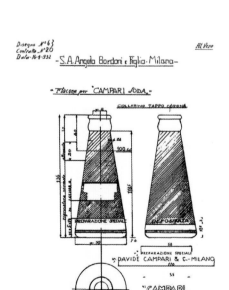

Bitter San Pellegrino Aperitif

San Pellegrino, San Pellegrino Terme (Bergamo);
now Nestlé Italiana, Assago (Milan)
1961

Bitter San Pellegrino, the first Italian single-serving non-alcoholic aperitif, made its debut in 1961—the year the patent was registered (no. 156194)—at the initiative of Giuseppe Mentasti, who took over from his father-in-law Ezio Granelli as director of the company *Terme di San Pellegrino spa* in 1957.

It was a blend of citrus extracts, spices and aromatic herbs, red in colour with a slightly bitter taste, and sold in an unusual glass bottle shaped like a triangular, but somewhat flattened prism, a form that would afford it immediate recognisability.

The genesis of the bottle is interesting because it demonstrates how the competition among soft drink manufacturers was sometimes independent of the design of its bottles. The Bitter bottle is the same bottle used by San Pellegrino for Rabarbaro, a drink it had produced since 1938, marking the debut of the Bergamo-based company on the market of premixed, slightly alcoholic single-serving drinks in response to the remarkable success of Campari Soda, introduced in 1932 in the special bottle inspired by Fortunato Depero (1892–1960).

Whereas the Rabarbaro San Pellegrino—which was also mixed with mineral water—was marketed for its beneficial medicinal qualities, Bitter, which was introduced during the economic boom years, appealed more directly to the fitness concerns of the time: as a result, it was alcohol-free and advertised as "L'aperitivo per gli sportivi," the aperitif for sportsmen. Following a series of memorable advertising campaigns developed by Armando Testa—who was responsible for the corporate image in those years—in 1975 the drink changed its name to Sanbittèr, and to accustom consumers to the new name, introduced the slogan "Sanbittèr, c'est plus facile," which accompanied the product throughout the eighties.

Archivio centrale dello Stato, Italian Patent and Trademark Office, no. 156194, filed 5.06.1961, reg. 9.08.1961.

→Rabarbaro S. Pellegrino, advertisement, 1952 (from *La Domenica del Corriere*, 2 March 1952).

→Arar, advertising poster, 1960s (Gruppo San Pellegrino).

l' aperitivo
degli sportivi

ARAR

Bitter

UNA
Novità!
S. PELLEGRINO

Bitter
ANALCOOLICO
S. PELLEGRINO

Aperitivo salutare

BITTER
S. PELLEGRINO

ANALCOOLICO
S. PELLEGRINO

L'APERITIVO VERAMENTE SENZA ALCOOL

Bertolini Yeast

Bertolini, Collegno (Turin); now Gruppo Cameo, Desenzano sul Garda (Brescia)

1911

Antonio Bertolini invented the single-dose packet of yeast in 1911, the year he founded his company in the Regina Margherita district of Collegno (Turin). Until then, homemakers had relied on an empirically-calculated pinch of baking soda to make their cakes rise, but from then on they could count on a pre-dosed packet. From the very outset the brand, which registered its trademark in 1922 with the slogan "the best cakes breads and doughnuts are made exclusively with vanilla-flavoured Bertolini Yeast" in the name of Droghificio Cav. Antonio Bertolini Torino (no. 23899), based its market and communication strategies on the concept of consumer service. One of the most interesting was the idea of the *Ricettario Bertolini*, a recipe book that came out in the thirties and was published uninterruptedly for over seventy years (it still exists today, not in printed form but as an e-book). And

to again convey the image of a company that could be a real help in the kitchen, the recipe book also featured material illustrating how to use the entire range of yeast products and other baking ingredients. In these publications, Antonio Bertolini addressed his customer directly as "dear Madam," illustrating how practical the yeast or vanilla-flavoured sugar was for baking better cakes. The advertising campaigns initially focused on great events that appealed to a mass audience, such as the parades of automobiles emblazoned with the images of the brand in the centre of Turin, publicized by announcements on the radio and film clips shown in movie theatres. After World War II came the company's famous jingle: "What does it take to make good cakes? it takes Bertolini!," whereas in 1970, the television show *Carosello* popularized the character

known as Mariarosa, a little girl created by the illustrator of children's books Maria Pia Franzoni Tomba (1902–1978), accompanied by the jingle "Brava brava Mariarosa anything you want you can do, life is always rosy if we are here with you!" which became indelibly etched in the memory of all the television viewers. The Bertolini brand is currently owned by the Cameo Group.

C. and G. Padovani, *Italia Buon Paese. Gusti cibi e bevande in 150 anni di storia*, Blu Edizioni, Turin 2011, pp. 76, 188–89; M.P. Moroni Salvatori, *Novecento in cucina*, Pendragon, Bologna 2014, pp. 153–54; Archivio centrale dello Stato, Italian Patent and Trademark Office, no. 23899, filed 23.05.1922, reg. 27.03.1924.

→Lievito Bertolini recipe book, 1930s (Private archives, Milan).

Spread 1

TORTA MARGHERITA - PAN DI SPAGNA

TORTA AL CIOCCOLATO - ZUPPA ROMANA

FOCACCIA PRIMAVERA - PANDOLCE GENOVESE

Piatto del giorno 7

GNOCCHI DI PATATE ALLA BERTOLINI

SANI - LEGGERI - NUTRIENTI - ECONOMICI
DIGERIBILI - VERAMENTE SQUISITI

Eccovi la famosa ricetta!

Lessate un chilo di patate, pelatele, schiacciatele e lasciatele raffreddare.

Unite un uovo intero, un pizzico di sale e per ultimo, 300 gr. circa di farina bianca alla quale avrete prima mescolato il contenuto di una bustina di LIEVITO BERTOLINI tipo speciale per GNOCCHI.

Formate quindi i gnocchi, lasciateli riposare per circa 5 minuti e poi cuoceteli in acqua bollente togliendoli non appena vengono a galla.

Conditeli subito con burro rosolato (colto) e formaggio parmigiano misto ad un cucchiaio colmo di zucchero; ed un altra presa di buona ricotta e di ottime spezie. Serviteli ben caldi ed ecco i complimenti dei Vostri commensali.

IL «LIEVITO BERTOLINI» TIPO SPECIALE PER GNOCCHI È IN VENDITA PRESSO TUTTE LE MIGLIORI DROGHERIE OGNI BUSTINA È DOSE SUFFICIENTE PER SEI PERSONE

9

Spread 2

KRAFFEN

Versare in un recipiente 60 gr. di burro sciolto e rimestando aggiungervi uno per volta 4 tuorli d'uovo, 30 gr. di latte, due cucchiai di zucchero, un pizzico di sale. Mescolare a parte 150 gr. di farina con 100 gr. di fecola di patate impastando una dose per mezzo kg. di Lievito Bertolini. Durante le manipolazioni incorporarvi una dose per mezzo kg. di Lievito Bertolini.

Fare quindi lo sfoglio dello spessore di un centimetro che si taglierà a dischi servendovi dell'orlo di un largo bicchiere. Unire questi dischi due per due dopo averli bagnati all'interno con un dito intinto nel latte ed imbottiti con mezzo cucchiaino di conserva di frutta. Friggerli in ottimo olio e servirli caldi impolverati di zucchero.

TORTA DI FRUTTA

Farina gr. 250, burro sciolto gr. 125, un tuorlo d'uovo. Impastare bene aggiungendovi poca acqua se l'impasto riesce troppo sodo ed incorporandovi durante la manipolazione una dose per mezzo kg. di Lievito Bertolini.

Con questa pasta imbottite il fondo ed i fianchi dello stampo poi aggiungetevi uno strato di buona conserva di frutta ed infine delle mele tagliate a fettine sottili bagnate nel rhum e impolverate di zucchero. Cuocere a forno moderato per circa un'ora. Ritirata dal forno e bagnate la superficie con una chiara già sbattuta a parte con due cucchiai di zucchero e mezza bustina di Zucchero Vanigliato Bertolini. Rimettiela subito al fuoco per altri 10 minuti e servirla preferibilmente calda. Desiderando si può guarnire di ciliege sciroppate.

TORTA REGINA

Si sbattono a schiuma 125 gr. di burro, si aggiunge 150 gr. di zucchero ed 4 tuorli d'uovo; quando tutto è ben mescolato, si aggiungono 250 gr. di farina, un bicchiere di latte e la neve delle 4 chiare, incorporando in ultimo una dose per mezzo kg. di Lievito Bertolini.

Stampo spalmato con burro e farina e passato subito al forno.

Entro circa mezz'ora, la torta è pronta.

SAVOIARDI — TORTA REGINA

PANETTONE ALLA MILANESE - PLUM-CAKE

CIAMBELLA ALLA ROMAGNOLA - BISCOTTINI VIENNESI

Spread 3

ROTOLINI DI MANZO

Preparate delle bracioline di carne tenera e ben battuta, riempitele con un trito di fegato di vitello, prosciutto, cipolla, trita molto fine, capperi e polpa d'acciughe sminuzzate; rotolatele facendo rientrare un poco le estremità nell'interno. Infarinatele leggermente e mettete i rotolini in salsiera; fateli colorire con olio, versatevi 1 bicchiere di vino bianco ed altrettanti e più d'acqua; aggiungetevi 2 cipolle a quarti, 2 carote, un gambo intero di sedano, sale e pepe. Cuoceteli per circa un paio d'ore e serviteli con gli stessi vegetali della cottura con il sugo sopra.

CUORE DI MANZO

Tagliatelo a fettine lunghe e sottili, infarinatelo. Mettete la padella su di un bel fuoco con un dito di olio, due spicchi d'aglio, e quando incomincia a dar fumo, gettatevi le fettine; fatele saltare leggermente, cospargetele di pepe e sale, impiattatele e copritele di Salsa di pomodoro (75) caldissima.

MANZO ALLA CERTOSINA

Mettete un pezzo di culaccio in casseruola con mezzo bicchiere di olio, e fatelo rosolare da tutte le parti, aggiungete 2 acciughe pestate e un battuto di funghi, cipolla, prezzemolo, finocchino, sale e spezie. Bagnate con un bicchiere di vino rosso e con brodo rifondendovene quanto basta per completare la cottura.

Prima di servirlo, levatelo dalla casseruola, digrassate e passate il sugo versandolo sulla carne. Contorno di Passato di patate (211) o Passato di lenticchie (206).

KRAFFEN - BIGNETTE

GALANI DI VENEZIA - FRITTELLE ALLA ROMANA

FOCACCIA SENZA UOVA - TORTA DI FRUTTA

Idrolitina
Carbonation Powder

Gazzoni, Bologna; now Prontofoods,
Montichiari (Brescia)

1911

A characteristic typology of the modernist artefacts is represented by additive or surrogate products, which define the character of foods through processes of transformation or substitution: from bouillon cubes to freeze-dried products. A special case in point were the powders made to add carbon dioxide to tap water, with the purpose of changing its taste and improving its substance to make it seem more like mineral water.

The first of its kind was Idrolitina, conceived in 1911 in the chemical-pharmaceutical laboratories of Arturo Gazzoni, located in Bologna; it was followed by a series of others that became quite popular (such as Idriz by Carlo Erba, Frizzina by Star or Cristallina by Ferrero). The reaction between the baking soda and the tartaric (or citric) acid contained in the packets, generated carbon dioxide ("fizzy" gas) and produced a solution of organic sodium salt with limited antacid properties.

This type of product was blandly "medical"; Gazzoni had in fact begun his production in the late nineteenth and early twentieth centuries, after running the Chianti restaurant in Bologna, patronized by many celebrities who later became early testimonials for Idrolitina, with foods deriving from medical research, such as the Antinevrotico De Giovanni (named after Dr. Achille De Giovanni who developed it in 1907) or the Pastiglie Re

Sole in 1917, liquorice drops made to sooth a cough.

Originally, Idrolitina was sold in an unsealed double blue and red bag (with the powders that contained, respectively, the base and acid principles), later replaced by the familiar yellow packet which remained unchanged over time, as did its *fin-de-siècle* graphic design. In order to mechanize the production of the packets, which were dosed and filled by hand by the women working in his factories, in 1924 Gazzoni encouraged his partner Gaetano Barbieri to found Acma (*Anonima costruzione macchine automatiche*, which is now part of the Coesia Group), the first company in Bologna to produce packing machines, basically setting the groundwork for a new sector that was destined to grow and prosper. The outcome was the design of the "713," the forefather of automatic machinery, which printed the packets, dosed the powder and packaged the product.

Arturo Gazzoni, who was also the author of forward-looking books on the subject of marketing and sales, laying a scientific basis for his pioneering experiences in the field, was one of the first, in the early twentieth century, to hire the great *affichistes* of his time to make his products more convincing and more attractive. They included Nasica (Augusto Majani, 1867–1959), who developed an original and ironic language that characterized

the company's advertising for a long time to come. In the early seventies, Gazzoni introduced new products such as Dietor, a sugar substitute, with the Dietorelle line, and Vantaggio foods (which now belong to the Swedish company Cloette, whereas Idrolitina is now a Prontofoods brand), which anticipated and interpreted, from a contemporary point of view, the everlasting consumer concerns about health and physical fitness.

B. Biancini, *Lo stabilimento A. Gazzoni & C. e l'industria della chimica-farmaceutica in Bologna*, Tipografia Mareggiani, Bologna 1927; A. Gazzoni, *Vendere, vendere, vendere*, Mondadori, Milan 1927; A. Gazzoni, *Lezioni di pubblicità*, Zanichelli, Bologna 1943; A. Berselli, *I protagonisti dello sviluppo industriale*, in *Bologna 1937-1987. Cinquant'anni di vita economica*, Cassa di Risparmio in Bologna, Bologna 1987, p. 142; R. Curti, M. Grandi (edited by), *Per niente fragile. Bologna capitale del packaging*, Editrice Compositori, Bologna 1997, p. 39 and ff. G. Pedrocco, "Bologna industriale," R. Zangheri (edited by), *Storia di Bologna*, Bononia University Press, Bologna 2013, book 4, vol. 2, *Bologna in età contemporanea 1915-2000*, edited by Angelo Varni, pp. 1052–53.

→Nasica (Augusto Majani), advertisement, 1911 (Gazzoni Historic Archives, Bologna).

Doppio Brodo Star Bouillon Cubes

Star, Muggiò (Monza-Brianza);
now Gallina Blanca Star
1952

Already an advanced process by the second half of the nineteenth century in countries that were more industrialized than Italy, the production of canned meat and bouillon mixes—developed in part to reuse the leftovers from the processing of meats—is a significant example of the symbiosis between scientific research in the field of nutrition and the technological advances made by industry.

In 1865, Justus von Liebig, a German chemist, invented the manufacturing process with George Giebert from Belgium, but it was Julius Maggi from Switzerland who began to market it in 1908 as a *bouillon kub*, after selling it in both capsule and granular form. Translated in Italian as "dado," after the word for dice, and available as both an imported product and, in the early years of the twentieth century, in various versions produced by Italian industries such as the *Società italiana dei prodotti alimentari Maggi* in Sesto San Giovanni, for example, or Arrigoni in Genoa (and later in Trieste), its strictly geometric form was an explicit reference to standardization, reflecting the Modernist period's aspiration to make artifice of nature.

After World War II, one Italian company became a synonym of this product: Star. In 1948 Regolo Fossati, a meat wholesaler, founded a company in Muggiò, in the Brianza region, dedicated to the production and packaging of canned meats and

bouillon cubes. The name of the company was *Stabilimenti Alimentari Riuniti*, but it soon became widely known as Star, which was both the acronym and the English translation of Stella, the name of the founder's wife. Well aware that it would be difficult to compete against established brands such as Simmenthal in Monza—a company dating back to the twenties—, Danilo Fossati (1928–95), who took over from his father, understood the commercial and competitive potential of this substitute for meat broth, which embodied two fundamental elements of home economics: it saved money, compared with the prohibitive cost of the original, and time, in the preparation of a traditional meal.

His collaboration with chemist Giovanni Nughes, who owned a laboratory in Robecco sul Naviglio (Milan), led to the sale of the exclusive rights for his formula for the production of bouillon cubes. Fossati began to develop a product with organoleptic properties that was well received compared to other brands distributed in Italy. The cubes were composed of meat extract, broth and yeast with the addition of flavourings, spices, salt and fats, enriched with a flavour enhancer, monosodium glutamate—which Nughes copied from the Swiss cubes that he had analysed, though they were hard to find on the Italian market due to customs restrictions.

Compressed into vacuum-dried cubes and wrapped in aluminium foil, each "dado" could make half a litre of broth. The first ones were distributed under the name of Hedelvais, previously used by Nughes (the brand was registered in 1951, no. 108033) and sold well through the distributors in his father's network.

But after 1952, thanks to the collaboration with Padua-based graphic designer Gino Pesavento, Dado Star acquired its own specific identity. First, to distinguish itself from the many other similar products on the market, such as Knorr, Liebig and especially Maggi, the shape of the product was modified: the "dado" cube, synonym of an artificial surrogate for another dish, was replaced by the "tab" that produced an original dish, an alternative broth, the Star "double broth" announced in the name, "Doppio brodo Star," with which it won recognition on the market (registered in 1954, no. 119219). Pesavento not only designed the company trademark using serifed letters with a thick contour around them, in 1952 he also designed the packaging featuring the portrait of the housewife that immediately became the company's signature icon. In addition to the intensive advertising campaigns ("Only Star knows the secret of the double broth"; "There are many broths but just one double broth," read the jingles), which continued insistently on television from the moment it went on the air, Star distinguished itself for the organization of its sales networks, which cut out wholesaler intermediation and mark-ups by establishing its own tight network of representatives, supported by warehouses and a fleet of delivery trucks to supply retail stores as quickly as possible.

To address the astonishing surge in demand, in 1953 the company was forced to upgrade the production capacity of its factories. The semi-manual production process was transformed with the introduction of automatic machinery, and at the end of the decade, the floor area dedicated to production increased with the new factory in Agrate (Milan), along the Milan-Bergamo highway, followed by the plants in Corcagnano (Parma), Sarno (Salerno) and Minerbe (Verona). In the late fifties, Star opened a factory in San Sebastian in Spain, and inaugurated the new brand Starlux. The bouillon cube, which had become the symbol of the brand, was followed by new products developed by the company in its own research labs for a mass consumer market, each of which interpreted more convenient yet qualitatively equivalent alternatives for preparing foods that would otherwise cost time and money, truly

obliging kitchen helpers. In 1955 the company introduced Sugo Star spaghetti sauce, Foglia d'oro Star margarine, a surrogate for butter, Gran Paradiso cheese servings, Frizzina, a powder to make water effervescent, Sogni d'oro instant camomile, Star Tea bags, along with Gran ragù meat sauce for spaghetti or Pummarò tomato purée, and many other lines of products that turned Star into one of the largest food industries in Italy.

The importance that the company attributed to communication is demonstrated by the creation of a dedicated company division called Pragma. After Pesavento, it was directed by Augusto Maestri, who restyled the trademark in 1965, then by Nuccio Bordoni who was also responsible for coordinating the agency and finally by Leo Burnett, who was in charge of advertising in the eighties. In 1987 the image of the housewife was restyled by Federico Bozzano, winner of the competition launched by Star for Italian illustrators.

In the seventies and eighties, as mass distribution flourished, Star purchased the Mellin, Mantovani and Tigullio brands, along with stock in Iri-Sme and Bsn-Danone.

Since 2006 it has been part of the

multinational food corporation Gallina Blanca Star. (fb)

D. Cimorelli (edited by), *Tutto il sapore di casa mia. Star 1948-1995*, Amilcare Pizzi, Cinisello Balsamo (MI) 1996; G. Piluso, "Impresa, mercato, consumi: la Star di Danilo Fossati fra autonomia e alleanze (1948-99)," *Annali di Storia dell'impresa*, 10, 1999, pp. 565–92; F. Fontanella, M. Di Somma, M. Cesar, *Come cambiano i marchi*, Ikon, Milan 2003, pp. 208–11; Paul H. Freedman, *Food: the History of Taste*, University of California Press, Berkeley 2007, pp. 241–44; Archivio centrale dello Stato, Italian Patent and Trademark Office, no. 108033, filed 13.11.1951, reg. 16.06.1952; no. 119219, filed 21.02.1954, reg. 24.08.1954.

on the previous page
→Bouillon-cube packaging department, Agrate (MI), c. 1995 (Star Historic Archives).

→Bouillon-cube packaging department at the Caldos Rapidos factory (later Starlux), San Sebastian (Spain), c. 11958 (Star Historic Archives).

→Advertisement (from *La Cucina Italiana*, September 1958, p. 846).

vi sono tanti brodi
ma solo
un doppio brodo

DOPPIO BRODO STAR

the design of the contemporary food product
1960–2000

Globalization and Genius Loci

Between the fifties and the sixties therefore, during the years of the economic boom in Italy, the significant changes in lifestyles and food habits led to a more "industrial" cuisine based on products made by a standardized mass production system. This trend intensified in the following decades, aided by the penetration of models imported from the United States and reinterpreted in the Italian style, based on *fast* (and/or *junk*) foods, not always perceived as such in terms of the quality of the food's form and content. The march of "taste" towards globalization triggered a process that challenged the naturalized and crystallized boundaries of the market, and led to a strong economic concentration, a disconnection between economic and sociocultural processes, an expansion of the communities of reference and the alteration of consumer routines.[1]

The decade of the eighties (which represented a critical phase for Italy and its social and economic status quo) was particularly controversial for the agricultural sector.

On the entrepreneurial front, the typical reduced concentration and large number of small manufacturing companies mentioned earlier remained unchanged, and was destined to persist over time. It is important to note the growing volume of pasta and baked dessert production, of meat processing and butchering, areas which "genuine industry was scarcely interested in pursuing, because these were processes that either did not contemplate technologies that could significantly raise productivity with respect to artisanal production, or else were more consonant to the direct involvement of farm labourers."[2]

Furthermore, the traditional entrepreneurial system was caught in a moment of transformation and crisis, leading to the divestiture of historic companies, changes in ownership and the participation of financial capital.[3]

Within this context, a significant role was played by government intervention and the State, which had long been exercising its responsibility for monitoring the entire system as well as individual companies

→Archizoom Associati, No-Stop City, Residential Parking, 1971 (Deganello Archives, Milan).

[1] "Standardization brings with it heterogeneity, globalization, localism," but this has opened up new possibilities because it "exposes local realities to the ample flow of global merchandise with the result that each local reality in the end may embrace a greater variety of possibilities" (R. Sassatelli, *Consumo, cultura e società*, Il Mulino, Bologna 2004, pp. 215–16).
[2] G. Gallo, R. Covino, R. Monicchia, *Crescita, crisi, riorganizzazione. L'industria alimentare dal dopoguerra ad oggi*, in A. Capatti, A. De Bernardi, A. Varni (edited by), *Storia d'Italia, Annali 13. L'alimentazione*, Einaudi, Turin 1998, p. 281. And further, "the forty largest

Italian food industries, excluding the groups, totalled a volume of sales in 1986 that was less than Nestlé alone" (ibidem).
[3] For example Ifil, owned by the Agnelli family (in retail with Gruppo Rinascente, Upim and Sma) or Cir, owned by Carlo De Benedetti (owner of the brands Perugina and Buitoni, Sasso, Vismara). Other events involved Montedison (owner of the Pai and Pavesi brands, formerly Edison, then Iri, Standa and Fininvest), the Ferruzzi group (sugar refineries and brands such as Eridania and Carapelli) and Enimont which, in various ways, would be implicated in the dramatic and exemplary political-judiciary crisis known as *Tangentopoli* in the early nineties.

→Ettore Sottsass, Living modules
for the exhibition *Italy the New
Domestic Landscape*, New York,
Kartell, Boffi, Ideal-Standard,
1972 (Kartell Archives,
Binasco).

and businesses. Starting in the sixties, with the intention of building a large and economically significant group, the government took control over a number of companies in the agro-industrial food sector (such as Cirio, Motta, Alemagna, Star, Surgela and the GS chain of supermarkets) under the wing of Sme (the holding company for the food sector of the *Istituto per la ricostruzione industriale* – Iri). This project foundered quickly—wrote Giampaolo Gallo, Renato Covino and Roberto Monicchia, because the "drive to reorganize the sector, the hypothetical economic policies and the attempt at public governance, which matured in the seventies and eighties, fell apart in the wake of agriculture's permanent state of crisis, of the mechanisms induced by growing European integration and market internationalization, the increased influence of finance on economic processes and the aggressive action of multinational corporations, with the processes of concentration that they provoked in this sector."[4]

Government management thus proved to be a rather controversial issue, and ended with the tumultuous "piece by piece" privatization of SME, which eventually led to protracted lawsuits, and favoured significant acquisitions by the major international corporations, including Unilever, Nestlé and Danone.

The presence of the multinationals later became consolidated at the global level and coexists today with historical or more recent Italian enterprises, which have been successful in addressing the economic, technological, social and cultural transformations by "thinking locally and acting globally."[5]

The Italian food heritage remained the brands, which sparked the interest and appetites of the major groups. The brand names (companies or products, later growing to include brand names for territories or for the certification of production system) became a fundamental element of identity for consumers, a sort of compass to help them get oriented within the extraordinarily vast array of products.[6]

In synthesis, it may be asserted that the modernisation of food in Italy was only partially accomplished, and this made it possible to maintain and preserve—not always consciously and deliberately, one might add—the ties to history, identity and tradition. Massimo Montanari writes: "This delay could well be reassessed today as a cul-

[4] G. Gallo, R. Covino, R. Monicchia, *Crescita, crisi, riorganizzazione...*, cit., pp. 284–85. Another government shareholding company with responsibilities in the food sector was Efim (through Sopal with the brands Alco, Colombani, Surgelati Brina, Terme di Recoaro).
[5] Ibidem, p. 28 and ff.; and in general M. Scoppola, *Le multinazionali agroalimentari*, Carocci, Rome 2000; L. Sicca, *Lo straniero nel piatto. Internazionalizzazione o colonizzazione*

del sistema alimentare italiano?, Egea, Milan 2002; F. Boccia, *Internazionalizzazione, multinazionali e settore agroalimentare*, Aracne, Rome 2009.
[6] Which prompted Carlo Petrini, the inventor of Slow Food, to say that in the end "industry sells an image not a food" (C. Petrini, *Il cibo e l'impegno*, in P. Floris D'Arcais, C. Petrini, C. Scaffidi (edited by), *Il cibo e l'impegno, Quaderni di Micromega*, 2, Gruppo editoriale l'Espresso, Rome 2004, p. 11).

tural resource," because it created new conditions for "the relationship with food in which paradoxically the height of modernity coincides with the rediscovery (or reinvention) of tradition."[7] The mid-eighties—amidst food scandals,[8] the crisis of historic entrepreneurs in the sector and the role of government, internationalization and the aggressive action of multinational corporations—brought with them new opportunities for the success of small to medium-size companies, which were becoming increasingly aware that they could design, produce and distribute for the very reason that they represented a different food culture, artisanal-local-typical, which guaranteed quality, safety, sustainability. This trend was also enriched and broadened in a series of exemplary experiences, in which food was simply part of a wider reflection that also embraced culture and politics: from Arci Gola (1986) to manifesto (1989) to the Slow Food Presidia (2000) conceived by Carlo Petrini; from the Salone del gusto at the Lingotto in Turin (1996) to Terra madre (2004), an international conference on the issues of food.[9]

The development of new systems to certify and protect food products must be understood within the context of a renewed interest in the Italian culinary heritage, and of the need for operative tools that could ensure effective action within the global agroindustrial and economic-financial sphere.

In this sense, the fundamental cultural, social and economic issue is bio-diversity, which is to say the reorganization of agrofood systems on a regional basis. It is no coincidence that Italy boasts 214 products protected by recognized designations of origin (Doc, instituted in 1963; Dop, Igp in the nineties, in conformity with legislation by the European Community), 4511 regional specialties, not to mention that the Mediterranean diet has been listed as a Unesco Intangible Cultural Heritage.[10]

→Ugo La Pietra, La casa telematica. Il pranzo TV, 1982 (La Pietra Archives, Milan).

[7] M. Montanari, *Identità italiana in cucina*, Laterza, Rome – Bari 2013, p. 72.
[8] 1986 was a symbolic year for the history of food in Italy, because of the scandal of methanol-based wine and other food alterations which led to the death of twenty-one people; see, among others, M. Montanari, *Identità italiana in cucina*, Laterza, Rome – Bari 2013, p. 72.
[9] "Slow Food may think of itself as a peasant revolution, but in many ways it is an expression of Italy's long tradition of city eating, its civilization of the table … urban Italians … use food to create identities for themselves … Petrini and his followers are trying to pioneer a new identity, a global form of citizenship that takes the politics of food as seriously as its flavor." (J. Dickie, *Delizia! The epic

history of the Italians and their food*, Simon and Schuster, New York 2010). Nor should the role of food culture magazines such as "La gola" (1982–92) founded by Giovanni Sassi, "Gambero rosso" (1992-), and "Slow" (1996–) be forgotten.
[10] A. Lupacchini, *Food design, la trasversalità del pensiero progettuale nella cultura alimentare*, List lab, Trento 2014, p. 69. In any case, it should be remembered that the designations "mainly regard "industrial" products, the first with the economic power to be recognized… sustained by public administrations and private capitals" (A. Capatti, "Oggi e domani," M. Montanari, F. Sabban (edited by), *Storia e geografia dell'alimentazione*, cit., p. 489).

→Gianni Sassi, *La Gola*, monthly
magazine of food and material
life techniques, I, 1, October
1982 (Private Archives, Venice).

Our contemporary condition therefore seems to have delineated two different but complementary directions. The first is the industrial system characterized by its international scope and economic and financial breadth, dominated by the multinational corporations which have instituted their own self-monitoring systems (necessary for the company's *reputation*) in order to address certain critical factors, such as the "increasing indeterminacy of the origins of food."[11] These companies are compelled to work within the logic of rapid consumption and a rapid changeover in products, with serious consequences for overall sustainability, and a controversial attitude towards experimentation with the artificial.[12]

At the same time, new opportunities have opened up for small high-quality food productions with recognizable local artisanal identities. This direction gained ground thanks in part to the organic and slow-food models ("international actor for the global promotion of the local"[13]), a "venue" where the regional-entrepreneurial body of knowledge meets and dialogues with the capabilities of design: from the content of the product to its form, communication and distribution. For example a forerunner, marking the dawn of market conditions open to different consumer cultures in Italy, was the company named Fattoria Scaldasole founded in 1981 by Marco Roveda. It proved to be an important vehicle for the diffusion of biodynamic agriculture, offering "safe and healthy" products (as the advertisements of the time sustained) such as yogurt, milk, puddings and fresh-squeezed orange juice.[14]

This direction was built with intelligence and with the purpose of enhancing the legacy of Italy's food culture, by initiatives such as Slow Food, and later by Oscar Farinetti with the Eataly stores (2006).[15] A particularly significant phenomenon for this experience was Eataly, the first "supermarket" for Italian food opened in New York in 2010,

[11] See G. Fabris, *La società post-crescita. Mangiare è un atto agricolo*, Milan, Egea 2010, p. 179. A situation that has also been closely monitored by the investigations of Oxfam International such as B. Hoffman, *Behind the Brands. Food justice and the 'Big 10' food and beverage companies*, Oxfam International, Cowley – Oxford 2013.

[12] On the theme of sustainability, see also S. Latouche, *Limite*, Bollati Boringhieri, Turin 2012. In 2000 Bosoni listed the new themes relative to the issue of food: "The physics of freeze-drying, the perception of dynamic food dyes, the aesthetics of frozen food, form and structure of pre-cooked foods... the new transgenic foods" (G. Bosoni, "Cibo: l'ingegneria genetica prende il comando, in G. Bosoni, F. Picchi (edited by), Food

design. Il progetto del cibo industriale," *Domus*, 823, 2000, p. 74).

[13] R. Sassatelli, *Consumo, cultura e società*, cit., p. 129.

[14] After ten years the company was sold and the entrepreneur began a new business that dealt in the themes of environmental sustainability, under the brand name Life Gate, radio, web portal and an intense cultural activity.

[15] See, among others, T. Venturini, *Il nostro pane quotidiano. Eataly e il futuro dei supermercati*, Cassa Risparmio di Cuneo-Slow Food, 2009. For a synthesis of the limits of distribution and the financial system see A. Belloni, *Food economy. L'Italia e le strade infinite del cibo tra società e consumi*, Marsilio, Venice 2014, pp. 115–22.

Spedizione
in abbonamento postale
gruppo III/70
Printed in Italy

1

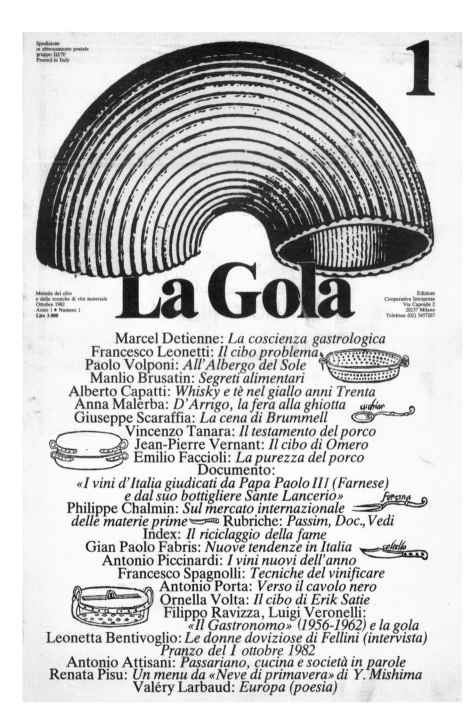

La Gola

Mensile del cibo
e delle tecniche di vita materiale
Ottobre 1982
Anno 1 ● Numero 1
Lire 3.000

Edizioni
Cooperativa Intrapresa
Via Caposile 2
20137 Milano
Telefono (02) 5457267

Marcel Detienne: *La coscienza gastrologica*
Francesco Leonetti: *Il cibo problema*
Paolo Volponi: *All'Albergo del Sole*
Manlio Brusatin: *Segreti alimentari*
Alberto Capatti: *Whisky e tè nel giallo anni Trenta*
Anna Malerba: *D'Arrigo, la fera alla ghiotta*
Giuseppe Scaraffia: *La cena di Brummell*
Vincenzo Tanara: *Il testamento del porco*
Jean-Pierre Vernant: *Il cibo di Omero*
Emilio Faccioli: *La purezza del porco*
Documento:
*«I vini d'Italia giudicati da Papa Paolo III (Farnese)
e dal suo bottigliere Sante Lancerio»*
Philippe Chalmin: *Sul mercato internazionale
delle materie prime* Rubriche: *Passim, Doc., Vedi*
Index: *Il riciclaggio della fame*
Gian Paolo Fabris: *Nuove tendenze in Italia*
Antonio Piccinardi: *I vini nuovi dell'anno*
Francesco Spagnolli: *Tecniche del vinificare*
Antonio Porta: *Verso il cavolo nero*
Ornella Volta: *Il cibo di Erik Satie*
Filippo Ravizza, Luigi Veronelli:
«Il Gastronomo» (1956-1962) e la gola
Leonetta Bentivoglio: *Le donne doviziose di Fellini (intervista)*
Pranzo del I ottobre 1982
Antonio Attisani: *Passariano, cucina e società in parole*
Renata Pisu: *Un menu da «Neve di primavera» di Y. Mishima*
Valéry Larbaud: *Europa (poesia)*

→Giorgio Giugiaro, working
drawing for the Marille, Voiello
pasta, 1983 (Barilla Historic
Archives, Parma).

→Enzo Mari, Cake for Case
da Abitare, 2003 (Enzo Mari
Archives).

rooted both in the local *genius loci* of food and in a comprehensive "industrial" system of strategies, distribution, design, communication and consumption.

For Franco La Cecla, "what is happening in Italian food with the *slow food* revolution and the presentation of the new Made in Italy (such as the Eataly stores) is a new arrangement of the codes. What was once the people's food, derived from a local glossary and spoken grammar, has now become a quality of origin brand, which uses local identity to make sure that the consumer participates in a meaning that often escapes him."[16]

Even though, as Ampelio Bucci sustains, "Italian food has always lacked and still lacks the "strategic planning" of a general policy,"[17] the Slow Food system may be considered as an attempt to pull together as a system and create a network. A project based on a cultural and political matrix which has given rise to an "alternative" system for business and the economy, sustained by instruments and approaches (cultural-editorial programmes, specialized trade fairs, social opportunities and so on) which in part offer alternatives to the traditional media and communication, as well as distribution systems. Besides, writes Roberta Sassatelli, it also opened more new opportunities: "Because it is becoming increasingly evident that there is nowhere else to go except the market and that the only thing to do is to intervene on its forms, boundaries and rules, new more evidently political forms of consumption are being developed."[18]

In recent years in fact, consumers have rallied to build a new agrifood system based on a "short chain" of production and distribution, with initiatives such as urban ruralisation, farmers' markets, local community buying groups, in contrast to globalized mass retail. Consumers and small producers have formed an alliance against standardization and globalization, demanding greater respect for the ethical aspects of large-scale production, which can make a difference in the choices of the multinational groups. Consumer boycotts, fair trade, local community buying groups for sustainable agriculture and ethical finance represent a far-reaching social and economic transformation.

This is a widespread, comprehensive and collective orientation, which has been widely embraced, but must still deal with a number of prob-

[16] F. La Cecla, "La forma che il cibo può assumere raccontano dell'Italia e delle su profonde differenze geografiche," monograph issue *Food*, suppl. to *Domus*, 913, April 2008, p. 47.
[17] Among other things, from the trouble in asserting the originality to the lack of international management, for example, of a typically Italian "product" such as espresso coffee, which has become a global industrial heritage thanks to Starbucks or Nespresso. See A. Bucci, "Dal prodotto alimentare all'offerta globale," *Diid-disegno industriale*, monograph issue *Food design*, 19, 2006, p. 15.
[18] R. Sassatelli, *Consumo, cultura e società*, cit., p. 221.
[19] M. Montanari, *Identità italiana in cucina*, cit., p. 73. And: "The Italian model… still functions on the principle of the network, as the circulation of local experiences that

lematic issues. Montanari writes: "The return to a regional and seasonal dimension... may also be seen as trendy."[19] Capatti believes that "the 'typical' product is a contradiction in terms: it may have a past that goes back centuries but in many cases the only existing version is the industrial one; add to that commercialization, which is one of its primary actions."[20] As they conform to the inevitable modality of contemporary communication-distribution-consumption, terms such as typical, tradition, artisanal, organic, not unlike the brand names Slow Food or Eataly, have (also) become "labels" that help to sell products. This is important because it guarantees general economies, but on the condition that they are not and do not become "empty" words, suitcase-words (to borrow Enzo Mari's considerations on design). For the present and the future, it is therefore important to pursue the safe and responsible direction now underway, implementing those aspects of information, service and quality that will benefit the consumer and the social-economic-environmental system as a whole.

Practical and ironic as ever, John Dickie sums it up in these words: "Less folklore traditions and clearer labels."[21] This is a direction in which the design culture can play an important part.

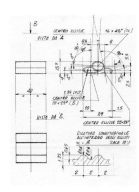

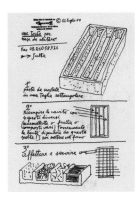

Nutritional Pluralism: Fast and Slow Food

"Today's industrial food sector needs no presentation, it is right here before everyone's eyes," sustained Carlo Petrini in 2005, "it produces every sort of edible food, it even offers traditional foods and conveys culinary cultures. At the supermarket you can buy frozen pizza, Mexican sauces and kits for *burritos*, a precooked *caciucco* or *paella* that you can heat in a pan, soups, broths and stews from all over the world. But there are also many products that have been "invented": chocolate snacks, potato chips, cheese slices... The brands on the brightly coloured packaging are more important than the contents, and the products are hard to associate, in terms of appearance, smell and taste, with anything that exists in nature."[22] The contemporary condition has witnessed the consolidation of a sort of "food polytheism,"[23] a "nutritional relativism," and we now live in a permanent "culinary tower of Babel": a model of rapid, unstable and artificial parsimony.[24]

maintain their own identity... diversity as a permanent datum of our national identity."
[20] A. Capatti, "Oggi e domani," M. Montanari, F. Sabban (edited by), *Storia e geografia dell'alimentazione*, cit., p. 489; he continues by sustaining that authenticity is a value established after the fact, as protection, it is "the modern answer to the loss of our heritage" (A. Capatti, "Oggi e domani," M. Montanari, F. Sabban (edited by), *Storia*

e geografia dell'alimentazione, cit., p. 493).
[21] J. Dickie, *Delizia! The epic history of the Italians and their food*, cit., p. 22;
C. Petrini, *Buono, pulito e giusto...*, cit.
[23] So sustained Giuseppe De Rita in A. Belloni, *Food economy...*, cit., p. 18.
[24] A. Morone, "Dall'artigianale all'industriale," *Diid-disegno industriale*, monograph issue *Food design*, 19, 2006, p. 34.

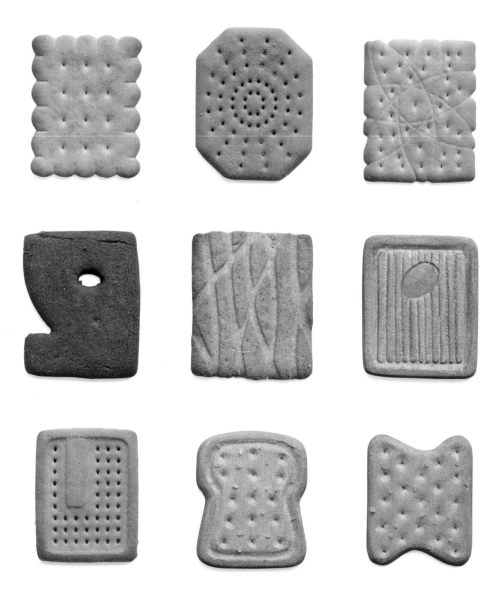

New patterns of behaviour have become consolidated. Among other things, there has been a massive exodus from the kitchen, as a result of the changing role of women; microwave ovens and frozen foods have been welcomed into the home; there is a new category of singles[25] with specific needs, new relationships have formed between parents and children, the former are less conservative, the latter more open to new food models. Furthermore, the interest in domestic or public conviviality is diminishing while the predilection for individual take-away foods[26] is in rapid expansion. A relatively standard eating pattern (breakfast, lunch and dinner) has given way to a deconstruction of the meal, or the prevalence of the single course, with a strong fragmentation between users, age groups, and social classes. An interesting perspective with a vast array of implications is offered by Claude Fischler: "As the third millennium dawns, food is less and less necessarily identified with the home."[27]

Contemporary phenomena such as the propagation of dedicated books, magazines and television shows appear symptomatic of a certain scarcity of information and competence. In the same way, public events built around food (such as trade fairs, festivals and conferences) denote an attempt to restore the minimal conditions of social interaction.

It is in this light that we must attempt to read the incompatibility, or better yet the hybridization between fast and slow food, two modes that in some ways have always existed, particularly in relation to the many different living and working situations.

In this sense, sometimes it seems more appropriate to distinguish between "fixed food" (that must be eaten at the table, perhaps with company) and "mobile food" (eaten quickly, frequently standing up and alone, for example fast-food items such as hamburgers, sandwiches, *piadine* or packaged snacks from a vending machine). Or we might describe it as the dialectic between global and local food.[28]

But in Italy it should always be remembered, as Sassatelli reminds us, that "culinary traditions have not been replaced by the development of the mass food industry… the diffusion of cheap fast food based on ground meat does nothing but promote the demand for health, authenticity and flavour… food scandals related to the techniques of mass production in the agroindustrial sector have in turn drawn consumer attention to "natural," "local," "traditional" products, from sustainable agriculture."[29]

→Giulio Iacchetti, Ti Voglio biscuits, Quality Food Group, 2002.

[25] As Luca Vercelloni anticipated: "The food habits of single men and women may be considered as a presage of far greater transformations, destined to expand" (L. Vercelloni, "Immaginario commestibile," M. Romanelli, M. Laudani, L. Vercelloni, *Gli spazi del cucinare, appunti per una storia italiana 1928-1957*, Electa, Milan 1990, p. 188).
[26] "The privatization of the relationship with food radicalizes certain of its conflicting and alienating aspects" (Ibidem).
[27] C. Fischler, *La macdonaldizzazione dei consumi*, in J.L. Flandrin, M. Montanari (edited by), *Storia dell'alimentazione*, Laterza, Rome – Bari 1997, p. 686.
[28] See also M. Montanari, *Il cibo come cultura*, Laterza, Rome – Bari 2004, p. 117 and ff.
[29] R. Sassatelli, *Consumo, cultura e società*, cit., pp. 217–18.

Contemporary Aesthetic Food Artefacts:
New Tastes and Patterns of Behaviour

The new economic-social-cultural conditions that emerged over the last decades of the twentieth century and the beginning of the new millennium were key to understanding and contextualizing the design of products, systems and services, for all sectors including food. Food artefacts have developed elements that interpret and consolidate existing conditions, but have also heralded growing trends and modalities, with significant elements involving the components of design. It may be useful to survey some of the more noteworthy aspects of this context, from the crisis in models of infinite growth and consumer spending to the "long tail" of the markets;[30] from the mandatory necessities of strategies and recognizable identities for companies and products to the new customized consumer experience; from the horizons opened by new technology for communication, design, distribution and of course production, in new digital forms made possible by computer networks, to the pressing demands on the design culture, which is called upon to take greater care of people, things and the planet.[31] Given these conditions, consumers (or at least some of them) are increasingly demanding an active role: they are selective, eclectic, competent, sensitive to problematic keywords, from sustainability to ethics.

Within society and the economy, different options, which are not mutually exclusive but complementary to one another, have been delineated for a better understanding of consumption and the markets, of doing business and developing design. Coexisting side by side are a "development-first" model, constrained by the impellent necessity of producing necessarily-new models and disposable products; and with it an idea of companies (and users) that are aware and responsible, sustained by a concept of "long term" project. In various and variable versions, design and *fast* products must therefore dialogue with *slow* possibilities. Whether one eats at McDonald's or at the finest of restaurants; whether one drives a supercar or an electric car, rides a bicycle or a bus, or goes on foot; whether one buys green products that can be disassembled and do not contribute to pollution, or chooses others that are more ephemeral and less environmentally aware; whether one designs for users or for technological performance or for luxury, the possibilities that are expressed are all legitimate and valid, each in its own way.

---

[30] On the contemporary consumer condition, see among others, G. Maione, *Le merci intelligenti. Miti e realtà del capitalismo contemporaneo*, Bruno Mondadori, Milan 2001; G. Fabris, *Il nuovo consumatore: verso il post-moderno*, Franco Angeli, Milan 2003.
[31] As Michel Maffessoli specifies, helping to focus on the theme of small things,

gestures and everyday behaviour and their relevance/irrelevance (in terms of economic or emotional value, or meaning): "This is the characteristic of all post-modern icons: the sense is never far away but lies in the meaning that must be given to all those little things that constitute the whole of existence" (M. Maffesoli, *Icone d'oggi, Le nostre idolatrie postmoderne*,

This confirms that, instead of opposing radically different alternatives ("one thing or the other"), it is possible for different positions to coexist ("one thing and the other"). We have evolved from the "either or" culture to the "and and" culture.

Immersed in these conditions, the food product is subject to the same mechanisms and dynamics as "aesthetic goods" within an "economy of symbolism,"[32] of an overall system that has (completely or in part depending on the product, as well as the contexts of the market, of society, the economy and geography) abandoned the rigid correspondence between cost and value, as well as the necessary correspondence of form and function, to experiment with more complex processes of creating value, in key words such as symbol-emotion-play-experience. Pierogiorgio Degli Esposti believes that "food habits are the result of a process of selection-adaptation that places great importance on the symbolic value of food"; and he continues "once the problem of the relationship between food and survival has been solved, we eat what we eat because we like it, we desire it, because it corresponds … to what we ideally strive for, to the customs of our social status and our group, actions that go well beyond the biological meaning of the act of eating."[33]

This leads us to recognize at least two directions in food product design that correspond to two different ideas of design-production-marketing. The first includes products that are historic, or have been totally redesigned within the logic of a long-seller, subject to constant processes of fine-tuning that frequently base meaning and value on the recognized qualities of timelessness or of research and design. The second refers to the products that respond to the demand for novelty and variety, for constant changeover based on a logic of rapid consumption, where the creation of value is generally a matter of marketing and publicity.[34]

Since they exist within this context, food products have frequently been the forerunners or emblematic embodiments of social, economic, cultural and design transformations, in regards to the capacity to develop new products or the organoleptic and visual aspects of taste (from Nutella to the Magnum ice cream bar), and to influence new patterns of behaviour, such as those that led, for example, to the popularity of the single-dose or single-serving product, or to the design based on new conditions of technology, preservation or pro-

→**Paolo Ulian, Finger Biscuit, prototype, 2004.**

→**Continuum, Tablò chocolate bar, Perugina, 2012.**

Sellerio, Palermo 2009, p. 63).
[32] See F. Carmagnola, *Vezzi insulsi e frammenti di storia universale. Tendenze estetiche nell'economia del simbolico*, Luca Sossella, Rome 2001, p. 29 and ff.
[33] P. Degli Esposti, *Il cibo dalla modernità alla postmodernità*, Franco Angeli, Milan 2004, p. 95.
[34] On the dynamics of (more or less) planned obsolescence and rapid change in the merchandise categories of food, see among others, N.D. Basile, *New menu Italia. La rivoluzione che ha cambiato la tavola degli italiani*, Baldini Castoldi Dalai, Milan 2009, pp. 43–46; more in general, F. Carmagnola and M. Ferraresi, *Merci di culto. Ipermerce e società mediale*, Castelvecchi, Rome 1999.

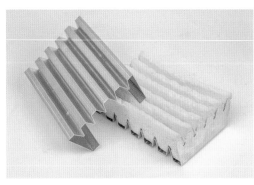

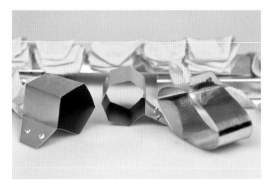

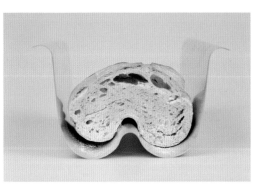

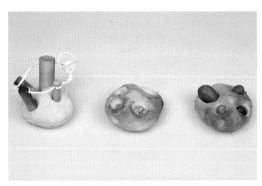

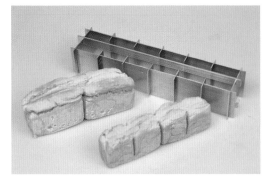

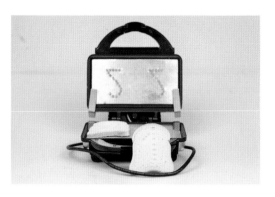

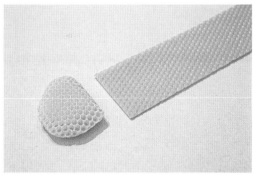

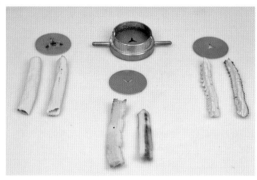

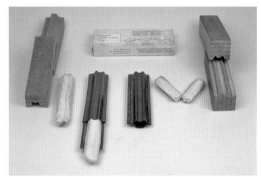

PANZUCCHERO

duction (from frozen to vacuum-packed to precooked foods), or the requirements of health and wellbeing.

The fact that the food product is presented and enjoyed in an integral and integrated dimension (all the constituent elements "exist" together at the same time) confirms the importance and/or predominance of the container over the content: the package is decisive to the identity of the product, it is a preferred space for research and experimentation on how to build the product's identity, confirmed for example by the longevity and recognisability of historical products such as the Coppa del nonno, Tic tac or Estathé, or more recently the design of bottles made out of PET for mineral water.

In fact, a new typology and design approach have recently emerged, exemplified by the pre-portioned coffee systems, centred on paper pods or aluminium capsules. What we have before us is a product-system and/or product-service strictly associated with a "machine," or a service that provides refill capsules in a sophisticated carefully-appointed boutique. This is an artefactual condition that has become quite common; just consider, as an example, the product-service relationship for a mobile phone (an object sold at low cost or given away in combination with the sale of a telephone contract or an application); or the preference for open or shared systems (from internet to sharing).[35]

Design and Food Product: Food Is not Just Food

The design of food artefacts over time was therefore the result of the convergence between many different design cultures (engineers, technicians, architects, designers and artists) and players (entrepreneurs, businessmen and managers, intellectuals, communicators), with products, systems and services that were mostly the outcome of complex and collective process. The designers frequently found it difficult to play a significant role within these dynamics, to fully capitalize on their potential and their skills.

In recent years, however, many projects have been developed within the sphere of *food product design* by name designers.[36]

In this book we will attempt to offer a synthetic analysis of some of the prevalent approaches—starting with the objective problematic issue of the relationship between the design and entrepreneurial cultures (artisanal and/or industrial)—but above all to examine the possibilities and available options.

[35] See, among others, A. Bassi, *Design. Progettare gli oggetti quotidiani*, Il Mulino, Bologna 2013.
[36] See C. Catterall, *Food, Design and Culture*, Laurence King, London 1999; S. Bureaux, C. Cau, *Design culinaire*, Eyrolles, Paris 2010; S. Maffei, B. Parini, *Food mood*, Electa, Milan 2010; B. Finessi (edited by), *Progetto cibo. La forma del gusto*, exhibition catalogue, Electa, Milan 2013; A. Lupacchini, *Food design. La trasversalità del pensiero progettuale nella cultura alimentare*, List, Trento 2014.

on the previous pages
→**Projects dedicated to bread and other local Italian food specialities by the students of the Industrial Design Studio held by Prof. Massimo Barbierato, Undergraduate Programme in Industrial Design, Università degli Studi della Repubblica di San Marino/Università Iuav di Venezia, 2014.**

→Thomas Bartoli, Carlo Piglione,
Eataly Smeraldo, Milan, 2014.

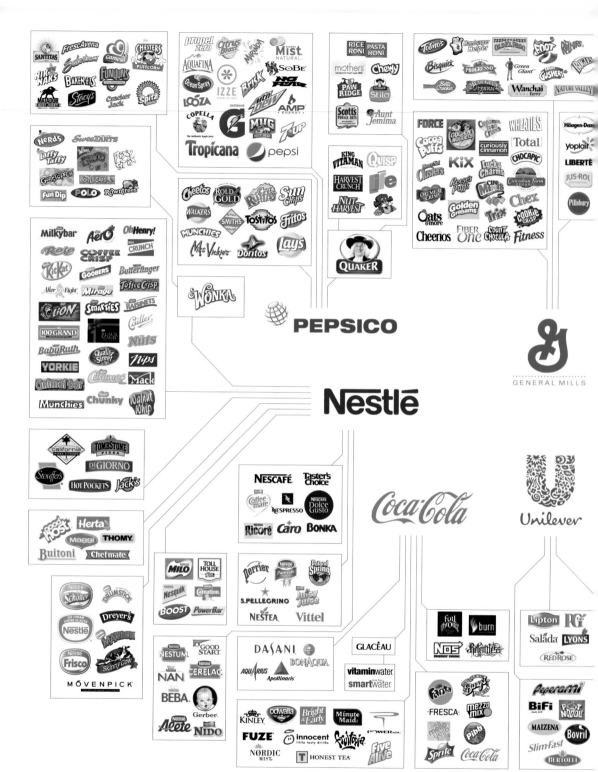

Kellogg's®

Associated British Foods plc

Mondelēz International
(formerly Kraft Foods)

DANONE

MARS

WRIGLEY

on the previous pages
→*Which brands belong to the "Big 10"?*, www. oxfamitalia.org/ scopriilmarchioJoki (redesign of Joki Gauthier's infographic for Oxfam 2012).

One of the first designers to try his hand at this theme was Giorgio Giugiaro with his design for the Marille pasta for Voiello in 1983; he was followed by others and especially by many young people in search of a subject to experiment with, that would be economical and easy to communicate.

Given the conditions, contexts and the demands of the client, often with little chance to explore methods and opportunities for production for a more comprehensive system-based approach, most of these designs appear to be based primarily on "language" and form. Few of them went beyond the one-of-a-kind piece or one-time limited edition, or past the phase of concept and/or prototype (which is frequently interesting but only partial), without ever becoming "real" products, put into production and sold on the market.

They are the result of a need or a legitimate and conceivable choice: they are fine for an exhibition, a museum, a magazine, a monograph or a competition, but they hardly ever have any real impact. Sometimes it seems that they lack a larger and more significant dimension, that takes into consideration the practical aspects of production but also explores more ample long-term approaches or scenarios.

Over time, there have of course been signals of greater possibilities, such as, to mention only a few examples that have become "historical" at this point, the Ti Voglio biscuits by Giulio Iacchetti (2002), or the Golosimetro chocolate bar by Paolo Ulian (2002), as ironic as his Finger biscuit for Nutella. It was much easier for packaging—because the theme was more consolidated and recognized, if anything—especially in the area of liquid containers: such as the bottles for mineral water designed by Sottsass associati (Lurisia), Pininfarina (Lauretana), Giugiaro (San Bernardo), Matteo Thun (Valverde), Hangar (Ferrarelle) and the aperitif bottle designed by Marco Zito (Negroni). More recently however, a number of new signals have appeared. We might mention—just to illustrate a few paradigmatic directions—the important honourable mentions at the Compasso d'Oro ADI (Associazione per il Disegno Industriale) won by the Campotti di Gragnano pasta by Mauro Olivieri (Pastificio dei Campi, 2014) and by the Tablò chocolate bar for Perugina by Continuum (2012); or the experimentation conducted with practical sense and a level of excellence within the Universities of design (such as the work of the students guided by Massimo Barbierato from the University of San Marino/Iuav University of Venice, which focused on the local identity of bread, 2014); or the experimentation with digital production systems, which remain controversial but must still be understood from the perspective of a "system," rather than as a manufacturing device; the Food design manifesto (Adi, 2014) and, in general, the development of a more

37 V. Cristallo, "Modelli di consumo del cibo," *Diid-disegno industriale*, monograph issue *Food design,* 19, 2006, pp. 45–46.

38 E. Morteo, *Grande atlante del design,* Electa, Milan 2008, p. 412. Belloni reports: "The food economy has an infinite

conscious and competent culture, embodied by the many associations and off and online magazines.

It seems possible to assert that a new phase has begun, based on the idea of design as a global shared process, that has an important role to play within the reality of the economic and social system, as the standard-bearer of innovation, meaning and values: "Design should not be seen as a demiurgic force that demands to intervene on everything, writes Vincenzo Cristallo, but as the possibility to possess the tools and methods required to interpret needs, distribute quality and give meaning to things."[37]

Enrico Morteo suggests: "The design of food (and even more of water) may be one of the greatest challenges to the design of tomorrow: it does not mean designing new hybrids between prunes and avocados but rethinking, with creativity and respect, the cycles of production and consumption, the rhythms of the seasons, the vocations of places, the waste of packaging and the processes of production."[38] One example that speaks for all is sustainability, which everyone is talking about, yet it has not been fully developed from the perspective of a new methodological approach. The issue is not just the use of natural or recycled materials—a frequent misunderstanding—but more substantially the analysis of the product's life cycle (LCA – Life Cycle Assessment), a complete review of the entire process of design/production/distribution/consumption/disposal. Within this logic, for example, the production process (energy consumed and materials used in the process, logistics management, etc.) is certainly important, but even more so are the design decisions. It makes a difference if a product is made with natural or recyclable materials that can be easily disassembled, if it is made sustainably, using non-polluting and non-toxic components, if it saves energy, if it is conceived with its disposal in mind and much more. It is also important that the project promote and lead to a virtuous and meaningful approach to the environment. A fundamental element is also the return of the idea of "getting by with less": the less material and elements are designed and used, the less energy, material and labour are consumed. And to analyse how products reach consumers: packaging has become a key factor in pollution, what with the hard shapes of plastic containers, and the less perceptible forms of the logistic effort to handle them.

Food is an important theme, vital for a large part of the world, because there truly is a "planet that must be fed." This field was a forerunner for advanced emerging cultural, social, economic and design dynamics, which established logics and patterns of behaviour open to the

number of possibilities. According to Andrea Illy its future lies in the acronym Save—sustainability, authenticity, variety and experientiality" (A. Belloni, *Food economy…*, cit., p. 132).

→R. Tramoyeres (GCLab)
and P. Morales, Food Printing
Machine, on display at the
exhibit *The Future in the
Making: open design Arcipelago*,
organised by *Domus* magazine
and curated by J. Grima,
Palazzo Clerici, Milan 2012
(© Domus/Courtesy Editoriale
Domus).

themes of usability, safety, health, sustainability or biodiversity (in terms of consumption and the market).

More in general, this goes to show how, within the system of contemporary artefacts-systems-services, there is a real and accessible economic, social and cultural space where it is possible to practice an alternative "model," alert to the issues of well-being for people and the planet. At this point the opportunities for the design culture appear wide open and in many ways unexplored: it can make a real contribution on specific issues or the great themes of our day.

Which means, for example, trying to understand if and why we should design, produce, communicate, distribute and manage the end of the life cycle; understanding how to act and building the best possible conditions so that our actions will respect the environment, jobs and people.

The way food and food products, systems and services have evolved— and the future possibilities of the sector, and those that are potentially open to other areas of design—makes it possible perhaps to reconsider the role of design as a strong cultural (and political) factor, remembering the words of Giovanni Klaus Koenig: "Design is real design only when it involves strong interactions between scientific discovery, technological application, good design and a positive social upshot."[39]

In this specific case, because, as Belloni writes "as many groups of innovators have already understood… know-how is no longer enough. Not even for food. The key ingredients today are the communication, marketing and brand's ability to tell a story, the search for investors and the ability to sell through internationalization, technology and the production process' capacity for innovation. Whether in culture or history, biology or chemistry, knowledge is the most valuable element of all, and that is why the Food Economy is no longer just food."[40]

[39] G.K. Koenig, "Design: rivoluzione, evoluzione o involuzione?," *Ottagono*, 68, 1983, p. 24.
[40] A. Belloni, *Food economy…*, cit., p. 12.

Nutella

Ferrero, Alba (Cuneo)
1964

If there is one universally renowned Italian food product, which has become synonymous for a synonymous for a new typology, which possesses a specific organoleptic identity that goes hand in hand with its unmistakable packaging, graphic design and overall image, it is surely Nutella.

Nutella went into production in 1964, but it was the outcome of the evolution of two earlier precedents. First, the Gianduiot, a sweet spread made of hazelnuts, cocoa and sugar in the shape of a loaf that could be sliced and spread on bread, which was developed by Pietro Ferrero (1898–1949) in his pastry shop in Alba (Cuneo). Created soon after World War II—the trademark was registered in 1949 (no. 93198)—with a wrapper featuring an image of the Piedmontese carnival character Giandoja, with two children and the Ferrero signature, it was followed by the Supercrema spread launched in 1951, made with hazelnuts, cocoa and vegetable oils, and registered as a trademark in 1951 (no. 107096). Pietro Ferrero came up with the idea of the hazelnut spread in response to a demand for inexpensive sweets, using ingredients that were readily available, such as the Langhe hazelnuts, and production processes befitting the postwar labour market. Michele Ferrero (1925–2015), son of Pietro, was responsible

for introducing Nutella on the market, with the intent to sell the product beyond the national borders as well. The name—registered in 1963 (no. 164196)—derives from the English word "nut," combined with the suffix "ella." The special jar, shaped vaguely like an inkwell—earning it the nickname Pelikan within the company—was patented on April 22nd, 1965 (no. 170128). Its form turned out to be particularly practical for display on supermarket shelves, and for the good grip it offered when opened. The trademark, which featured the lower-case "n" in black and the others letters in red using the Helvetica Medium typeface, was designed by Carmelo Cremonesi and Gian Carlo Rossetti of Studio Stile, and was completed with the picture of a slice of bread with Nutella on it to illustrate the contents of the jar. In the sixties, the company introduced single-portion packs made of plastic and containing 30 grams each, the perfect amount to spread on a slice of bread.

From the very beginning, the success of the product was sustained by memorable advertising campaigns such as "Tutti per uno, Nutella per tutti" in the late sixties; the series of television commercials featuring the cartoon character Jo Condor in the seventies or "What kind of a world

would it be without Nutella" coined by Fulvio Nardi in the nineties. As an incentive to buyers, Ferrero also sold the product in reusable glass containers that constituted entire sets of jars or drinking glasses decorated with silkscreened images and characters.

Storia di un successo. Ferrero la più grande industria dolciaria del MEC, Aeda, Turin 1967; G. Padovani, *Nutella. Un mito italiano*, Rizzoli, Milan 2004; C. Padovani, *Mondo Nutella. 50 anni di innovazione*, Rizzoli Etas, Milan 2014; A.M. Sette, *Disegno e design. Brevetti e creatività*, exhibition catalogue, Fondazione Valore Italia, Rome 2010, pp. 322–23; Archivio centrale dello Stato, Italian Patent and Trademark Office, no. 93198, filed 7.11.1949, reg. 18.12.1949; no. 107096, filed 3.10.1951, reg. 21.04.1952; no. 164196, filed 9.10.1963, reg. 16.03.1964; Archivio centrale dello Stato, Italian Patent and Trademark Office, no. 170128, 22.04.1965.

→Advertising label, 1950s.

→Patent no. 170128, 22 April 1965.

→Equipment for the production of Nutella (Ferrero Archives, Alba).

di corsa
a scuola
ma
non
dimenticate mai
i **PRODOTTI**

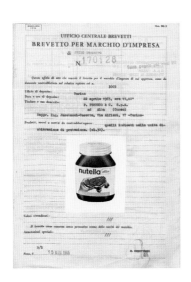

Kinder Surprise

Ferrero, Alba (Cuneo)

1974

Kinder Surprise, known in Italy as Ovetto Kinder, was created in 1974 on the basis of Michele Ferrero's (1925–2015) idea to put a little toy surprise inside a small chocolate egg. The intention was to transform the chocolate egg, generally sold for specific holidays such as Easter, into an everyday product. An idea that was quite similar—but with far more impact—to the concept that prompted Motta or Melegatti to market *panettone* and *pandoro* as something more than a "holiday cake."

The Kinder egg consists in an outer layer of milk chocolate and an inner layer made out of a milk icing, a recipe patented for Ferrero in 1974 by Amilcare Dogliotti (no. 3961089), who also designed the box for Tic Tac mints, and held dozens of other patents. Inside the egg, a plastic capsule-shaped casing contains a surprise: a little toy, generally made out of plastic or wood or a metal alloy. The capsule, with its unmistakable yellow colour, is deliberately difficult for a child to open, a measure conceived to make it safe, and at the same time to involve adults in the game as well. Another of Dogliotti's patents, dated 1976 (no. 4106657) reads as follows: "Container suitable for small playthings and to be inserted into an Easter egg or any other hollow product."

The surprises, which soon became collectors' items, were inspired by a vast typology of toys, and developed a variety of different themes over a period of more than forty years. Since 1974, at least 8000 different toys have been designed, many of them in pieces: part of the game actually consists in assembling them, following the instructions contained inside.

The development of the products in the seventies led to a full-fledged delineation of the structure responsible for the ideation, design, engineering, and patenting processes, as well as the design of the corporate identity and naming, the communication and advertising of the Ferrero food products, which came to full realization over the following decades, contributing decisively to making this one of the largest and most innovative companies in the international confectionery industry.

The insights and ideas of every generation of the Ferrero family were thus implemented in a complex and comprehensive design process that was directly guided, managed and controlled by the company, committed with all of its research, development and design resources which at the present time also include Soremartec, a division of the Group that—as the company advertising explains—"provides services, information and conducts research studies for the entire Ferrero Group, in the fields of technical and marketing research, to invent and launch new products and ensure a continuous process of innovation and improvement in our existing products."

E.M. Formia, P.P. Peruccio, *Il punto di vista del designer. Progettavamo per non fare sorprese indigeste. L'ingegner Alfredo Zanellato Vignale spiega le complessità legate all'ideazione delle sorpresine degli ovetti Kinder*, in "Il giornale dell'architettura," 55, 2007, p. 2; United States Patent, *Method of manufacture of hollow chocolate articles*, priority 30.07.1973; reg. 24.07.1974, publ. 1.06.1976; *Container usable as a toy construction element*, no. US 4106657, priority 17.09.1975; reg. 19.07.1976, publ. 15.08.1978.

→Patent, no. US 3961089, 30 July 1973.

→Machinery for the production of the Kinder Surprise (Ferrero spa Archives, Alba).

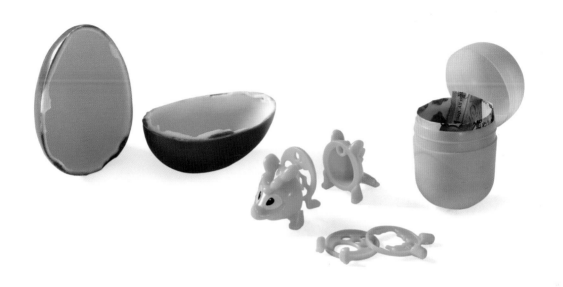

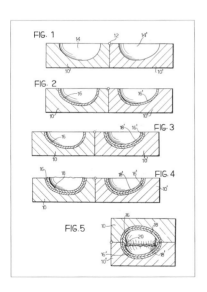

FIG. 1

FIG. 2

FIG. 3

FIG. 4

FIG. 5

Mulino Bianco Cookies

Barilla, Parma
1975

The Mulino Bianco line of bakery products was introduced by Barilla in 1975, representing a departure with respect to the Parma-based company's traditional pasta sector. During a rather complex phase in Italian history—marked by political and social conflict and economic crisis, which culminated in the period of austerity caused by the oil crisis in 1973—the company sought to rekindle the values of the preindustrial age and an idyllic, simple, natural and reassuring society. In an effort to bring back the idea of this undoubtedly fictitious lost identity, the first advertising campaigns, which would be elaborated in an ample succession of commercials broadcast on television, read: "When the windmills were white the cookies tasted like butter, milk and wheat." The central element of Mulino Bianco is the design of the trademark, a combination of three elements: ears of wheat and flowers as an expression of nature; the small mill that embodies the values of tradition; the name as the synthesis of the values of nature and the past. On the basis of the original trademark layout by graphic designer Gio Rossi, the final version was perfected by Cesare Trolli, illustrator and chromolithographer for the cookie packaging.

The typology, morphology, image and name of the different varieties of cookie are meticulously planned: the functional, aesthetic and communicative aspects are delineated and translated into prototypes; after being tested and regulated, they move easily into the process of standardized production. Though they are produced industrially, they are made to look like country-style biscuits, just a touch *naïf* and irregularly shaped, deliberately bringing to mind the home-baked cookies of the past. "Our cookies—writes Gio Rossi—were to be different from the industrial culture and the contemporary culture, as an understated reflection of the dream of fine craftsmanship that lies dormant in our stratified personal subconscious ... So the cookies did not look anything like all the rest, but exactly like the ones your "great-aunt" use to make, with a cookie-cutter and a wood-fired stove."
Mulino Bianco occupies a fundamental position in the history of food products, and more generally in the history of Italian society and culture, because the characteristics of its products captured lifestyles and tastes during a significant phase of transformation for the economy and consumer buying, offering a somewhat nostalgic but

reassuring vision which definitely paved the way for new scenarios and modalities that were of great inspiration to many. This tendency and approach to product design were substantially analogous to those that arose in other fields, from furniture to car design, variously labelled as "the design of memory," retro-design or, to use a more cultured term coined by Clino Trini Castelli, "transitive design." As sustained by Valeria Bucchetti, a historian of communication, "Mulino Bianco ushers in a new approach to advertising. The product is not simply described or displayed, it becomes the object of a narration built around a world that serves as an ideal context, a setting in which the actor-product performs and to which it must belong."

V. Bucchetti, *Un'immagine globale*, in A. Ivardi Ganapini, G. Gonizzi (edited by), *Barilla. Cento anni di pubblicità e comunicazione*, Barilla Historic Archives, Parma 1994, pp. 317–22; *Mulino Bianco Story (1973-1993)*, in ibidem, pp. 282–322.

→Production of the Mulino Bianco Pan di Stelle biscuits, 1987 (Barilla Historic Archives, Parma).

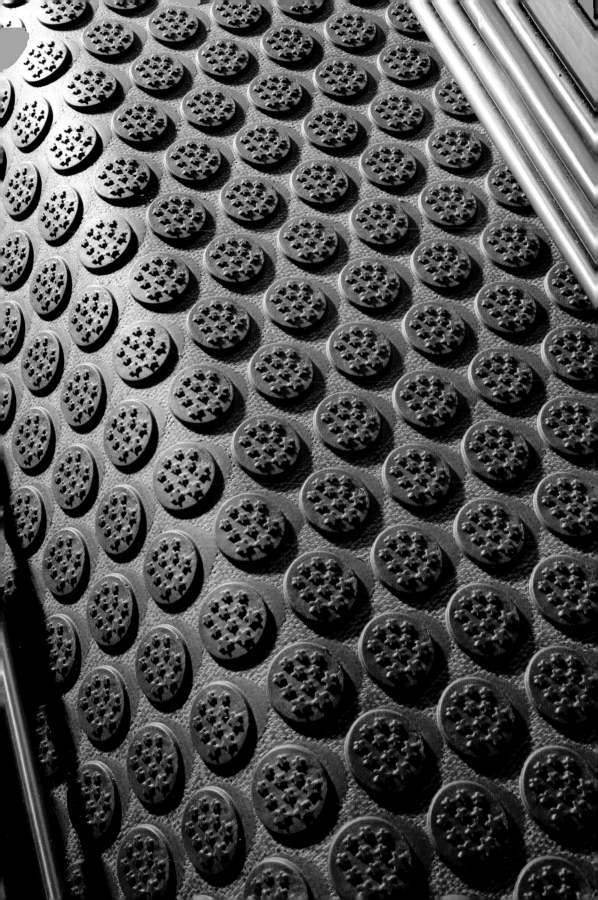

→Gio Rossi, drawings
with proposals for the shape
of Mulino Bianco biscuits,
mid-1970s (Barilla Historic
Archives, Parma).

**the design of the
contemporary food product**
1960–2000

**/ new tastes
and lifestyles**

Coppa del Nonno Ice Cream Cup

Motta, Milan; now Nestlé Italiana,
Assago (Milano)
1973

The packaging of food products is an extremely important area of design, which serves to communicate the product and its qualities, relying on a cutting-edge visual language or proudly upholding a more old-fashioned image in order to consolidate its recognition factor. In other cases, the packaging is irremediably associated with the food product itself, and is completely identified with it. One of the products that has built an inseparable relation between food and package—in a sector such as industrial ice cream which has produced such a wealth of inventions—is the coffee ice cream cup Coppa del nonno Motta. This was one of the first times that packaging was given its own shape and colour, breaking away from the anonymity of the paper cup in which industrial ice cream had always been sold since it was introduced in the fifties—the name was registered in 1954 (no. 121346).

It was designed in 1973 by Salvatore Gregorietti, who had been associated with Bob Noorda and Massimo Vignelli at Unimark International, and later worked as a visual designer for Benetton, Prenatal and Fabrica. "Working for the Motta group in the seventies, he recalled, I happened to design the container for the "Coppa del nonno." In its simplicity, this project entailed solving a series of rather challenging problems posed by the highly industrialized production, the low cost and the ergonomics of the object. Hardly anyone knows who actually designed it. Nevertheless, I don't believe I have ever been as proud of a project which, apart from a few minor adjustments, has remained unchanged over the years and has been produced in a number of pieces that I couldn't possibly estimate." He continued: "Because it was coffee ice cream, the idea of putting it into a container that evoked the shape of a coffee cup was so obvious it felt right."

The problems that arose concerned the possible production techniques. Cardboard, the material of choice until then, did not have the flexibility required to change the traditional form of the open cup. Injection-moulded plastic offered greater freedom, but in consideration of the expected quantities, it was important to develop an optimal configuration that would require a simple mould, with no undercuts, to optimize the speed and cost of production. Equally important was the ergonomic solution for holding the cup: placing the index finger under the handle and the thumb on top provided a secure grip.

"Credit must be given to Motta for demonstrating uncommon bravery for the time, concluded Gregorietti, by promoting and accepting a "different" solution for a mass-produced product, including the colour brown, which the marketing gurus considered to be inappropriate for food." Though it recently underwent a slight restyling, it has been in production continuously since then.

Salvatore Gregorietti: "Cosa c'è di più piacevole e gratificante del superfluo," *Alidesign*, the Magazine of the Association of Industrial Design Alumni, Politecnico di Milano, 3 October 2002, p. 6; Archivio centrale dello Stato, Italian Patent and Trademark Office, no. 121346, filed 23.09.1954, reg. 8.02.1955.

Magnum Ice Cream Bar

Algida, Rome; now Algida-Unilever,
Rome – Naples
1989

Within a specific typology such as ice cream bars on a stick, which has had its share of long-sellers and has produced an endless variety of different versions, it is no easy task to come up with a creative intuition capable of generating new products that have the potential to become standards, setting new benchmarks and reshaping hierarchies and the way we eat ice cream. Magnum succeeded in this undertaking, and changed the image of ice cream as something to eat on-the-go, a recreational pastime, to give it a new, more glamorous and exclusive standing, by focusing first on the product's attractiveness in terms of appearance and flavour, and second, by building a strong image and identity for the product. This comprehensive project began by giving form to the object, in coordination with a strategy for market positioning and relevant advertising approaches.

Magnum Algida was conceived in 1989 as an ice cream bar on a stick, with a milk chocolate coating over vanilla ice cream, only to be developed through the years in an ample spectrum of different versions. The form seems inspired by a certain language, somewhat playful and "overblown," that was also developed in product design in the eighties (for example in the colourful plastic objects designed by Stefano Giovannoni for Alessi), with their rounded shapes and "fun" iconography/imagery.

The decision to oversize the product compared to the archetypes of ice cream bars on a stick, such as the Pinguino or Mottarello, was just one step in a development process that also experimented with the taste and the variety of flavours. Magnum is creamier and sweeter than other chocolate-coated ice cream bars and furthermore, its chocolate coating is thicker and breaks with more of a crunch than traditional ice cream bars. The communication of the trademark was vigorously oriented towards an emphatic reinforcement of the brand—culminating in the large iconic M that appears on the packaging and is embossed on the body of the ice cream bar itself—but it also played up the sensorial component of the experience.

→Product and production systems.

Calippo Ice Pop

Eldorado, Milan – Naples;
now Algida-Unilever, Rome – Naples
1980s

Eldorado was one of Italy's largest industrial ice cream manufacturers. Founded in the early fifties, with offices in Milan and in Naples, the brand gave a strong imprint to a number of ice cream bars that were very popular with teenagers and children from the sixties to the eighties, such as Camillino, Piedone, Fior di Fragola, Gommolo, Cucciolone, Nembo Gel or the unforgettable Miniball, a plastic container filled with ice cream that looked like a football, and opened by removing one of its hexagons. With Calippo, the typology of the ice pop, which was easy to produce at home with the cheap and ubiquitous plastic moulds for the freezer and was included in most manufacturers' collections of ice creams bars, was revolutionized in its shape and the way it was eaten. Doing away with the stick altogether, the new product was shaped as a cylinder, and contained in a sturdy paper package that offered a new interpretation of the traditional cup. The package was also a cylinder that flattened towards the bottom so that it could be easily gripped and squeezed to push the ice out gradually, as it melted in contact with the heat produced by the hands. It could be eaten without a spoon, and had the further advantage of preventing the melted ice from dripping down onto one's hands and clothes, because it trickled directly back into the package, ready to be slurped when the ice was finished.

"The ice cream in a tube," which was designed with particular attention to ergonomics, was initially presented as a fun and playful reinterpretation of the ice pop, and was targeted to children and teenagers, consistently with established brand policies that preferred the visual and narrative language of cartoons—from Cocco Bill and the startling cartoons by illustrator Jacovviti (Benito F.G. Jacovitti, 1923–1977) to Eldoleo drawn by Silver (Guido Silvestri, 1952) and later by Giorgio Cavazzano (1947).

The company, which entered into an alliance with Spica in the sixties, was bought by the English-Dutch group Unilever which, in the mid-seventies, acquired a series of Italian brands in the industrial ice-cream sector, including Toseroni—a company founded in Rome after World War II—and Algida. Calippo, in fact, is currently marketed under the Algida brand. (fb)

→Advertisement, 1991.

Liuk Ice Pop

Eldorado, Milan – Naples;
now Algida-Unilever, Rome – Naples
1991

In 1991, the Eldorado brand—which had been purchased by Unilever, owner of the Algida brand—presented a new version of the ice pop which, like the Calippo ten years before it [**Calippo Ice Pop** p. 262] brought genuine innovation to the typology. Liuk is a lemon-flavoured ice cream that, while based on the typology of the ice pop which had been explored over the years in varying styles and flavours by every brand, is a "totally edible project," and a significant example of food packaging. By substituting the traditional wooden stick with a liquorice stick, the ice pop may be eaten in its entirety, thereby eliminating almost all waste, except for the wrapper. Furthermore, by combining liquorice with lemon, not only does it bring back the flavours of tradition, it also offers a pleasing chromatic combination of black and white. Nicknamed "Steccolecco," it is both fun and delicious at the same time, attracting and intriguing children as well as adults, alluding to that strand of fairy tale culture that features many edible objects such as the cookie cottage in the tale of Hansel and Gretel by the Brothers Grimm, the Gingerbread Man, borrowed by Dreamworks for the animation film *Shrek*, or those necklaces and bracelets that, instead of beads, are made out of coloured candy strung on elastic thread.

P. Tamborrini, *Design sostenibile. Oggetti sistemi e comportamenti*, Electa, Milan 2009, p. 84.

Big-Babol Bubble Gum

Perfetti, Lainate (Milan);
now Perfetti Van Melle, Lainate (Milano)
1978

In 1946 the brothers Ambrogio and Egidio Perfetti founded their own company in Lainate (Milan), the Dolcificio Lombardo, which changed its name to Perfetti spa in 1970, after conquering the national and international market with its famous Brooklyn chewing gum, named after the bridge. The new chewing gum was first produced in 1955 (the trademark was registered as no. 124085), a rapid response to the popularity of chewing gum after World War II, when the American lifestyle was massively introduced into Italy.

Brooklyn was a huge commercial success, the result of excellent design decisions and communication strategies, to which the work of graphic designer and advertiser Daniele Oppi (1932–2006) contributed significantly: from the sixties advertising campaigns that featured the slogans "la gomma del ponte," and "the long-lasting flavour of quality," to the package and stick format of the chewing gum, borrowed from the 1893 American archetype Wrigley's Spearmint Chewing Gum. In the wake of Brooklyn's consolidated success, in 1978 Perfetti introduced Big Babol bubble gum: it was cube-shaped, rather soft in consistency, made big bubbles, had an intense strawberry flavour and was bright fluorescent pink. A "pop" product, both ironic and playful, which deliberately distorted the name and logo, inspired by the culture and languages of the seventies which reinterpreted the nineteenth-century American stick of gum in a contemporary key. "Softer, juicier, larger, longer-lasting flavour, bigger bubbles," recited the advertisements, which in the seventies starred showgirl Daniela Goggi in print and on the posters, and in the television commercials as well.

In 2001 Perfetti changed its name to Perfetti Van Melle after its acquisition by the Dutch company Van Melle, which made it one of the largest and most important confectionery industries in the world.

Archivio centrale dello Stato, Italian Patent and Trademark Office, no. 124085, filed 3.01.1955, reg. 10.06.1955.

→Advertisements for Brooklyn and Big Babol (Perfetti Historic Archives).

Estathé Ice Tea

Ferrero, Alba (Cuneo)

1972

With its special single-serving plastic packaging shaped like a 20-centilitre drinking cup, sealed with a membrane that could be perforated with the attached straw, Estathé was a drink made from a tea infusion, launched by Ferrero in 1972. The name combined the concept of summer, "estate" in Italian ("Sete di Estate, sete di Estathé," read the advertising jingle in the eighties) with the idea of cool and thirst-quenching ice tea, and was the Alba-based company's first venture into this sector. Ferrero's decision to invest in the ice tea typology went against the prevailing trend of carbonated soft drinks, and at the same time gave the company a marketing alternative for the summer season, when sales of chocolate decline drastically.
Its interest lies in the transformation of a what was typically a home-made drink, brewed tea left to cool, into a product that was the outcome of a design and production process within an industrial and marketing system. Furthermore, the single-serving pack, which was easy to use thanks to the straw that came attached to it—conjuring up images of summertime and a carefree "young" lifestyle—also encouraged drinking the tea on the move. Estathé anticipated and intercepted some of the fundamental consumer trends that began to emerge in the late sixties, and which thanks to innovative designs for packaging made out of new materials such as plastic and aluminium, began to popularize single-serving products (snack cakes, such as the Buondi, savoury snacks such as crackers, or canned soft drinks), reflecting new eating habits that often meant eating meals on the move or juggling increasingly fast-paced and more stressful lifestyles.

Findus Frozen Fish Sticks

Findus Italia; now Iglo Foods Group,
Cisterna di Latina
1967

Frozen foods represented the next pivotal step—after the discovery of canning, food preservation in glass jars and vacuum-packing—in the evolution of food practices and habits. They made cooking faster and, compared to more traditional consolidated methods, offered new possibilities for organizing the home and everyday life in general. They introduced a new way of relating to food, by making concepts such as fresh or even natural relative and/or outdated, by virtue of the obviously artificial nature of frozen products, from the way they look to the way they are preserved.

In 1964, when freezers were not yet common in Italian homes, Findus Italia (an Italian company involved at the time in joint ventures with international corporations Nestlé and Unilever, owners of the Findus brand, which changed hands many times over the years, until 2010 when it was sold by Unilever to Iglo Foods) began to produce frozen foods in their facilities at Cisterna di Latina, starting with vegetables and fresh products, then expanding to pre-cooked foods. "And just like after the Cirio revolution in the nineteenth century, the housewives of Italy learned to cook vegetables out of season," summarize Clara and Gigi Padovani. In 1967, Findus introduced its cod fish sticks, characterized by the design of their "rational" rectangular shape, in response to the requirements of the industrial production, storage and preservation systems. Their success was undoubtedly boosted by the massive advertising campaigns that, over an extended period of time from 1967 to 1998, starred Capitan Findus (the rest of Europe knew him as Captain Iglo and Great Britain as Captain Birdseye, a tribute to the naturalist and inventor Clarence Birdseye, who perfected freezing techniques after observing the Inuits in the Labrador regions, where he was sent on a US government mission in the 1910s). Findus conquered the hearts of mothers by making it easier to convince their children to eat fish, and substantially contributed to the change in Italian eating habits by cutting the time it took to prepare meals, a necessity of modern lifestyles. Over the years the range of Findus frozen foods increased, sustained by unrelenting advertising campaigns on every media and on television in particular, contributing to the introduction of new eating habits, routines and standards: from the Sofficini in 1975 to "4 Salti in Padella" in 1996, to dishes that promised even shorter cooking times, especially after the advent of the microwave oven.

C. and G. Padovani, *Italia Buonpaese*, Blu Edizioni, Turin 2011, p. 245.

266   **the design of the**   / **new tastes**
        contemporary food product   **and lifestyles**
        1960–2000

Tavernello Wine

Corovin, now Caviro, Faenza
(Ravenna)
1983

When it hit the market, this low-alcohol wine in a cardboard box was considered scandalous—and in some ways still is today. Without venturing to assess its quality or taste, the story of Tavernello certainly deserves recognition as the result of a precise strategy, project and organization by a company that, in the space of a few decades, has become one of the largest producers at the international level. What is interesting for the purposes of this book, in particular, is the correspondence between the food product-wine (targeted for a specific price and market segment) and the signature design of the box with its relative communication strategy. Tavernello, the first wine to be sold in a brick carton in Italy in 1983, delves its roots in the growing phenomenon of wine cooperatives, which arose in the Romagna region in the sixties for the purpose of selling cask wine. With the aim of finding access to the market and building customer loyalty, in 1966 nine wineries joined forces to found the Consorzio Corovin (renamed Caviro in 1985), and built a plant to house both the bottling and distilling processes. The transition that was then taking place from the small scale of the farm, to the large scale of the vineyard, led the wineries to adopt industrial organizations and systems for growing grapes and producing wine, and to strongly increase market appeal.

This entailed a significant optimization of the processes, a traceable supply chain and tracking throughout the production process to guarantee overall quality, and maximum availability in mass distribution retail points. This is the context in which the idea for an alternative to the glass wine bottle was developed. At the end of the year 1980, Corovin, in collaboration with Tetra Pak and the University of Bologna, began its experimentation and produced the first brick cartons, which until then had been used to contain milk, mineral water and the first fruit juices. The response of the wine to the cartons made of poly-coupled paper was good and in 1983 the consortium approved the motion to begin packaging wine in brick cartons, in two different formats, one quart and one litre. The carton was very practical, occupied very little space in the refrigerator, but above all was cheaper and did not require the return of empty bottles. The choice of the name was deliberately evocative: "Given that the product was unquestionably innovative, perhaps even too innovative for the time—sustains Giordano Zinzani, the company oenologist during that delicate phase—we wanted the name to embody the idea of tradition; hence the reference to the tavern, and the name Tavernello."
This interest in new modalities for drinking wine continued with

the development of Bag-in-box, in the 5 or 10 litre size, which contains the wine in a plastic bag enclosed within a cardboard box equipped with a pour spout.
The product's diffusion was aggressively supported by television and media advertising campaigns, directed since 2002 by the Armando Testa agency. "Being considered back then as the desecrators of the nobility of wine— declared Secondo Ricci, president of Caviro—proved to be Tavernello's good fortune." The cooperative is currently one of Italy's largest wineries with a turnover of 327 million euro; it boasts 32 wine cooperatives in seven regions of Italy (from the Friuli in the north to Sicily in the south), 13,500 farms and in 2013 sold 173 million litres of wine.

S. Williams, *Il caso Tavernello. Un successo del modello imprenditoriale cooperativo*, Edizioni Homeless Book, Faenza 2014; G. Dell'Orefice," La coop del Tavernello si compra una griffe dell'Amarone," 6 February 2014, in http://food24.ilsole24ore. com/2014/02/la-coop-del-tavernello-si-compra-una-griffe-dellamarone/; "Caviro trent'anni di vino col Tavernello," 30 July 2013 in http://www.settesere.it/ it/n2640-economia-caviro-30-anni-di-vino-col-tavernello.php.

→Product packages, 2014.

Illy Paper Coffee Pods

Illy, Trieste

1974

The contemporary condition of product design has produced new typologies of artefacts that exist beyond their actual physical component or require a strict symbiosis with others that mutually substantiate one another. Respectively known as service-products or system-products, their value is measured primarily by the performance they offer users (for example a bike-sharing project) or the role they play within a complex and interrelated structure of elements.

The latter is the case of most food products, starting with the pre-portioned systems for making espresso coffee at home. The product consists in both the capsule or pod filled with coffee, and the espresso machine. The distinguishing (and profitable) element, contrary to the past, is not however the machine, but the pod-capsule: not the hardware but the software, to use terms borrowed from Information and Communication Technology, the typological field of reference that in some ways triggered this "philosophical" transformation of objects. All told, the physical product (computer, mobile phone, etc.) is relatively inexpensive or free, whereas the computer programmes or applications are always for sale, frequently upgraded and marketed with advertising designed to increase their appeal.

In recent decades, the market for pre-portioned coffee has developed considerably from an economic standpoint, affecting social behaviour as well; but most of all, it has influenced methods and criteria for attributing value to consumer goods. Purchasing pre-packaged capsule-pods with a highly polished and "branded" image in luxury shops has become an evident sign of status or personal style

(hardly anyone still sustains that this is just a passing trend). However, apart from the case of food products alone, this phenomenon is destined to impact the overall sustainability of the system—with regards to the quantity of material and the energy required for production, transportation, etc.—, which seems unable to rationalize, and on the contrary tends to increase, the material component of consumer goods.

Considering this series of elements and their relevance in understanding certain contemporary dynamics, it is worth briefly reconstructing the origins of pre-portioned coffee systems.

Illy was the first company to file a patent, in 1974, for a technological system to produce espresso coffee, called *Easy serving espresso* (Ese), based on coffee machines that were designed to use pre-portioned pods, containing roasted coffee, ground in just the right amount and pre-compressed to an optimal state, sealed between two thin layers of filter paper. Ernesto Illy (1925–2008), who counted around thirty employees at the time, was inspired by a number of electric coffee machines he observed on the Anglo-Saxon and American markets, which made coffee automatically by pouring the boiling water over coffee grounds contained in a funnel-shaped filters made of paper similar to the paper used for teabags. He simply had to adapt this idea of using individual portions of espresso coffee by fitting them into the industrial chain, hence the development of a long strip of paper pods sold directly with the espresso machine.

In 1996 Illy liberalized the Ese patent with the aim of creating a unified industrial standard. It should be noted that this is a sector that offers both

closed and open systems: the machines in the closed systems only use capsules produced by the manufacturer of the machine; the open systems use universal capsules that can be of any brand or model, as long as they are compatible, available in a range of prices. By making the patent available to everyone, Illy created the only open system in the field of espresso coffee prepared with paper pods, advancing the industrial development of espresso coffee and creating a brand of machines and pods, guaranteed to be compostable.

The transformation of the domestic coffee market began, not coincidentally, in the nineties when the first metal capsules were introduced and strongly endorsed by multinational groups such as Nestlé or Italian manufacturers such as Lavazza, Vergnano and even Illy. This led to the transition from a "world" dominated by coffee pots towards other instruments, but above all, these different and more recognizable methods of fruition (similar to those of a vending machine) preluded to a dimension of global marketing.

F. and R. Illy, *Dal caffè all'espresso*, Mondadori, Milan 1989; M. Giuli, F. Pascucci, *Il ritorno alla competitività dell'espresso italiano*, Franco Angeli, Milan 2014, pp. 169–83; conversation by the author with Furio Suggi Liverani, director of research and innovation at Illy, 11 December 2014; United States Patent, *Coffee machine*, no. US 4253385 A, priority 3.05.1978, reg. 27.04.1979, publ. 3.03.1981.

→Patent, no. US 4253385 A, 3 May 1978.

→Box of paper espresso coffee pods.

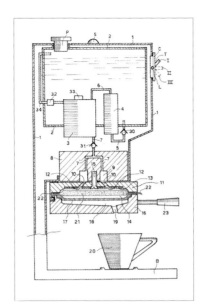

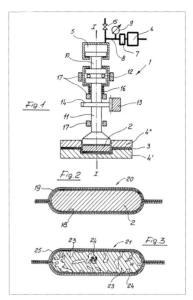

essential
bibliography

AA.VV. (edited by), *Brevetti del design italiano, 1946-1965*, Electa, Milan 2000

AA.VV., *Necessario indispensabile. Oggetti ed eventi che hanno cambiato la nostra vita 1952-1991*, Arnoldo Mondadori Arte, Milan 1992

G. Andrews, *Slow food una storia fra politica e piacere*, Il Mulino, Bologna 2010

A. Bagnato, *L'industria agro-alimentare italiana. Impresa familiare, cooperative, multinazionali*, L'Albatros, Rome 2004

N.D. Basile, *New Menu Italia, la rivoluzione che ha cambiato la tavola degli italiani*, Baldini Castoldi Dalai, Milan 2009

A. Bassi, *Il design anonimo in Italia. Oggetti comuni e progetto incognito*, Electa, Milan 2007

A. Belloni, *Food economy. L'Italia e le strade infinite del cibo tra società e consumi*, Marsilio, Venice 2014

M. Boot e M. Casciato (edited by), *La casalinga riflessiva. La cucina razionale come mito domestico negli anni '20 e '30*, catalogo della mostra, Multigrafica Editrice, Rome 1983.

G. Bosoni, F. Picchi (edited by), "Food design. Il progetto del cibo industriale," *Domus*, 823, 2000

J.-A. Brillat-Savarin, *Physiologie du goût*, A. Sautelet et Cie libraires, Paris 1826)

V. Bucchetti, *Packaging, design storia, linguaggi e progetto*, Franco Angeli, Milan 2005

S. Bureaux, C. Cau, *Design culinaire*, Eyrolles, Paris 2010

P. Camporesi, *La terra e la luna. Dai riti agrari ai fast food. Un viaggio nel ventre dell'Italia*, Garzanti, Milan 1995

A. Capatti e C. Colombo (edited by), *Occhio al cibo, immagini per un secolo di consumi alimentari in Italia*, Coop, [Milan] 1990

A. Capatti, M. Montanari, *La cucina italiana, storia di una cultura*, Laterza, Rome – Bari 2005

A. Capatti, A. De Bernardi, A. Varni (edited by), *Storia d'Italia, Annali 13, L'alimentazione*, Einaudi, Turin 1998

C. Catterall (edited by), *Food, Design and Culture*, Laurence King Publishing in association with Glasgow, London 1999

A. Corbin, *Storia sociale degli odori*, Bruno Mondadori, Milan 2005

R. Curti e M. Grandi (edited by), *Per niente fragile. Bologna capitale del packaging*, Editrice Compositori, Bologna 1997

A. de Bernardi, "L'industria alimentare: una storia di lungo periodo," C. Petrini, U. Volli (edited by), *La cultura italiana. Cibo, gioco, festa, moda*, vol. VI, Utet, Turin 2009, pp. 202–19

P. Degli Esposti, *Il cibo dalla modernità alla postmodernità*, Franco Angeli, Milan 2004

J. Dickie, *Delizia! The epic history of the Italians and their food*, Simon and Schuster, New York 2010

B. Finessi (edited by), *Progetto cibo. La forma del gusto*, exhibition catalogue, Electa, Milan 2013

J.L. Flandrin, M. Montanari (edited by), *Storia dell'alimentazione*, Laterza, Rome – Bari 1997

T. Favarelli Giacobone, P. Guidi, A. Pansera, *Dalla casa elettrica alla casa elettronica. Storia e significati degli elettrodomestici*, Arcadia Edizioni, Milan 1989

P. Floris D'Arcais, C. Petrini, C. Scaffidi (edited by), *Il cibo e l'impegno, Quaderni di Micromega*, 2, Gruppo editoriale l'Espresso, Rome 2004

Food, monograph issue, suppl. to *Domus*, 913, April 2008

Food design, monograph issue, *Diid-disegno industriale*, 19, 2006

A. Lupacchini, *Food design, la trasversalità del pensiero progettuale nella cultura alimentare*, List lab, Trent 2014

S. Maffei, B. Parini, *Food Mood*, Electa, Milan 2010

S. Maffei, B. Parini, *Más allá del gusto. Alimentar una (r)evolución de la alimentación con el diseño*, in *Experimenta*, 67–68, 2015

D. Mangano, *Che cos'è il food design*, Carocci, Rome 2014

A. Mariani, *La struttura dell'industria alimentare in Italia*, Franco Angeli, Milan 1990

A. Marzo Magno, *Il genio del gusto. Come il mangiare italiano ha conquistato il mondo*, Garzanti, Milan 2014

M. Montanari, *Il cibo come cultura*, Laterza, Rome – Bari 2004

M. Montanari, *L'identità italiana in cucina*, Laterza, Rome – Bari 2013

M. Montanari, F. Sabban (edited by), *Storia e geografia dell'alimentazione*, Utet, Turin 2006

M.P. Moroni Salvatori, *Novecento in cucina. Bibliografia gastronomica italiana, 1900-1950*, Pendragon, Bologna 2014

B. Munari, *Good design, All'insegna del pesce d'oro*, Scheiwiller, Milan 1963

A. Murcott, W. Belasco, P. Jackson (edited by), *The Handbook of Food Research*, Bloomsbury, London 2013

Musei del gusto, mappa della memoria enogastronomica, Carsa Edizioni, Pescara 2007

G. Origlia (edited by), *Album. Annuario di progetto e cultura materiale diretto da Mario Bellini, 1, Progetto mangiare*, Electa, Milan 1981

PackAge, storia, costume, industria, funzioni e futuro dell'imballaggio, exhibition catalogue, Lupetti, Milan 2001

C. and G. Padovani, *Italia Buonpaese. Gusti, cibi e bevande in centocinquant'anni di storia*, Blu Edizioni, Turin 2011

M. Panella, *Il cibo immaginario, 1950-1970 pubblicità e immagini dell'Italia a tavola*, exhibition catalogue, Artix, Rome 2013

C. Petrini, U. Volli (edited by), *La cultura italiana. Cibo, gioco, festa, moda*, vol. VI, Utet, Turin 2009

C. Petrini, *Slow Food, le ragioni del gusto*, Laterza, Rome – Bari 2001

C. Petrini, *Buono, pulito e giusto. Principi di una nuova gastronomia*, Einaudi, Turin 2005

M. Romanelli, M. Laudani, L. Vercelloni, *Gli spazi del cucinare, appunti per una storia italiana 1928-1957*, Electa, Milan 1990

P. Sardo, *Il buon paese. Inventario dei migliori prodotti alimentari d'Italia*, Arcigola Slow Food, Bra (CN) 1994

M. Scoppola, *Le multinazionali agroalimentari*, Carocci, Rome 2000

A.M. Sette (edited by), *Disegno e Design. Brevetti e creatività italiani*, catalogo della mostra, Fondazione Valore Italia, Rome 2009

W. Schivelbusch, *Storia dei generi voluttuari. Spezie, caffè, cioccolato, tabacco, alcol e altre droghe*, Bruno Mondadori, Milan 1999

L. Sicca, *L'industria alimentare in Italia*, Il Mulino, Bologna 1977

L. Sicca, *Lo straniero nel piatto. Internazionalizzazione o colonizzazione del sistema alimentare italiano?*, Egea, Milan 2002

G.E. Simonetti, *Fuoco amico, il food-design e l'avventura del cibo tra sapori e saperi*, DeriveApprodi, Rome 2010

P. Sorcinelli, *Gli italiani e il cibo. Dalla polenta ai cracker*, Bruno Mondadori, Milan 1999

V. Teti, *Il colore del cibo: geografia, mito e realtà dell'alimentazione mediterranea*, Meltemi, Rome 1999

D. Villani, *50 anni di pubblicità in Italia*, Editrice l'Ufficio Moderno, Milan 1957

L. Vercelloni, *Viaggio intorno al gusto. L'odissea della sensibilità occidentale dalla società di corte all'edonismo di massa*, Associazione Culturale Mimesis, Milan 2005

K.L. Yam, *The Wiley Encyclopedia of Packaging Technology*, John Wiley & Sons, Hoboken, NJ 2010

photographic credits

AA.VV. (edited by), *Due dimensioni*, Editype, Milan 1964, n.pag.: p. 141
AA.VV., *Ecco Milano*, Nuova Mercurio Milano, Milan 1958, p. 377: p. 173 bottom
Agazzi: p. 72
Algida-Unilever: p. 260
Archivio Citterio: p. 35 top
Archivio storico Majani 1796, Valsamoggia: p. 195 top
Archivio Salvatore Gregorietti: p. 259
Aldo Ballo: p. 151
Elio Basso: pp. 109 bottom, 154 bottom, 156–57, 161, 162–63, 185, 190, 191 bottom, 194 bottom, 200, 205 right, 222, 223, 252, 254, 255 bottom, 262 bottom, 265
Riccardo Bucchino & Paolo Brignone: p. 245
G. Celant and G. Dorfles, *Armando Testa, una retrospettiva*, Electa, Milan 1993, pp. 73, 91: pp. 135, 210 right
R. Curti and M. Grandi (edited by), *Per niente fragile Bologna capitale del packaging*, Editrice Compositori, Bologna 1997, pp. 28–29: p. 61 bottom right
dcm associati: 214 right
A. Giusa (edited by), *Cinquant'anni per il San Daniele. Storia del Consorzio del prosciutto di San Daniele 1961-2011*, Consorzio del prosciutto di San Daniele, Udine 2011, pp. 269, 126: p. 56
Gruppo San Pellegrino: pp. 127 top right, 213 bottom
Illy Caffè: pp. 86, 88, 269
Longoni: p. 113 top
L. Menegazzi, *Il manifesto italiano*, Electa, Milan 1995, pp. 206, 262: pp. 127 top left, 147 right
Molinari: p. 146
Diego Motto: p 174
Museo del prosciutto e dei salumi di Parma, Musei del cibo della provincia di Parma, Langhirano: p. 35 bottom
M. Panella, *Il cibo immaginario, 1950-1970 pubblicità e immagini dell'Italia a tavola*, Artix 2013, pp. 93, 151, 105, 98: pp. 103 in alto, 136 right, 194 top, 253 top
Matteo Piazza: p. 150
G. Origlia (edited by), *Album. Annuario di progetto e cultura materiale diretto da Mario Bellini*, 1, *Progetto mangiare*, Electa, Milan 1981, p. 48: p. 32
San Carlo Unichips: p. 206
Studio Giulio Iacchetti: p. 238
P. Tamborrini, *Design sostenibile. Oggetti sistemi e comportamenti*, Electa, Milan 2009, p. 84: p. 263
Tavernello-Caviro: p. 267
Bruno Vaghi: pp. 26, 168
Luigi Vaghi: pp. 15, 42 bottom
A. Valeri, *Pubblicità in Italia. Storia, protagonisti e tendenze di cento anni di comunicazione*, Edizioni Il Sole 24 ore, Milan 1986, p. 95: p. 108
D. Villani, *La pubblicità e i suoi segreti*, Editoriale Domus, Milan 1946 (anastatic reprint, 1993), p. 136: p. 147 left
Stefano Zardini: pp. 29 bottom, 256, 257

acknowledgments

Aiap / Lorenzo Grazzani
Algida-Unilever / Desirée Sigurtà (jesurum lab)
G.B. Ambrosoli
Armando Testa Archives
Auricchio / Enza Bassini
Massimo Barbierato
Barilla Historic Archives, Parma / Roberto Pagliari
Olga Barmine
Umberto Bartocci
Alessandra Bassi
Annalisa Bassi
Elio Basso
Buitoni-Nestlé Historic Archives / Silvia Ferrata, Maia Lottersberger, Sara Pecchielan (Edelman Italy)
Sergio Brugiolo
Fiorella Bulegato
Caffarel / Benedetta Mele (MilleEventi srl)
Giorgio Camuffo
Betty Caorsi
Fratelli Carli / Sabrina Calonaci;
Barbara De Micheli (Barabino & Partners)
Ginette Caron
Cedral Tassoni / Alessandra Bodei, Elio Accardo, Barbara Reverberi
Civica raccolta delle stampe Achille Bertarelli, Castello Sforzesco, Milano / Antonella Casali, Giovanna Mori
Cirio Historic Archives – Conserve Italia / Gianluca Pilo
Civico archivio fotografico raccolte grafiche e fotografiche Castello Sforzesco, Milano / Giuseppina Simmi
Club amici del chinotto / Emanuele Breveglieri, Giovanni Landolfi
Gruppo Colussi / Monica Carbonio
Consorzio del Prosciutto di San Daniele / Giovanna Barbieri
Consorzio Grana Padano
Consorzio Parmigiano Reggiano
Continuum / Emanuele Teobaldo
Pietro Costa
Giovanna Crespi
Francesco Dal Co
Anna Dalla Via
Davide Campari – Milano / Simona Grosso
Paolo Deganello
Elena Dellapiana
Deoleo / Mariella Cerullo, Cristina Sacco
Eataly / Simona Milvo, Silvia Ramella
Editoriale Domus / Carmen Figini
Esselunga / Saverio Gennaro, Raffaella Iodice
Fabbri 1905 / Alessandro Bizzotto (Lead Communication)
Ferrarelle / Alba Abbinante
Ferrero / Emiliano Laricchiuta
Florio / Cecilia Cazzani (MCS&Partners)
Fondazione 3M archivio fotografico / Daniela Aleggiani, Francesca Stefanachi
Fondazione Fiera Milano Historic Archives / Andrea Lovati
Fondazione Isec / Giorgio Bigatti, Alberto De Cristoforo
Gelati Motta – Nestlé / Rossella Digiacomo (Found srl)
Gelati Pepino 1884 / Mattia Giardini
Giorgio Giugiaro

Fabrizio Gomarasca
Giancarlo Gonizzi
Salvatore Gregorietti
Gruppo Sanpellegrino Historic Archives
Laura Guidetti
Giulio Iacchetti
Illy Caffè / Angelica Anzilotti, Furio Suggi Liverani, Christine Pascolo, Adriana Spada
Kartell museum Archives / Elisa Storace
Krumiri Rossi / Nicola Molghea
La cucina italiana Archives /
Ettore Mocchetti
La Metallurgica / Luigi Bianchi
Ugo La Pietra
Lurisia / Danila Lombardi (dcm associati)
Luxardo / Piero Luxardo
Majani 1796 / Nicolò Canova
Enzo Mari
Antonio Mattei / Vania Bini, Angela Giancaterino
Melegatti / Alessandra Malizia
Gruppo Montenegro / Simonetta e Isabella Seragnoli
Giovanni Mucci / Mario Mucci
Musei del cibo della provincia di Parma
Museo della liquirizia Giorgio Amarelli
Mutti / Sara Pecchielan, Giorgia Amarotti (Edelman Italy)
Nonino / Elisa Ellero, Giannola Nonino, Antonella Nonino, Barbara Manzini, Daniela Tessaro
Mauro Olivieri
Oxfam Italia / Mariateresa Alvino, Joki Gauthier, Demostenes Uscamayta
Pastiglie Leone / Elisa Mereatur
Perfetti Van Melle /Anna Re
Perugina-Nestlé historic museum Archives / Maia Lottersberger (Edelman Italy)
Sergio Polano
Saclà / Lucia Ercole
Sammontana / Vanessa Marsana (Weber Shandwick)
San Carlo Gruppo alimentare – Unichips Italia / Dalila Agrati
Saporetti Immagini d'Arte / Roberto Mascaroni
Sabrina Sciama
Maddalena Scimemi
Gianni Sinni
Paolo Tamborrini
Tavernello-Caviro / Giovanna Nonni
Federica Tommasi
Paolo Ulian
Andrea Vecera
Marco Zito

documentary research
Sabrina Sciama

editorial coordination
Giovanna Crespi

copy editing
Laura Guidetti

translation
Olga Barmine

design
Tassinari/Vetta

layout and cover
Anna Dalla Via

technical coordination
Andrea Panozzo

quality control
Giancarlo Berti

This volume was printed for Mondadori Electa S.p.A.,
at Elcograf S.p.A., via Mondadori 15, Verona, in 2015